MW01097752

BETWEEN LAND AND SEA

BETWEEN
LAND AND SEA

A COLD WARRIOR'S LOG

REAR ADMIRAL PHILIP A. DUR, USN

LIONCREST
PUBLISHING

Between Land and Sea: A Cold Warrior's Log

Hardcover ISBN: 978-1-5445-2692-8
Paperback ISBN: 978-1-5445-2690-4
Ebook ISBN: 978-1-5445-2691-1

Library of Congress Control Number: 2021925380

For my shipmates at sea and my colleagues ashore who helped chart the course I sailed and the roads I took while in the uniform of my country and the navy.

CONTENTS

FOREWORD

John Lehman, former Secretary of the Navy

As secretary of the navy during the Cold War's last decade, I and the rest of the service's leadership depended on the navy's superb cadre of officers with a subspecialty in strategy and planning. We leaned on them heavily to conceptualize, craft, disseminate, and advocate for policies, strategies, and concepts that would further our nation's interests and those of our allies, especially through the optimal use of our naval power. Their at-sea assignments as line and intelligence officers—often in combat in and over Vietnam—gave them professional naval knowledge, experience, and credibility. Their specialized education, staff assignments, and broad range of contacts throughout the international security community gave them the insights, bureaucratic skills, and polish to fight the internal Pentagon, White House, Hill, and Alliance policy battles—as well as spar with the Soviets. They not only could talk the talk—in offices, classrooms, and conference halls—but then they could turn around and walk the walk, as seamen and naval diplomats, on quarterdecks and bridges, helping to implement what they had assisted in conceiving, before returning yet again to headquarters and schoolhouses to use what they had just learned and demonstrated out in the real world.

Populated primarily by very bright and dedicated surface warfare officers and maritime patrol aviators, this community, and the navy, benefited from an array of long-established navy advanced education programs that had sent them to the finest war colleges and graduate schools at home and abroad. More importantly, they were astutely managed—informally but successfully—by experienced senior flag officers who had often come up the same way. They were commonly, but not exclusively, to be found in the OPNAV Directorate for Plans, Policy and Operations (OP-06), as Phil Dur was periodically, under the leadership of flag officers such as Bob Hilton, Don Engen, Bill Crowe, Art Moreau, Sam Packer, Ace Lyons, Hank Mustin, and later Phil himself—admirals who were themselves usually serving their third or fourth tours in that office.

Preeminent among these warrior-strategist-diplomats throughout the 1970s, '80s, and '90s was Philip Alphonse Dur, the author of this book. His saga, like that of his fellow subspecialists, demonstrates how, with proper motivation and understanding, a talented officer could rise in a field that the navy and the nation sorely needed. The essential factors were proper motivation and understanding on the part of his superiors, the acquisition of operational experience and leadership in the fleet as well as shore duty, and above all, aptitude and passion.

The requirement for officers with Phil's experience, knowledge, skillset, and judgment is no less today than it was during the often-dark days of the late Cold War. An often-missing element recently, however, is the mentorship—example-setting and career management—that was available to aspiring naval strategists and policy experts of Phil's and my generation, and that we in turn imparted once we were called on to serve in senior positions in the navy's hierarchy. It is a particular concern of mine that this invaluable corps of naval policy gladiators has now been all but disbanded, a situation in part driven by the requirement for years of joint duty. Moreover, I sense a periodic lack of oversight to ensure that more of today's appropriately educated and experienced navy political-military/strategic planning officers are actually assigned to billets, and repeat tours, that use their strategic knowledge and political-military experience and acumen, as he did—cogently talking the talk and also energetically walking the walk.

Publication of Phil's *Between Land and Sea* provides ammunition to help turn this around. It lays out how one motivated Cold War and post-Cold War officer was able to pursue a demanding and highly successful career at sea—reaching the pinnacle of professional accomplishment as a battle group commander—while at the same time contributing enormously to the defense policy of the nation and its ability to develop and wield its naval power effectively—strategically and operationally, as well as tactically.

I crossed paths with Phil periodically when I was secretary of the navy. (He appears periodically in my book *Oceans Ventured*, as I do in this book of his.) This was not by accident: It's fairly normal for officers of his education, bent, and caliber—the navy's strategic cadre—to interact with very senior officers and officials who relied on them. I was aware of Phil and his shipmates in OPNAV and OSD when I was a consultant for Chief of Naval Operations, Admiral Jim Holloway. We were all struggling with the perverse attitudes toward effective use of US naval power by many in the Carter administration. In OPNAV—as he relates—Phil drafted seminal naval and allied concept papers that would later underpin the Reagan administration's Maritime Strategy. Furthermore, while in OSD, Phil successfully argued for a robust official definition of "maritime superiority"—something always high on my own agenda list.

Later, I met him again on board his destroyer command, USS *Comte de Grasse* (DD-974), anchored off Yorktown during a ceremony commemorating that epic battle, along with then-Vice

President George H. W. Bush and Vice Admiral James A. "Ace" Lyons, commander of the US Second Fleet. Like myself, Phil had returned a few months earlier from participating at sea off Soviet Northern Fleet bases in VADM Lyons's exercise OCEAN VENTURE, the Reagan administration's opening salvo at sea against a Soviet Navy that had become dangerously accustomed to a free ride in northern waters.

When Phil moved on to serve on the National Security Council staff (which I helped facilitate), our interactions increased, both directly and indirectly. They increased even more when later he became Ace Lyons's executive assistant (EA) when Ace was OP-06. Now in his second tour in OP-06, Phil was able to build on his previous related tours to effectively assist Ace (who was himself on his fourth OP-06 tour, at least), the Chief of Naval Operations, and myself from that influential and demanding position. Then he was off to become commanding officer of USS *Yorktown* (CG-48), our second Aegis cruiser, where he famously closed the last chapter of the Cold War at sea during his steadfast 1988 Black Sea cruise, asserting freedom of the seas in the face of Soviet naval intransigence. That event I learned about from the newspapers, having stepped down from office as secretary the year before. If you read no other chapter in Phil's book, be sure to read Chapter 10.

Phil still had more years of public service ahead of him. He went on to use his prodigious knowledge and skills to serve as EA and senior naval aide to one of my successors, Secretary of the Navy Will Ball. Then, fluent in French and Spanish, he was appointed US defense attaché in Paris to solidify our alliance with France and its own important armed forces, which proved to be so useful during the Gulf War. Then he was back to sea again, this time flying his flag as commander of the *Saratoga* battle group in the Mediterranean. He closed out his naval career as a two-star admiral, serving as director of the Naval Strategy Division (OPNAV N51, in the old OP-06[1]) and then as assistant deputy Chief of Naval Operations for Plans, Policy and Operations (as key deputy to OP-06, and as "deputy operations deputy" for the navy).

His final monument and gift to the naval service and the nation while he was in uniform was his fostering of the naval strategic concept *Forward...from the Sea*, published in 1994,[2] one of the most important strategy documents in the history of our navy, and the consummation of a full career of experience and service "between land and sea." That publication, signed out by the secretary of the navy, the Chief of Naval Operations, and the commandant of the Marine Corps, was primarily meant to inform and influence the then-current generation of national defense leaders at the very highest levels, as they considered various policy options. And it did so.

This book, however, is primarily meant to inform and influence the *next* generations of mid-grade and junior officers and midshipmen as they consider the options available to them for successful careers in the navy. If they've got a passion for leading and operating at sea—and an equally strong passion for naval strategy, national defense policy, and international affairs—Phil shows them here by his example how those passions once were, and can be again, pursued successfully in the United States Navy. The book is much more than just another navy flag officer's log or memoir; it's also an inspirational and practical manual on what a modern US Navy career as an operator-strategist should look like. Unlike other books on recent navy strategy, this one, uniquely, illustrates the role of strategy in the personal and career formation arenas, as well as in functioning as a consummate

1   Now N3/N5.

2   US Navy and US Marine Corps, *Forward...from the Sea*, 1994.

professional at top policy and operational levels. It's a master-ful description of the kind of career that any top-flight navy strategist-operator should aspire to have. As such, it should be required reading in the strategy curricula at the Naval Academy, the Naval War College, and the Naval Postgraduate School; for every Federal Executive Fellow cohort; and for anyone whom the navy sends to civilian grad schools in national security affairs, government, international relations, political science, or history. They, the navy, and the nation will all benefit from Admiral Dur's willingness to recount his example-setting naval career for us.

PREFACE

After I completed my naval career, I often reflected on my years in uniform and the many opportunities and challenges I was afforded, during and after my retirement from the navy. A second retirement from an exhausting stint as president of Northrop Grumman Ship Systems following my naval service finally afforded the opportunity to reflect and record experiences over thirty years of the Cold War. The chapters of my life that may be of interest are those that I believe made my career experiences exceptional if not unique.

I begin with an explanation of my choice for a title to describe a career divided between assignments at sea and ashore. Atop the highest hill on the Cap Ferrat, between Villefranche-sur-Mer and Beaulieu in the South of France, a plaque that adorns the entrance to a chapel dedicated to Our Lady features a prayerful poem titled "Entre Terre et Mer." That poem, which I discovered as a young officer during the first of many visits to Villefranche, served to inspire me during my career. It reads:

> Le hasard d'une promenade vous a conduits
> à cette chapelle au bout du monde;
> Derrière l'abside c'est le large,
> derrière le porche, l'abri d'une rade.
> Vous êtes entre Terre et Mer,
> Là où s'apaise la longue course
> des vagues de Levant ou de Ponant.

Ici tant de marins sont venus
la veille de lever l'ancre.
Tant de femmes ont gravi la colline
pour trouver la force
d'espérer leur retour.
Vous êtes entre Terre et Mer.
Faites halte
Faites silence
Et que monte de votre cœur,
rejoignant la prière millénaire,
Votre adoration
vers Dieu, le créateur
de la Terre et de la Mer.

My translation:

By chance, a stroll brought you to this chapel on the
*   far side of the world. Facing the Apse is the open*
*   ocean, behind the chapel lies the shelter of a bay*
You are between Land and Sea, where after long
*   reaches, waves from the east and west calmly wash*
*   ashore. It is here that so many sailors have come*
*   on the eve of weighing anchor. And where so many*
*   women have climbed to find the strength to await*
*   their return*
You are between Land and Sea,
Pause, be silent, and summon from your heart the
*   millennial prayer*
Your adoration for the Creator of the Land and of the Sea

The educational experiences afforded me by the navy are important in explaining the assignments that followed, especially my years at Harvard pursuing a PhD, studying under acclaimed academicians and confronting angry anti-defense crowds.

Command at sea, the goal of every line officer, looms large among my proudest accomplishments. Commanding a destroyer, a cruiser, and a carrier battle group were the culmination of long preparatory assignments at sea under outstanding mentors and role models from whom I borrowed heavily. The hundreds of officers, chief petty officers, and blue jackets I met and befriended on this journey were the foundation for my good fortune. The reader will appreciate my description of the circumstances surrounding a collision of my cruiser with a Soviet destroyer in the Black Sea in 1988, accurately described as the last incident of the Cold War. Similarly, it seems incumbent on me to explain the tragic and accidental missile firings by my flagship, the USS *Saratoga*, on a Turkish destroyer in the Aegean Sea in 1992.

Assignments ashore provided altogether different opportunities. I am especially mindful of my work in the Office of the Secretary of Defense, which contributed to winning Secretary of Defense Harold Brown over to accepting the objectives of an offensive maritime strategy and a commitment to maintaining a margin of maritime superiority over the Soviet Union. Two years on the staff of the National Security Council (NSC) put me in a ringside seat and gave me a role in advancing the Reagan administration's foreign policy and security objectives in the Middle East. I will note for the record that I worked diligently to promote what I knew firsthand to be President Reagan's objectives, despite determined opposition from the secretary of defense and the chairman of the Joint Chiefs of Staff (JCS). I will treasure the many personal encounters with a man I admire as the greatest president of my generation.

As the defense attaché at our embassy in Paris as the Cold War ended and a hot war erupted in the Middle East, it was my good fortune to befriend and work closely with the senior military advisor to the president of France. We worked closely to advance our countries' common interests and objectives in a world beset with convulsive geopolitical changes. I am especially proud of the opportunity to have discussed our goals and progress in the Gulf War with President of France François Mitterrand.

Finally, you will understand that I left the navy sooner than I would have preferred. I loved my years in uniform, and I feel that I still owe an explanation to family, friends, and my shipmates who wondered why I left the field. I hope that they will come to appreciate "the rest of the story."

INTRODUCTION

DIPLOMATIC ROOTS

I was born to Philip Francis Dur and Elena Delgado Dur on June 22, 1944, in Bethesda, Maryland, while my father was serving as a cryptologist intelligence officer and Japanese linguist in the Office of Naval Intelligence (ONI). My mother, who had immigrated to the United States in 1938, was born of Spanish parentage in Camaguey, Cuba, in 1914. Owing to my mother's native Spanish and my father's absence during and immediately after the war, I was raised in the Spanish language. In 1948, at the age of four, my father took his young family (we were four children) on what became an eleven-year odyssey across both oceans. This was the setting of my earliest memories of the Cold War.

Upon arriving in Le Havre, France, in June 1948 aboard the SS *America*, there were hundreds if not thousands of manifestants—striking dockworkers protesting the shipment of US food aid and farm machinery to the war-impoverished French people. The noise of the crowd was deafening, and there were gendarmes and police wielding batons. My father explained that the protesters were communists who hated America and the help it was sending to France. This was rough stuff for a four-year-old just conscious of what it meant to be an American in postwar France. Yet, apart from that incident, we were often celebrated as liberators. Even my young school chums often expressed their admiration for America and what we had done during the war.

Almost two years later, while living in Saint Cyr au Mont D'or on the outskirts of Lyon, I was enrolled in a parochial school,

École Libre, speaking schoolboy French. The male teacher had me obtain a large map of the United States from my father, which he posted on a wall. (Forty years later, while I was the defense attaché in Paris, I was invited to visit my alma mater, where I presented gifts in the form of ball caps from the USS **Comte de Grasse** to all the students. I was pleasantly surprised to note that the school has hung a portrait of me in the entrance.)

Although my brothers and sisters and I were conversant in French, our English suffered due to limited exposure. Our mother generally spoke to us in Spanish, and our father and all the servants in our household spoke only French. One morning in June 1950 while in the library of our spacious French country home, Villa des muguets, I was with my dad, who was listening to the Voice of America on a short-wave radio. During what was a loud news flash, he yelled an expletive in English that I will never forget: "Goddamn!"

Somewhat shocked, I asked him what was the matter.

"*Les communistes ont envahi la Corée*," was his reply: the communists have invaded Korea. And so, for the second time in my young life, I came to understand that the communists were indeed bad actors in my father's view of things.

We left France in 1951 and moved to Germany, where my dad was posted successively to three different diplomatic missions. Germany was the setting for several more Cold War events, as I came to know them. The first was during rising tensions in Berlin, the divided former capital of Germany, which was occupied by American, British, French, and Soviet forces. I remember, while attending a movie at our army base in Bremen, a newsreel piece that described a fractious meeting of foreign ministers on the subject of Allied access to the city through Soviet-occupied East Germany. I was struck by how malevolent the Soviet foreign minister appeared while yelling at his Allied counterparts.

Movies at the US military theaters in Germany always began with a newsreel, followed by clips of military bands playing the national anthems of the four victorious allies. We all had to stand for anthems but only for the "Star-Spangled Banner," "God Save the King," and the "Marseillaise." For the Soviet anthem, on my father's signal, we sat back down quickly.

While living in Bremen, my parents also joined a pilgrimage by American Catholics living in occupied Germany to Rome. My older sister Elena and I accompanied them on this adventure, which began with a three-day voyage in a long train pulled by a steam locomotive from the most northern part of Germany to the middle of the Italian Peninsula. Our route took us through Austria, and there occurred a dramatic moment in my memory of the Cold War. As the train entered the Soviet-occupied zone, it came to a screeching halt in the middle of the night. My mother awakened my sister and me and instructed us in a loud voice to get dressed immediately and put on our warm coats. We did as instructed and stepped out onto the cold platform. There, Soviet soldiers yelling in loud, uncomplimentary German forced all the "pilgrims" in our car onto the platform while they examined passports and searched our car for "contraband," as my father explained it. It seemed like hours in the cold before we were allowed back in the train so we could continue our journey through friendlier zones of Austria.

When we arrived in Italy, our first stop was in Bologna, and a sea of red hammer-and-sickle flags of the Italian Communist Party (PCI) greeted us as we entered the station. I asked my father why these red flags were flying in a country that he had told me was Catholic and friendly to Americans. He explained that there were a few communist Italians who admired the Soviet Union. I became anxious that we might not be as welcome in Rome as we had been told. There were other instances of a communist presence when we got to Rome, especially large posters every-where of Togliatti, the leader of the Communist Party, who was running for election to the Italian Parliament at the time.

A final Cold War memory from our time in Germany coincided with an awards dinner held for my Cub Scout pack. We were gathered with parents and families to receive our promotion badges and arrows, and as we waited for the ceremony to begin, a loud buzz came over the dinner. The ceremony stopped suddenly, and the master of ceremonies took on a grave tone, announcing the sudden death of Joseph Stalin, the leader of the Soviet Union. The news overtook the proceedings, and all the adults present seemed delighted with this announcement.

After a posting in Koblenz, Germany, followed by a two-year assignment as American consul in Colón, Panama, my dad was transferred to Yokohama, Japan, in the fall of 1955. At the time, there were still two hundred thousand US Army troops posted at the Kishine Barracks on the outskirts of Yokohama. This rather massive military presence was a vestige of the US occupation of Japan and the uneasy truce that had settled over the Korean Peninsula after the war ended in 1953. For the two summers that I attended Boy Scout camp, Camp Motosu, I counted exactly seventy-two different army, navy, air force, and Marine Corps bases, camps, and installations in Japan.

As described earlier, my father's example and the interests he passed to me were pivotal in my formation, but one trait that I developed on my own was leadership. My experience in scouting was the foundation. Of all the extracurricular activities open to me while living in Japan, Boy Scouting offered the most rewards. The military provided the facilities, the equipment, and most importantly, the volunteer leaders. In the three years we were in Yokohama, I devoted all my spare time to scouting. In the process, I learned to motivate, inspire, and reward others for achieving goals and meeting standards. To my great disappointment, my father was reserved in recognizing my progress. Scouting was not something he cared much about. My mother, by contrast, came to every Court of Honor and proudly wore the miniatures of every rank I attained. The lessons learned in scouting ultimately inspired my choice of professions.

When a typhoon threatened the camp in Hakone National Park, marines in full combat gear aborted a training exercise in Camp Fuji, packed us onto trucks, and whisked us away to the safety of their base in the Japanese Alps. In any event, the tension of Cold War military presence and constant maneuvers by all the US armed forces in the Far East were a reminder of the dangerous times we were living in. For instance, my memories of high school in Yokohama include drills that required us to dive under our desks in response to simulated nuclear attacks. We were also reminded constantly to avoid "snake dance" demonstrations in front of military and consular housing areas by pro-communist unions protesting our presence.

Our family returned to the Washington, DC area in 1958, and my dad was assigned to the Japan desk at the State Department. The last three years of high school in McLean, Virginia were relatively uneventful, but for a growing consciousness among those of my generation, crises in the Taiwan Straits, Laos, and Indonesia did not bode well for the future.

Cuba became a family concern. During my high school years, my mother was greatly concerned for her siblings still living in Cuba as revolution engulfed the country of her birth. In January 1959, we watched Fidel Castro and his rebels riding triumphantly through the streets of Havana on captured tanks after the overthrow of Batista. It was indeed a sad moment for Cuba and for my mother, as she literally wept over Cuba's fate: "*Ay Cuba, tus hijos lloran*" (Oh, Cuba, your children are crying).

One high-water mark during this troubled time was the election of John F. Kennedy. With a storied war record as a naval officer, he encouraged my generation to think optimistically of the contributions we could make in the promotion of American ideals. His inaugural address in January 1961, which I attended with many of my high school classmates, was inspiring. To this day, I can recall my favorite lines: "With history the final judge of our deeds, and a clear conscience our only sure reward, let us go forth to lead the land we love, asking His blessing and His help, but knowing that His work here on earth must truly be our own."

It is easier with the benefit of hindsight to understand how experiences in childhood and adolescence shape goals and even careers. My abiding interest in international affairs and foreign languages was formed by exposure to life in other countries and my father's assignments as a diplomat. Dinner conversations in our household centered on interpretations of history and current events. Those discussions were often quite lively as my siblings and I challenged my father's conservative views.

In my last year of high school, my father encouraged me to apply to the College of Engineering at Notre Dame. I was surprised, but his explanation was that the Soviet success with Sputnik in 1958 had made studies in engineering a patriotic obligation. Since my high school grades and my SAT scores suggested I could succeed in math and applied science, I dutifully complied with his preference for me. After five semesters of engineering and physical science courses and a summer as an engineering intern at the Lockheed Missiles and Space Company in California, I understood that engineering was not my calling. In the middle of my junior year, I changed majors and increased my course load to graduate in four years with a major in political science (styled as "government and international affairs"). I was also the first undergraduate in the department to qualify for a certificate in Soviet East European affairs.

As part of my undergraduate experience, I learned the Russian language and studied Russian history, Marxist economics, and philosophy. I was enthralled by the Russian literary giants Dostoevsky, Tolstoy, and Turgenev. I also studied under several distinguished professors who had emigrated from Eastern Europe after World War II when Soviet armies invaded Czechoslovakia, Poland, Hungary, and the Balkans. These learned refugees, Stephen Kertesz, Ivan Ivanus, Boleslaw Szczesniak, and Cyril Czech, were passionate anti-communists, determined to educate students on the risks of communism when explaining the fate that had befallen Eastern Europe. Their stories of the draconian treatment of their former countries by the Soviets were chilling.

My college years were formative on many counts. Of lasting importance to my future was my status while enrolled as a Navy Reserve Officers Training Corps (NROTC) midshipman and a student of naval science. Our classes, labs, and drill periods provided the focus, if any were needed, on the challenges confronting us in the darkest days of the Cold War. The intervention in Vietnam developed while I was in college, and although the news and accounts of progress in the war seemed optimistic at first, our instructors were keen to prepare us for the dangers and challenges we would face. By the time we graduated in the summer of 1965, the country's involvement in Vietnam was massive, and dissent was already brewing among members of our generation. Nevertheless, I enjoyed my NROTC days and managed to win the distinguished company award in my senior year while serving as a company commander. No doubt, my adolescent experience with the Boy Scouts helped lay the foundation for these early leadership skills.

Another memory that looms large from this era was the Cuban missile crisis of 1962. As the crisis mounted, my classmates and I gathered in front of the single black-and-white television in the basement of Cavanaugh Hall, our freshman dormitory, to hear President Kennedy's address to the nation. We all felt that we were at the precipice. The president finished his remarks at about 7:30 p.m. As if on cue, many of my fellow students and I headed for the confessionals in Sacred Heart Church or to the Grotto of Our Lady. I wanted to call my family, who had moved back to Nagoya, Japan, to share my concern that war might begin suddenly. Unfortunately, even the cost of a three-minute call was prohibitive.

After the president issued his ultimatum to the Soviets, subsequent developments gave the navy remarkable responsibility in the conflict in resolving the crisis and wide play on the national news. We midshipmen took great pride as our patrol planes found Soviet subs and forced them to surface and our destroyers intercepted ships carrying missiles bound for Cuba. Those of us in the NROTC unit were given a classified preview of tactics and rules of engagement (ROE) applicable to naval blockades.

After completing all the requirements for my bachelor's degree in 1965, I was awarded a one-year fellowship to continue my studies at Notre Dame toward a master's degree in Soviet East European studies. I extended my studies of the Soviet government, communist ideology, and the Russian language and completed all the requirements for the degree in June 1966.[3] The following month, I left South Bend, Indiana to begin my service at sea. My academic preparation at Notre Dame would prove a valuable investment.

---

3   My master's thesis was titled "Sakhalin: The Focus of Russo-Japanese Confrontation, 1805–1905."

CAREER FORMATION

A meaningful attempt to describe a career in uniform requires the explanation of one's choice of service and decisions on warfare specialty. It is often assumed that progression in a naval career conforms to the navy's established career patterns and that assignments are made pursuant to the "needs of the service." Those assumptions are only partly true. To be sure, a successful career will conform to certain requirements and is dependent on demonstrated performance in key assignments. For unrestricted line officers, those requirements are for the most part "at sea" billets. Progressive increases in responsibility in sea duty assignments are the *sine qua non*. Some fifty years ago, Adm. James Calvert observed that the course of assignments is intended to prepare, qualify, and even test unrestricted line officers for the stated goal: command at sea.[4] However, in my case, this path took a much more circuitous and unconventional route.

My first inspiration in my choice of career was parental. My father had served as an intelligence officer in the navy during World War II; he'd attained the rank of lieutenant commander. A Japanese linguist, he had aided in the decryption and translation of Japanese naval communications. He was kept on active duty after the war and assigned to the Central Intelligence Group (precursor to the Central Intelligence Agency [CIA]), where his work included translating myriad Japanese war documents, which I found fascinating. In 1947, he accepted a lateral appointment to the Foreign Service, where he could apply his fluent mastery of four foreign languages. Before entering the navy, my father had completed a PhD in history at Harvard University with the intent of pursuing an academic career. He explained to us that the later decision to undertake a career as a diplomat was to continue his public service in foreign affairs. As I matured and observed his

4   Rear Admiral James Calvert, *The Naval Profession* (New York: McGraw-Hill, 1965), 32, 52.

dedication, my own aspiration to serve in government grew. On reflection, I never considered any career beyond those in public service; his example was that compelling. The story told to me was as follows. On the occasion of my expected arrival, my dad was away, and so the chauffeur that night was the Cuban consul general, Mr. Pepe Sera, a friend of my parents. While en route to the Naval Hospital in Bethesda, Maryland, Mr. Sera predicted to my mother that she would be delivering a "future admiral." At the ceremony at which I was eventually promoted to rear admiral in May 1989, I remember her whispering to me in Spanish as she put the gold board on my shoulder, "*Todo esto ha sido ordenado!*" (This has all been ordained!).

Another important factor in my decision to enter the NROTC was the fact that young men coming of age in the '60s were subject to the draft by the Selective Service. Inasmuch as I was bound for college in 1961, it seemed logical to enroll in an officer training program, which would postpone military service until after graduation. Receiving an appointment as an NROTC midshipman at the University of Notre Dame, the navy became an important part of my undergraduate formation. I thoroughly enjoyed the experience, including the rigorous course work, summer training cruises, and most importantly, the opportunity to lead. This last consideration was something that had become important to me earlier, in scouting when I spent six years advancing through the Boy Scouts until attaining the rank of Eagle before my fourteenth birthday. Those experiences gave me the confidence that I could lead others to purposeful ends.

Whereas the choice of service may have been ordained, choosing the branch or specialty within it was more complicated. Having studied international relations, specialized in Soviet East European area studies at the bachelor's and master's levels, and attained a working knowledge of Russian, I initially asked for an assignment in the Office of Naval Intelligence (ONI). Like my father, I had some facility learning foreign languages and an abiding interest in international affairs. As it had to him, the choice of intelligence as a specialty appealed to me. After receiving my preference card, my "detailer," or assignment officer, in the Bureau of Naval Personnel (BuPers) explained that I would first have to complete a tour at sea in an unrestricted line billet. Thereafter, assuming that openings were available, I might apply for a transfer to the "restricted line" with a naval intelligence designator. By "restricted," the navy means that officers with these designators are not eligible for command at sea.

I arrived aboard my first ship, the USS *Little Rock* (CLG-4) in the fall of 1967, where I was assigned as the radio officer, communications watch officer, and Operations Communications (OC) division officer. The *Little Rock* was flagship for the Sixth Fleet in the Mediterranean. That assignment caused me to think hard about my initial plan for a career in intelligence, as the allure of fast-paced operations and the challenges of sea duty gradually eroded my earlier intention to seek opportunities in intelligence.

As a communications watch officer in a flagship, I came to know the embarked admiral, William Martin, and his staff rather well. After a little more than a year, I transferred from the Communications division and was assigned to the Operations division of the admiral's staff (N-3) as the assistant fleet scheduler. The change brought me into even closer contact with senior line officers: destroyermen, aviators, and submariners. Many of these officers had commanded ships and squadrons and others were aspiring to command at sea.

Among the most influential of these were two destroyermen, Captain (later Rear Admiral) William Clifford and Lieutenant Commander (later Captain) Rudolph (Rudy) Daus. Rudy described with fondness the thrills, challenges, and what sounded like awesome responsibilities accorded to junior officers in destroyers. We stood many night watches together on the flag bridge, and while watching the destroyers in our formation maneuvering at high speed, he would ask rhetorically, "Who do you think is driving that Greyhound tonight? Bet he's not an intelligence officer." It was not until I was well into the first year of my next assignment, the long-sought intelligence billet in Washington, that I came to realize Rudy was right: my earlier intention had been misplaced.

I had also considered a career in the Foreign Service following the navy, and so, while in Washington, I briefly explored that possibility. I applied to take the Foreign Service exam and got an appointment to speak with an official responsible for recruiting. After listening to his description of typical career tracks, I took special note of the practice of assigning junior officers to "challenging tours in hardship posts." When I inquired about the possibility of more graduate study and pursuit of a PhD in political science while in service, the personnel officer was not encouraging. "The Foreign Service doesn't need PhDs; we get ours on the job," he said bluntly. I decided that I was not willing to abandon the ambition to continue my graduate studies and earn the PhD. My interest in the practice of diplomacy waned accordingly.

Coincidentally, while at ONI, I was assigned temporary additional duty as a recorder for a selection board convened at the BuPers to select lieutenants for promotion to lieutenant commander. Having this vantage point was valuable because it provided access to hundreds of service records of officers under consideration for promotion, and as an eyewitness to the proceedings, I could see what qualities and accomplishments were most highly regarded by the board.

During the several weeks the selection board was in session, I spent long hours collecting records and recording the board's proceedings. Having rethought my earlier interest in a career in intelligence, I was now more inclined to—and felt myself better suited for—the unrestricted line and destroyer duty. Were I to remain on active duty in the navy, my new and abiding ambition would be working toward command at sea.

Over a lunch he hosted on the last day of the board's proceedings, Captain Albert Sackett, who was the president of the board, took me aside to discuss career opportunities in the surface line. Capt. Sackett was also a senior captain in the Officer Distribution Division, directly responsible for the development and management of officers in the surface navy. The captain made the following proposal: I would apply for admission to Destroyer School (Sackett was about to take command of the Destroyer School), and he would waive the Officer of the Deck, Fleet Operations (OODF) prerequisite and send me to sea for four months on a deployed destroyer where I could earn the required qualifications. I would then enroll in Class 30 at the Destroyer School, which would convene in January 1970. Following my department head tour, he "would see to it" that if it were still my choice, I would be assigned to continue my studies for the PhD.

As it happened, I nevertheless earned my OODF qualification in USS *C. H. Roan* (DD-853) while deployed in the Mediterranean. But then, as Sackett had proposed, I completed Destroyer School as a member of Class 30 in July 1970 and was assigned as operations officer aboard USS *Knox* (DE-1052), homeported in Pearl Harbor, Hawaii.

On completion of that assignment and after selection for promotion to lieutenant commander, I took Rear Admiral (formerly Captain) Sackett up on his earlier offer: I applied to Harvard University and, receiving a Littauer Fellowship from the Kennedy School, enrolled in August 1972 with the intent of obtaining a PhD.

This summary account of early career decisions and of the help of mentors and seniors is important for understanding the many opportunities and good fortune that came my way over the course of a thirty-year career spent between land and sea, which I describe in this book. Those who steered me to assignments in destroyers (and cruisers), and the men with whom I served in seven ships, provided the inspiration and indescribable sense of accomplishment that followed. Serving under eight commanding officers (COs) before assuming command of my own destroyer taught me more about leadership, management, and the importance of mentoring younger generations than any collection of textbooks on these subjects could ever have. Simply put, I learned from these officers how to lead others, often in incredibly stressful situations. Just as importantly, I took note of the pitfalls of misguided leadership that I wanted to avoid. I will readily concede that my own leadership style was an eclectic one, born of experience.

A rather common and even trite admission made by senior officers, but never truer than in relation to my experience, is this: to the extent that I succeeded while serving and especially while in command, I owe that good fortune to incredibly talented, dedicated officers, chief petty officers, and blue jackets with whom I was privileged to serve. Their own devotion to the country and the navy was at once my inspiration and the driving force behind my own motivation to succeed with them. One measure of the talent and dedication of those with whom I was privileged to serve will serve to illustrate. Six officers in a wardroom of twenty-four officers assigned to USS *Yorktown* while I was in command were ultimately selected to Flag rank. Two others would certainly have made the cut but for events beyond their control that shortened their careers.

Each assignment provided the foundations and afforded me the experiences so necessary for those that followed as I rose in seniority. My two-year assignment to the staff of the National Security Council (NSC) while a commander was a pinnacle in the career of a political-military subspecialist in the navy. Observing closely and participating directly in the formulation and execution of the nation's foreign and national security policies under President Ronald Reagan were honors that—to use an overworked adjective—qualify as truly exceptional.

In sum, the experiences recounted in the chapters that follow were largely the result of a determination to structure my career. Mine was a somewhat uncommon but certainly not exclusive example of the opportunities open to young people contemplating careers in the service of their country. Understanding one's interests and passions and developing realistic, ambitious but attainable goals are irreducible minimums in professional development.

An example of choice in selection of assignments ashore was my assignment to the staff of the NSC. In that case, I made a calculated choice. Admiral William Crowe, a future Chairman of the Joint Chiefs of Staff (CJCS), had nominated me for assignment to the Strategic Studies Group (SSG). This was a small and very select group of captains and commanders charged with developing strategic options for the navy that reported directly to the Chief of Naval Operations (CNO). As Admiral Crowe explained to me in a phone call, members of the SSG were "the brightest and most promising group of officers, destined for brilliant futures." At that same time, an opportunity to serve in the White House suddenly arose. That appointment, though also prestigious, would take me out of the navy's reach into unfamiliar surroundings. It was also fraught with risk in that I might be asked to participate in actions not to the Defense Department's liking—with possible consequences. This was certainly the case, as things turned out, but I made the choice to take the position at the White House pursuant to my interest in national security affairs and policy making.

Similarly, several sea duty assignments offered some choice. My strong preference, due to my French heritage, to command a destroyer with a connection to France resulted in orders to command the USS *Comte de Grasse*. Having been screened to command a destroyer, my performance in qualifying assignments was such that I was competitive to command one of the newest class of ships, the *Spruance* class. The specific ship was a matter of choice and timing.

As Admiral Calvert argued more than fifty years ago, there are established career templates and requirements that are ordained. That said, many assignments are still the individual's to choose among a number of possibilities. The following chapters will describe how one naval officer balanced personal goals and objectives with the "needs of the service," including successive commands at sea and participation in the development of political-military plans, national security policies, and naval strategies.

CHAPTER 1

NAVAL OPERATIONS, STRATEGY, AND CRISIS DIPLOMACY IN THE MEDITERRANEAN

USS *Little Rock* (CLG-4) and Staff, Commander Sixth Fleet

I reported aboard the USS *Little Rock* (CLG-4), homeported in Norfolk, Virginia, in November 1966. I was assigned as the ship's radio officer, as a communications watch officer, and as a division officer responsible for sixty radiomen. Following refresher training at Guantánamo, Cuba, and a series of gunnery exercises at Culebra Island in the Puerto Rican Operating Area, the ship sailed independently to Rota, Spain. There, we relieved another cruiser, the USS *Springfield* (CLG-7), as the flagship for the Commander of the US Sixth Fleet (COMSIXTHFLT).

Springfield had been homeported in a beautiful site on the French Riviera, Villefranche-sur-Mer, located just east of Nice and about ten miles from Monte Carlo. Sadly, by the time I reported, we in *Little Rock* were bound for a new homeport in Italy, a consequence of President De Gaulle's decision in 1966 to pull France out of the North Atlantic Treaty Organization (NATO) military command structure.

It is important to note here for the record that President De Gaulle did not "throw the US Navy out of Villefranche" as is often alleged. He offered to allow our continued use of the port as a homeport for the Sixth Fleet flagship, but he insisted that the United States would have to obtain diplomatic clearance to enter French waters each time the ship returned from operations at sea. In short, he insisted that the United States formally acknowledge French sovereignty in matters concerning the entry and departure of foreign warships.

Nevertheless, the US government, through the State Department, registered what can only be described as a fit of pique over the proposed change of status.[5] Having declined De Gaulle's offer, the United States moved COMSIXTHFLT, his staff of eighty officers and men, and the fourteen-hundred-man crew of the *Little Rock* to Gaeta, Italy, where we arrived in late January 1967. This explanation of the reason for the move is critical because of the myth that prevailed for years in the navy.

Our new homeport was scenic but not quite as idyllic as Villefranche. Nonetheless, the blue Tyrrhenian, with a backdrop of the Apennine Mountains, made Gaeta a picturesque home for the flagship as well as the staff and their families. *Little Rock*

---

5   For a detailed discussion of De Gaulle's reasons for leaving the NATO military organization, see John Newhouse, *De Gaulle and the Anglo Saxons* (New York: Viking, 1970), 277, 281–283; see also Maurice Couve de Murville, *Une politique étrangère 1958–1969* (Paris: Librairie Plon, 1971), 79–80.

was required to moor to a large buoy in the harbor because the NATO fueling pier there could not accommodate a ship of that size and draft.

Above the city, there was a large castle that commanded a view of the old city and the strategic harbor. The castle in 1967 was serving as a military prison holding two Nazi war criminals: Walter Redder, an Austrian SS commander, and Herbert Kappler, a German Army lieutenant colonel. Both officers had been convicted in 1944 of the war crime of executing hundreds of Italian men in response to partisan attacks on German troops. On many trips to the top of the mountain, we could witness these prisoners exercising in the courtyard of the castle. To the generation I represented, it made World War II seem a little closer.

Not long after the *Little Rock* was moved to Gaeta, the ship sailed west on what would be a two-month-long tour around the western Mediterranean. As had been the practice for several years, the flagship would make at least two trips around the western basin and at least as many around the eastern basin. (A line connecting the island of Malta, the Strait of Messina, and the city of Taranto on the heel of Italy provided the division between the eastern and western Mediterranean.) Among the goals of the biannual western swings were exercises with several other NATO navies: the French, Italian, and the British. Although Spain was not a NATO member, exercises with its naval and air forces were also routine.

These exercises were typically bilateral in nature. In the NATO command arrangement for the Mediterranean, the ships of the other European navies operated under the Commander in Chief of Allied Forces Mediterranean (CINCAFMED), who was the British and Allied commander in Malta. The French were simply reluctant to operate as a NATO component under British command. Many familiar with the history of the period conclude that the withdrawal of the French Mediterranean fleet from forces assigned to NATO in 1959 and the move of major naval forces to the Marine Nationale's (French Navy) Atlantic headquarters were the result of Allied criticism incident to the war in Algeria. (With history as our guide, one is left to wonder whether the Hundred Years' War, the Napoleonic campaigns, and Dunkirk gave rise to the antipathy and mistrust that still hover over Franco-British relations.)

Interestingly, although France was no longer a party to NATO's military organization, the Marine Nationale continued to maintain close relations with their US counterparts. To that end, since 1966, there had been a permanent billet for a US liaison officer on the staff of the French commander of their Mediterranean Fleet (ALESCMED). During this visit, the staffs of COMSIXTHFLT and ALESCMED met to develop plans for future exercises.

From France, we continued west into the Alboran Basin, where we conducted an exercise with the Spanish Navy and Air Force as a unit of Carrier Task Group 60.2. Here again, the exercise was strictly bilateral because Spain, then ruled by Generalissimo Francisco Franco, was not a member of NATO. In fact, at the time, it was generally regarded as a pariah by the other European NATO members, especially the British, who were critical of US-Spanish ties.

The exercise with the Spanish was elementary in comparison with those we had conducted with NATO countries in the Mediterranean. We had a stark reminder of the Spanish government's checkered past when a large formation of Spanish Messerschmidt ME-109 fighters dived toward and then flew over our task group at low altitude, making a terrifying noise. These aircraft, which had been acquired by the Spanish nationalists from Nazi Germany in the late 1930s during the Spanish Civil

War, remained in service and were apparently still in good operating condition as late as 1967.

A visit following that exercise to the beautiful port city of Barcelona gave me yet another glimpse of Spain under Franco. Because I spoke Spanish, I was assigned duties as a shore patrol officer while in port. My responsibilities were to patrol the city's bar districts and other attractions frequented by *Little Rock* sailors. The idea was to get those in obvious need back to the ship before problems arose. On the few occasions when inebriated sailors were arrested by the Spanish gendarmes or the Guardia Civil, our boys came to understand that the shore patrol was a much better and safer bet.

Among the sites I was assigned to patrol in Barcelona was the main bullfighting ring in the Plaza de Toros. On our arrival at the amphitheater, the local Spanish police directed us to a seating area in the stands reserved for law enforcement. I was startled to find myself in the company of about twenty Guardia Civil members, several of whom were manning .30-caliber machine guns with an almost 360-degree field of fire! I wondered then and still wonder now what sort of calamity would have triggered machine gun fire into a crowd of spectators watching a bullfight.

A port visit to Valetta, Malta was also included in this swing. Although independent, Malta was still under the weighty tutelage of the British, but a nationalistic movement, led by Dom Mintoff, was causing problems for our British allies, who still maintained headquarters for the British Mediterranean Fleet and an important Royal Dockyard there.[6]

By June 1967, the logic of force reductions prevailed; the flag of the British Mediterranean Fleet commander was hauled down, and in Valetta, the Royal Navy Dockyards were subsequently transferred to the Maltese government. The sun

6 "Dom Mintoff, Malta's Political Giant Passes Away," *Times of Malta*, August 9, 2016.

had indeed finally set on this island fortress of the empire. With the British command of NATO naval forces terminated, the command was retitled Naval Forces Southern Europe (NAVSOUTH), headquartered in Naples under the command of an Italian admiral.

Although Malta had been strategically important to the British, it had also been and continued to be important to the United States as late as 1967. In the 1950s and into the 1960s, we had made good use of the Royal Navy Dockyards. We used Malta extensively as a base for our maritime patrol aircraft. Additionally, our carrier aircraft frequented several excellent bombing ranges, our marine battalion conducted amphibious landing exercises on isolated beaches, and we used the unpopulated islet of Filfla for live naval gunfire training.

These facilities were uniquely important for the combat readiness of our ships and aircraft squadrons. When I moved to the assistant fleet scheduling office in 1968, I was responsible for scheduling the visits and training of our ship in Maltese waters. I knew how important our access was. When the British left, pressure from the Mintoff government effectively limited our access to Malta and its hospitable and friendly public.

Before leaving my recollections on the Sixth Fleet's relationship to the British and the Royal Navy (RN) in the Mediterranean, another anecdote will illustrate the situation in 1967.

On our way to a port visit in Lisbon (from which we would sail hurriedly), the admiral and the flagship made a call in Gibraltar, then a Royal Crown colony. Our visit came several months before a referendum to determine the peninsula's political future: either continued British sovereignty, reversion to Spanish control, or a form of independence. The situation regarding Gibraltar's future was tense and most awkward for the United States. After all, the British were allies, and the Spanish government, though not a party to NATO, had an important bilateral basing agreement with the United States.[7]

As the ship entered the channel into the Port of Gibraltar, the *Little Rock* commenced a twenty-one-gun salute in honor of Her Majesty, the Queen of England. The salute was answered round for round by a battery at the British naval station. Amazingly, a Spanish saluting battery in Algeciras also began answering each round of our salute. So, in effect, we were taken as saluting both British and Spanish sovereigns. At the time, Franco's Spain was not reconciled to British rule in Gibraltar. The sailors manning the Spanish saluting battery meant to demonstrate that much to the visiting US admiral.

Later, another amusing incident occurred at a reception hosted by the British Flag Officer Gibraltar (FOG). I was seated at a table with the wife of Rear Admiral Michael Fell, RN, who was the FOG. At another table, COMSIXTHFLT, Vice Admiral William I. Martin, stood up for a traditional toast, at the conclusion of which he offered a joke. It was a mildly off-color story, which he attributed to a source in his hometown in Booger County, Missouri. He delivered it with an Ozark drawl, and his English was certainly not the King's English.

When the admiral sat down amid hushed laughter, Mrs. Fell turned to our table and remarked that it seemed "incredible" to her that someone from that "sort of background could accede to the command of the Sixth Fleet!" A somewhat inebriated member of our staff, Lieutenant Commander Maurice "Tex" Treiber, the flag secretary, retorted in his own heavy drawl, "Ma'am, that's why we fought y'all during our Revolution and again in 1812!" A silence ensued as the lieutenant commander's remarks carried well beyond our table.

---

7   The US-Spanish agreement, the 1953 Pact of Madrid, gave the United States access to four major bases in Spain: the Zaragoza, Torrejón, and Morón Air Bases and Rota Naval Base.

Only months after our return to our homeport in Gaeta, a series of crises would keep us at sea for the better part of 1967.

The first crisis was in reaction to the Greek coup in April 1967, which spawned multiple crises for the Sixth Fleet. On April 21, King Constantine was forced into exile by Colonel Papadopoulos and a group of rebellious Greek Army officers. The coup effectively ended the constitutional monarchy and suspended democratic rule in Greece. It was staged in reaction to concessions made by the monarchy to the Socialist government, which the military regarded as a prelude to the type of chaos Greece had suffered following the end of World War II. Of grave concern for the United States and the Sixth Fleet was the status and safety of US nuclear weapons in Greece, which in keeping with NATO agreements, were under "dual key." Practically speaking, they were now under Hellenic Army control.

At the same time the coup was underway in April 1967, the *Little Rock* was conducting a port visit in Lisbon, Portugal. While I was on watch in the Communication Center, a FLASH message was received from the Commander in Chief US Naval Forces Europe (CINCUSNAVEUR) in London, directing the admiral to get his flagship underway immediately and rendezvous with our carriers in the eastern Mediterranean. Interestingly, the flagship had made a protocol visit to Athens a few months before, and Admiral Martin had welcomed His Majesty for a visit and a briefing on the situation in the eastern Mediterranean.

The overarching concern conveyed in any number of messages to the Sixth Fleet commander from the US embassy in Athens and the State Department, which I handled while on watch, was the specter of a communist countercoup. In the anxious days following the takeover, *Little Rock* steamed south of the Peloponnese in anticipation of an ordered intervention to secure the US nuclear weapons at several Greek bases. In addition to these special weapons, there was also a more general concern for the safety of US bases and installations in Greece.

The Sixth Fleet, for example, relied on a chain of Naval Communication Stations (NAVCOMMSTAs) across the Mediterranean to provide high-frequency (HF) radio communications and effective command and control for a widely dispersed fleet of almost fifty ships. One such station was at Nea Makri near Marathon. Inasmuch as the fleet at the time relied exclusively on HF communications for long-haul traffic, the loss of NAVCOMMSTA Greece alone might have compromised fleet communications to a large extent. There was also the advance base and a NATO air facility at Souda Bay on the island of Crete. It is no exaggeration to state that both bases were nearly indispensable to support fleet operations in the eastern Mediterranean. Souda Bay also housed a large NATO fuel depot and an ammunition magazine where war reserve munitions were stocked.

Following direction from the London headquarters of Admiral John S. McCain in response to the Greek crisis, the fleet's two carrier task groups concentrated their operations in the Aegean Sea. In addition, the Amphibious Task Force (Task Forces 61/62) with its embarked Marine Battalion Landing Team moved to the vicinity of Greece. Those task forces were readied to secure nuclear weapons and evacuate US military personnel in case the situation deteriorated.

With the crisis abated and the security of our personnel, equipment, and facilities assured, the fleet retired.

But just as one emergency subsided, another replaced it. In May 1967, the month prior to the outbreak of the Arab–Israeli Six-Day War (also known as the June War), tensions in the eastern Mediterranean increased dramatically. A month earlier, first a French submarine and then an Israeli submarine had disappeared mysteriously while at sea in the Mediterranean. There was a concern that the Soviets acting on behalf of the Egyptians had sunk the Israeli and French subs; the cause of those incidents has never been adequately explained, but we know now that they were not related. Owing to the presence of Soviet submarines in the Mediterranean at the time, the Soviets were suspect.

In response to Jordan's closure of the Straits of Tiran to Israeli shipping on May 23, 1967, the United States concentrated the principal forces of the Sixth Fleet: the Sixth Fleet flagship was hurriedly deployed eastward to the waters off the Levant, where it rendezvoused with the USS *America* (CVA-66) and the USS *Saratoga* (CVA-60) task groups. Then came the announcement on May 30 that Jordan and Egypt had created an alliance in the form of a joint defense agreement, clearly aimed at Israel.

This crisis also marked the onset of close and continuous Soviet Navy surveillance of Sixth Fleet operations in the Mediterranean. On June 3, CINCUSNAVEUR informed COMSIXTHFLT that the Soviets had declared their intent to move twenty warships, including nine submarines, through the Bosporus into the Mediterranean. The same message instructed Admiral Martin (COMSIXTHFLT) to keep US ships and aircraft one hundred nautical miles from the coasts of Egypt, Syria, Israel, and Lebanon and twenty-five nautical miles from Cyprus. Since the presidency of Nasser, the Soviets had become a de facto ally of Egypt and Syria, partners in the United Arab Republic.

When crisis exploded into hostilities on June 5, intelligence received in our Communication Center aboard *Little Rock* confirmed that the Egyptian and Royal Jordanian Air Forces had been decimated by the Israeli Air Force in the first few hours of the war, while most of the Arab aircraft were still on the ground. Indeed, the results were so striking that the Egyptian government, citing Soviet intelligence, claimed that strike aircraft launched from the two US carriers had contributed to the Israeli aerial offensive. This was patently false, and the Soviets knew it.

While I was on watch as the communication watch officer, a radioman handed me a "flash" message from the Commander in Chief US European Command (USCINCEUR) in Stuttgart, directing CINCUSNAVEUR and COMSIXTHFLT to suspend all routine flight operations while maintaining a high state of alert. This was clearly motivated by the Egyptian claims of US attacks, even though the state of alert and the flight activity that we had conducted were intended to guard against hostilities directed at our ships. Consequently, flight operations from the carriers were stopped on June 6, and several Soviet warships took screening positions literally in the formations of both US carrier task groups.

Early in the morning of June 8, I assumed the watch in the Communication Center. Shortly thereafter, the bells began ringing on the sixty-words-per-minute teletype, which was connected to a dedicated direct communication link with CINCUSNAVEUR headquarters in London. The message, which was garbled by static interference on the HF radio circuit, was a FLASH-precedence operation order from the Joint Chiefs of Staff (JCS) in Washington. It directed COMSIXTHFLT to reposition the USS *Liberty* (AGTR-5), a communications intelligence ship, from her current position just outside Egyptian territorial waters to an operating area one hundred miles off the coast of Egypt—beyond implications that she was party to the conflict. That message had a date time group of 080110Z (8:10 a.m. Washington time).[8]

When I finally received a legible version of the message, I hurried two decks up to the ship's Flag Plot (the flagship's tactical and navigational control room). There, I handed the high-precedence

8 JCS Message DTG 080110Z Jun 67.

top-secret movement order to Commander Dick Slusser, the staff watch officer, telling him that I thought the admiral would want to see this message immediately, given its content. Cdr. Slusser told me that he would take care of matters and waved me off. I learned later that Cdr. Slusser had tried unsuccessfully to get the message to the assistant chief of staff for operations, Captain Robert Kasten, because Kasten was in a meeting regarding the restrictions on US aircraft operations discussed above.

While I was on watch again that afternoon, we received desperate voice reports from the *Liberty*. The transmissions were relayed to COMSIXTHFLT through the NAVCOMMSTA in Greece. The voice reports on the high command network (HICOM) described the attacks the lightly armed ship was under from hostile aircraft and motor torpedo boats. I called the staff watch officer in Flag Plot, who informed Adm. Martin. The admiral, his chief of staff, and four other captains then crowded the small space of radio central, where I was communicating on a relayed voice circuit with the *Liberty*. The admiral asked me to query the radioman calling regarding the identity of the attackers. We were all certain that it was the Egyptians. The response was startling: Some of the attacking aircraft had a blue-and-white Star of David under their wings, and the torpedo boats were flying the Israeli flag.

As the attacks continued, Adm. Martin ordered Rear Admiral Larry Geis, the carrier task force commander, to launch aircraft to protect *Liberty* and repel the aerial and torpedo attacks. Both carriers in Task Force 60 launched attack aircraft: F-4B *Phantoms* and A-4C *Skyhawks* from the *America* and A-1D *Skyraiders* from the *Saratoga*.

I distinctly remember the sound of the general quarters alarm on the *Little Rock* shortly thereafter. I later learned that the bridge watch was reacting to what appeared to be preparation for conflict with the Soviet ships in the midst of our formations. Alarms on the Soviet ships had apparently sounded when the aircraft were launched from our carriers; the ships were observed to then accelerate to high speed, and it appeared that Soviet sailors were scurrying to battle stations.

Before the defending aircraft could arrive on the scene of the attacks on the *Liberty*, the Israeli government transmitted "abject apologies," insisting that the attacks were a case of mistaken identity. The responding aircraft were therefore recalled at the direction of the JCS.

The message from CINCUSNAVEUR to move *Liberty* had not come to Admiral Martin's attention until almost 11:00 a.m. local. As a result, the direction was not received by that ship until after the Israeli attacks.[9] I remember thinking that had the message been successfully delivered to the admiral earlier, he would certainly have ordered the ship to move away immediately. Alas, had the message ordering *Liberty* to move been processed earlier, the disaster that befell the ship and the loss of some thirty-nine sailors might have been avoided.

The *Little Rock* came to flank speed after the attack and rendezvoused with the stricken ship early in the morning of June 9. It was quite a sight and a testament to the fury of the attack the lightly armed ship had sustained. There were hundreds of shell marks around the bridge area and large gaping holes on her beam that were open to the sea. Helicopters and small boats began transferring the one hundred critically wounded sailors to the *America*, *Saratoga*, and *Little Rock* sick bays.

The incident is still troubling to me, given the sequence of events and the content of the messages I had been privy to in the days and hours before and during the Six-Day War. Although Israel was subsequently absolved of responsibility for

9   COMSIXTHFLT Message DTG 080917Z Jun 67.

a premeditated attack on a US ship, many—myself included—
were not convinced by the offered explanation that it was a case
of mistaken identity. One conjectured motive is that an Israeli
attack on a US ship might have been attributed to Egypt, resulting in US retaliation against that country. It is still difficult to
accept that, given the state of Israeli military intelligence and the
prominently displayed "holiday" ensign (an oversized American
flag) flown by the *Liberty*, the attacking aircraft, and especially
the attacking torpedo boats, did not recognize their quarry.

In the year following the June War, new crises in the Levant
repeated as the tense cease-fire took tenuous hold and as the
Israelis consolidated their gains in the Sinai, on the Golan Heights,
on the West Bank, and in Jerusalem proper. The Soviets, for their
part, extended their presence and activities in Egypt and Syria
following the Six-Day War.

Among the most serious developments for the Sixth Fleet was
the emergence of the Fifth Eskadra, the Soviet Mediterranean
squadron. Drawing on logistical support from the Soviet Black
Sea Fleet and now using facilities in Egypt and Syria in addition
to those in the Crimea, the Soviet Eskadra and aerial activity
grew apace. The causal connection between the increased Soviet
presence and Israel's spectacular victory over its Arab enemies,
who were already aligned with the Soviet Union, was confirmed
in late 1967 by the first deputy commander of the Soviet Navy,
Admiral of the Fleet Kazatonov, who claimed that Soviet warships
entered the Mediterranean to consolidate international peace
and security in conformity with the interest of the Arab States
who are victims of Israeli aggression.

Certainly, following the June War, and long after my departure from the *Little Rock* in August 1968, the ubiquitous and
continuous Soviet naval threat in our Mediterranean (*mare
nostrum*) became a preoccupation. Some twenty to fifty Soviet

warships and submarines routinely shadowed our carrier task groups in the Mediterranean. Soviet ships visited Alexandria and Port Said in Egypt and Latakia in Syria.

To make a serious point, when the Israelis staged a maneuvering exercise in the Sinai Peninsula in October 1967, a Soviet spokesman announced preemptively that Soviet forces would repel any attacks on their naval units in Port Said. Our aircraft carriers were routinely overflown by TU-95 *Bear* aircraft based in the Crimea, and by TU-16 *Badger* bombers and MiGs (piloted by Soviet crews) flying from bases in Egypt. In response, the Sixth Fleet was on a near-combat footing and all ships were required to maintain their crews in Readiness Condition III when operating east of the Malta-Messina-Taranto line. Perceptions of the severity of the Soviet threat were such that our ships manned antiaircraft weapons even when conducting port visits or while at anchorages in the eastern Mediterranean.

The US reaction to the greatly expanded activity of the Soviet Union was particularly sharp. Our position was that the Soviet deployments were "destabilizing" and dangerous because the commingling with our ships and the routine harassment of US carriers conducting flight operations might spark confrontations.[10] Moreover, the Soviet presence was meant to signal support of the revanchist and confrontational Arab states committed to the destruction of Israel. (After the June War, the United States began describing Israel as an "ally" while simultaneously declaring that the security of Israel had become a "vital" interest for the United States.)

Little Rock remained in the Aegean Sea for more than a month following the Six-Day War. In September, the flagship

10 Admiral W. I. Martin, COMSIXTHFLT, interview with *Rome Daily American*, July 27, 1967. The admiral's strident reaction to expanded Soviet naval activity in the Mediterranean came to the attention of the State Department. Subsequently, it earned him and his public affairs officer a rebuke from his superiors.

participated in Display Determination, a major NATO exercise in the Aegean Sea; following those operations, we sailed for Istanbul, Turkey for a protocol visit by the fleet commander.

A memorable incident occurred there on October 7 at the fleet landing near the Dolmabahçe Palace, where sailors on liberty disembarked from tenders. A large and unruly group of hundreds of rock-throwing Turkish students gathered to confront the sailors at the landing, resulting in several injuries. Although order was restored by scores of Turkish gendarmes, the incident was widely publicized, and the port visit was shortened as a precaution.

The immediate assumption was that this was a reaction to US involvement in the Arab–Israeli War. However, according to an expert on Turkish foreign policy, the demonstration was also a result of a significant downturn in US-Turkish relations in connection with the smoldering Cyprus dispute between Greece and Turkey.[11] The United States had tried to mediate the crisis in 1964 without appearing to favor either of our NATO allies. However, during that mediation effort, President Lyndon Johnson had sent a letter to the Turkish president, warning that should Turkey intervene militarily to protect the Turkish Cypriot community, the country's continued membership in the NATO alliance would become problematic. The Turks had reacted badly to the implied threat, which was highly publicized at the time and continued to be brought up at times by the Turkish press, including shortly before *Little Rock*'s arrival.

The turbulent political and military environment in the Mediterranean for most of 1967 was fascinating for a student of international affairs and Soviet foreign policy. My duties in the communications department had provided detailed information

11 George S. Harris, *Troubled Alliance: Turkish-American Problems in Historical Perspective, 1945–1971* (Washington, DC: AEI-Hoover Policy Studies, 1972), 169–171.

on the critical developments and the navy's response thereto. To my great delight, I was invited to join the operations division of Adm. Martin's staff in January 1968. I would remain officially a member of ship's company, detailed to the admiral's staff.

Little Rock's commanding officer (CO), Captain John J. Mitchell ("Black Jack" seemed a fitting nickname given his brusque manner and the strict discipline he dispensed), cautioned me that a move to the admiral's staff was not a good choice if I contemplated a career as an unrestricted line officer. In contrast, as my CO, he could improve my prospects on that career trajectory. Mitchell called me into his cabin and said, "You know you could remain a full member of ship's company, stand bridge watches, and take a collateral assignment as the ship's intelligence officer." I understood that my loyalty was being tested. I acknowledged his observations politely and took my leave.

As the admiral's chief of staff had explained to me, one of the principal reasons Adm. Martin wanted me to join his staff was my Russian-language ability. And because I was contemplating my next assignment as an intelligence officer in the restricted line, the opportunities it offered were preferable to remaining a member of ship's company aboard *Little Rock*. My decision to move was made easier because I knew that the chief of staff would overcome any opposition from Captain Mitchell to my transfer. I accepted the new post.

In April 1968, not long after I joined Adm. Martin's staff, a dramatic incident, witnessed by virtually every member of the staff and much of *Little Rock*'s crew, led to Capt. Mitchell's relief as CO of the flagship. Adm. Martin had received a request from a German news network requesting permission to film Sixth Fleet carrier flight operations. Permission was granted, and the film team embarked aboard *Little Rock*, which was steaming in company with the carrier *Saratoga*. As many of us watched from the signal bridge, the ship was ordered to take a station three hundred yards on the port (left) beam of the carrier while she launched and recovered aircraft. I remember distinctly hearing the flagship order a speed of thirty knots when in her assigned station, just as the carrier began launching aircraft.

With the launch complete, *Saratoga* adjusted her course to port about ten degrees to optimize the wind over the deck as she began recovering aircraft. The change was apparently *not* signaled to **Little Rock**, which continued steaming at thirty knots on the previously signaled course. What happened next was nearly tragic.

Given the speed of both ships and the difference in the courses they were steering, the distance between them closed suddenly to less than one hundred yards and a collision appeared imminent. The camera crew dropped their equipment. Loud voices were heard on **Little Rock**'s bridge, and in what seemed like an instant, the cruiser was in a hard turn to starboard, crossing the carrier's bow. The ships did touch very briefly as the *Saratoga*'s bow knocked a fitting off the stern of the cruiser.

Those of us on the signal bridge that afternoon will never forget the sight of the enormous bow of the *Saratoga* passing over **Little Rock**'s superstructure as she heeled heavily to port while at maximum speed. There were at least a dozen senior officers on the signal bridge that afternoon, collectively representing many years at sea; several had commanded their own ships. As I glanced around, all were on the deck holding on to the rail for dear life. I followed suit! The risk that can befall a ship maneuvering around an aircraft carrier was a lesson I never forgot. In this instance, stopping the cruiser or turning to port might have been a prudent reaction.

My first assignment in the surface operations division of the admiral's staff required a transfer by helicopter to the USS

America (CVA-66). I was to serve as an interpreter in the event the AGI Soviet trawler[12] shadowing the carrier to collect intelligence attempted to impede operations during the impending celebration of the twentieth anniversary of the establishment of the Sixth Fleet. On several occasions, the AGI did maneuver precariously, and I communicated with the Soviet ship via very-high-frequency (VHF) radio. I received no reply each time, and the ship continued to harass *America*, crossing her bow while she was launching and recovering aircraft. Evasive maneuvers were successful, but the close calls could be measured in only tens of yards. I was disappointed that my mission to warn the ship had been such an abject failure.

Soviet interference with carrier flight operations had become almost routine by this time, and we expected a Soviet combatant to join our tactical formations on a regular basis. In fact, we often remarked with amazement that the intruders would execute coded tactical maneuvering signals with such precision. There was little doubt that our putative enemy had studied our operations and knew just when and how to interfere.

In addition to my normal duties, I prepared several point papers for the admiral on subjects such as the Montreux Convention, governing passage through the Turkish Straits and its applicability to US warship transits. On one occasion, in response to a discussion about the feasibility of conducting port visits in the Black Sea beyond those we made routinely to Turkey, I wrote a paper explaining why communist Romania might welcome a visit from ships from the Sixth Fleet.

Since the early 1960s, Romania had been treated as the black sheep of the Warsaw Pact. The Soviets were extremely critical of the relations Romania had established with several NATO European nations and, more alarmingly, with the People's

12 AGI was the US Navy's official designation of such ships as Auxiliary, General Intelligence.

Republic of China! My paper explained that Romania had earned the wrath of Soviet leaders for having left the Soviet-led commercial alliance COMECON and for raising new "issues" regarding Soviet-Romanian frontiers. I wrote that the stated logic for potential US visits to Romania might be as a response to the Soviet Navy's entry into the Mediterranean and the visits of Soviet ships to Syrian and Egyptian ports after the Six-Day War. In other words, we in turn could begin challenging the Soviets by operating and conducting ship visits to Romanian ports in their backyard, the Black Sea. The admiral wrote me a nice note remarking that he had enjoyed my point paper and that he would work with the State Department to arrange a ship visit to Romania.

These experiences in applying my academic interests and receiving encouragement from my seniors rekindled an interest in another goal: further graduate schooling in political science and economics. I recognized that higher education and advanced degrees enhanced credibility in policy-making circles. In September 1968, with a good departure fitness report from the chief of staff, I left Gaeta and reported to Naval Intelligence Headquarters in early September 1968.

CHAPTER 2

LEARNING WHILE OPERATING IN THE PACIFIC

Operations Officer, USS *Knox* (DE-1052)

The Office of Naval Intelligence (ONI) proved an interesting assignment, particularly in the frantic activities of my section following North Korea's seizure of the USS *Pueblo* and the imprisonment of her crew. (We did not realize at the time how damaging the loss of cryptographic machines would be if someone with current codes were to provide them to the Soviet Union, an ally of North Korea. The Walker spy scandal, years later, confirmed how serious the loss of *Pueblo* was for our national security.)[13]

ONI, however, was the consummate military bureaucracy, with responsibility to advise and analyze but never to exercise command of operating forces. As I previously discussed, my planned one-year stint at ONI was foreshortened because I decided to opt instead for a career as an unrestricted line officer

---

13 The seizure of *Pueblo* and its cryptographic equipment provided North Korea with the hardware necessary to process encrypted telegraphy. The transfer of the keying material by the Walkers provided the requisite software.

and as a destroyerman; the conversations with Captain Sackett had opened my eyes to how much more attractive a career with a command opportunity would be.

I also recall my many discussions with a mentor on the Sixth Fleet staff, Commander Rudy Daus.[14] Rudy had risen to command of a destroyer escort as a young lieutenant commander. He would often describe the exhilarating challenges and opportunities for officers in destroyers as we watched ships in our task group maneuvering to station or refueling alongside fleet oilers.

In July 1969, less than ten months after my arrival in Washington, my young family and I packed up and moved to Newport, Rhode Island to prepare for my destroyer training at the Naval Destroyer School (DesTech).

In my career, I had not seen service on a destroyer, which was a basic requirement for course entry; I therefore needed to qualify as an Officer of the Deck, Fleet Operations (OODF) in destroyers before I could enroll. Accordingly, I checked into the school six months ahead of the start of the course scheduled to begin January 1970.

I was assigned to destroyers deploying to the Mediterranean in order to earn my qualification. I served in two *Gearing*-class destroyers, the USS *Stickell* (DD-888) and the USS *Charles H. Roan* (DD-853) from early August until just before Christmas. I stood watches in both ships and served as the Combat Information Center (CIC) officer during characteristically high-tempo Sixth Fleet operations. It was a fast-paced deployment, and I came home to Newport with my OODF letter, ready for the challenges ahead.

Destroyer School (since renamed Surface Warfare Officers School Command) provided a six-month course of instruction

---

14 Rudy has written a fascinating autobiography; see Rudolph Halouk Daus, *The Crescent Odyssey* (Bloomington, IN: Universe, 2010).

that, by 1970, had become a prerequisite for duty as any destroyer department head. Before completing the course, each student filled out a preference card indicating his preferences. The exact job, the type of ship, and the homeport assigned after graduation were decided, however, by the Bureau of Naval Personnel (BuPers), based on class standing. The result was intense, high-pressure competition among ninety lieutenants (and several lieutenant commanders) for high marks.

I suppose that it was because my time at sea in destroyers was considerably less than that of classmates, on enrollment I was marked as a "graduation risk." To improve my prospects, I was assigned a tutor, Commander Merget, the weapons department head. A nice, soft-spoken officer, he was to mentor me and help me with the rigors of the courses.

I applied myself diligently, studied hard, and finished second in my class. Most gratifying was election by my classmates to win the Admiral Arleigh Burke Leadership Award. (Admiral Burke was the storied commander of Destroyer Squadron [DESRON] 23, the "Little Beavers," which was the only DESRON of World War II to be awarded a group Presidential Unit Citation.) Hard work had paid off.

My transfer orders from BuPers reflected my first choice of jobs at graduation (operations), in my preferred class of ships (the new *Knox*-class DEs), in my chosen homeport: Pearl Harbor, Hawaii.

* * *

When I reported aboard USS *Knox* (DE-1052) in July 1970, it was only two months before the ship was scheduled to deploy to the western Pacific on her maiden voyage, which would include combat operations in Southeast Asia. Our ship was the first in a new class of destroyer escorts, so we were going to demonstrate her fitness for duties assigned! As this would be her first deployment, the challenges were clear, and there was a lot of work to do before we sailed.

On arrival, I recall being impressed that everything on the ship appeared new. Like a new car, the paint was fresh throughout, the accommodations were spacious for all hands (particularly when compared the World War II ships to which I had been assigned for OODF qualification), and everything seemed to work as designed. I was also impressed with our crew. The sailors—many of whom had been specially selected for duty in a new construction ship—seemed motivated and determined to make their ship deserving of her exalted status as a class leader. The chief petty officers were another important group, and I was similarly impressed with the breadth of their technical and leadership experience.

Our officer complement, comprising twenty young men of varied experiences and backgrounds, included a chief engineer from Massachusetts who was a Harvard alumnus, and a weapons officer from rural West Virginia who had attended a small teacher's college. My roommate on the upper level of "officers' country" was a Dartmouth graduate whose father had served in destroyers in World War II and was now the president of Hormel, the giant food company in the Midwest. I digress to note that since the end of the draft, constructive diversity—measured by educational, geographic, and socioeconomic attributes—of our young officers has declined. The wardroom in *Knox* in 1970 was a microcosm of the best candidates the country could produce. For example, our executive officer (XO), Lieutenant Commander Chris Nelson, was a graduate of the University of Colorado and a mining engineer with remarkable leadership skills.

The ship's design was distinguished by a single gun (other destroyers mounted two guns) and only one-half of the propulsion plant characteristic of ships of this size, 4,100 tons. On the other hand, and to our advantage, we carried the most sophisticated anti-submarine warfare (ASW) sensor afloat, the SQS-26CX sonar!

To my chagrin, however, although we were to deploy to the war zone, we lacked the navy's newest electronic warfare (EW) system designed to spoof incoming enemy cruise missiles, the AN-ULQ-6C. Not content to wait until the next regular overhaul to have it installed, I discussed a plan with my commanding officer (CO), Commander Estel W. Hays, to have the equipment delivered to us before we sailed. I argued that it might be installed during several maintenance periods scheduled at the Ship Repair Facility in Subic Bay, the Philippines. I'd already confirmed that the facility was up to the task and that we were already scheduled to spend a considerable amount of time there in the coming six months.

Captain Hays was a "by-the-book" type of naval officer. A Naval Academy graduate and an experienced Washington hand, he understood and accepted the bureaucratic processes required to effect changes in a ship's armament. His subspecialty was weapons engineering. The captain agreed that I should proceed, but he cautioned that it would be a "long shot," given the small amount of time that remained before we sailed. There was also the attitude of the responsible officers at the Type Commander Headquarters in San Diego. He said, "Go ahead and try to change their minds, but you will hit a brick wall when you talk to the staff in San Diego. They always know better."

After hours on the phone with literally a dozen different officers in different bureaus, I wore them down, and within a week—literally the day before we sailed to the western Pacific—I was happy to meet the arrival of the requested equipment on the pier at Naval Station Pearl Harbor. My first success as a department head, however, awaited a successful installation in the Philippines and the systems tests that followed.

* * *

The deployment to the western Pacific began with a long voyage to New Zealand via American Samoa in the company of only one other destroyer, the USS *Hamner* (DD-718). The refueling stop in Pago Pago, the capital of American Samoa, was memorable, both socially and operationally. The island's population had not seen many visits by warships since World War II and the welcome we received, with dancers greeting us and a band playing on the pier, was friendly and most impressive. We stopped there only overnight to refuel after the long transit from Pearl Harbor. The refueling operation featured taking NSFO (black oil) by gravity feed from a tank high on a hill above the port. The operation, which normally took a few hours when transferred by pumps, took the entire day. We left Samoa with full tanks destined for New Zealand.

En route to New Zealand, we participated in LONGEX (70), an ASW exercise organized by the Royal New Zealand Navy, involving destroyers from the United Kingdom, Canada, Australia, the United States, and of course, New Zealand. The Royal Australian Navy provided the submarine opposition in the form of two diesel electric boats. We aboard *Knox* had the superior ASW equipment, and I remember how proud we were that we made most of the detections with the new low-frequency sonar mounted in the bow of our ship. Another takeaway from this exercise was how well the group of ships operated together using NATO procedures. Although the Australians and New Zealanders were not members of the Atlantic alliance, they had Allied code books and the tactical publications that surface ships and aircrafts used to prosecute submarines. I assume that we or the British had provided them the materials.

Our visit to Auckland with all the other destroyers was a good opportunity to socialize and compare notes with junior officers of the other English-speaking navies. One event organized by our Kiwi hosts was a bus tour of the New Zealand wine industry, which was in its infancy in 1970. On the long bus ride and after too much sampling of the local vintages, we had a humorous and friendly allied exchange. Several RN officers broke out with a spirited rendition of "Britannia Rules the Waves," the RN's fight song. The rest of us listened to several verses without joining the chorus. After a quick conversation with the others, I suggested a song that might be a fitting sequel. Following a quick lesson from the USN group, we and our fellow Canadian, Australian, and "Kiwi" officers chimed in on a verse from Johnny Horton's hit, "Battle of New Orleans," which celebrated Andrew Jackson's routing of the British Army in 1814. The Americans provided most of the lyrics, but all joined in the refrain. Our British colleagues seemed rather surprised that these citizens of the Commonwealth would join Yankee "rebels" in this retort.

From New Zealand, we sailed north to our first visit in the Philippines, transiting the famous San Bernardino Strait, where US and allied destroyers had fought the Imperial Japanese Navy a quarter of a century before. On arrival in Subic Bay, we began the installation of the EW suite received earlier. The installation was completed in record time and tests were successful.

Before leaving the Philippines, we were tasked with participating in a ceremony celebrating the liberation of this island in the

Philippines in the small town of Hinobaan, located on Asia Bay not far from Bacolod, the capital city of the province of Negros Occidental. The ship could not enter port, so we anchored and the villagers transported us onto a beach at the edge of the village in bamboo rafts made especially for the occasion. It was a sight to behold as young, brawny Filipinos swam while pulling four bamboo barges laden with officers and men in bright white uniforms. The festivities ashore included pig roasts in open pits and native dancers stepping agilely between long bamboo poles that were clacked together synchronously with accompanying native music. A main attraction was a beauty contest judged by members of our ship, including yours truly.

In late November 1970, while in Subic Bay, we received orders to hurry "buttoning up" our engineering plant to join the USS *Hancock* (CVA-19) task group. Transiting at high speed and under cover of night and under strict emission control, we were instructed to stop transmitting radars and to secure transmitting on all high-frequency (HF) circuits. The mission was classified "Secret"; we soon learned it was to provide cover for the attempt to liberate US POWs from the Son Tai Camp in North Vietnam. Alas, the attempt failed: the camp had been evacuated hours before the inserted army force could complete the assault and liberate the prisoners.

* * *

The ship headed off to war in the Gulf of Tonkin. This was the first deployment for all the officers in our wardroom with the exception of the captain. We spent some time reflecting on the missions we might be assigned and the risks we might encounter.

On balance, we were all confident that we and *Knox* were up to the tasks that lay ahead—we because of the training we had received, and the ship because of her condition and readiness.

Arriving in the Gulf of Tonkin, I had my first opportunity to conn (control the engines and the heading of the ship) the *Knox*, alongside a huge (800 foot) replenishment ship, the USS *Camden* (AOE-2). Thankfully, my training in the Mediterranean allowed me to make a good first approach on the *Camden*, and I succeeded despite heavy seas in keeping our ship alongside at the prescribed distance while we took on fuel and transferred stores. In the early '70s, all officers of the deck (OODs) in destroyers were required to keep a log of their watches and evolutions at sea, including time at the helm during replenishments. Captains of surface combatants in the Pacific Fleet were required to annotate and grade the performance of their bridge watch officers. After this particularly challenging evolution, I was encouraged by a congratulatory entry in my own logbook from the captain.[15]

In the Gulf of Tonkin, we had a ringside seat to the navy's participation in operation Rolling Thunder, the aerial bombardment of North Vietnam. As a plane guard destroyer for many days, we took station 1,500 yards astern of carriers operating on Yankee Station in the northern Gulf of Tonkin, following the carriers to be in position to rescue pilots in damaged aircraft. In awe, we watched thousands of launches and recoveries of strike, fighter, and reconnaissance aircraft, including the A-4 *Skyhawk*, the A-6 *Intruder*, the A7 *Corsair II*, the F-4B *Phantom*, the F-8B *Crusader*, the RA-5C *Vigilante*, and the A-3 *Skywarrior*. Every watch on the bridge featured an airshow.

---

15 This grading of seamanship evolutions was a useful and instructive practice that lapsed in the late '70s. After recent collisions involving destroyers in the Pacific Fleet, the log has been reinstated.

Especially poignant were the recoveries of damaged aircraft hit by flak and missiles while over North Vietnam. On many occasions, we scrambled to a "ditching" site to recover an air-crew that had ejected from a damaged airplane. On most of these occasions, we were outhustled by the carrier's "angel," the SH-3 *Sea King* rescue helicopter, but there was one incident in which we recovered the crew of an A-4C *Skyhawk*. Thankfully, the pilot, though obviously shaken, was not seriously injured.

When not in a plane guard station behind a carrier, we were assigned as an escort destroyer in a search-and-rescue station, designated North SAR, just east of the North Vietnamese port of Haiphong. There, we provided gun cover for the ship designated to operate rescue helicopters in the northern gulf. The North SAR picket ship[16] was a guided-missile ship, usually a frigate (DLG; later reclassified as cruisers), also tasked with intercepting any enemy aircraft in hot pursuit of our egressing strike aircraft. That ship, and our ship as escort, also provided vectored air intercept control for navy fighters in the Barrier Combat Air Patrol Stations just off the coast of North Vietnam.

Those stints on the North SAR station were never boring as we scoured our radar scopes and EW screens for enemy PT boats, threatening flights of MiG aircraft over North Vietnam and the occasional trawler that intelligence sources told us was carrying weapons bound for the Vietcong in South Vietnam.

One night in February 1971, having been replaced by another destroyer, on the North SAR station, we took up surveillance of a trawler leaving Haiphong. That particular trawler had been observed loading weapons and munitions from a pier adjacent to one used by Soviet ships. We waited for her to leave port and

---

16 A picket ship is radar equipped and used to increase the radar detection range around a naval force to protect it from surprise attack, typically from the air.

then followed her for three days out of visual range. We reported her position frequently to "Market Time," the command responsible for surveillance and interdiction of these ships supplying the Vietcong. When the trawler crossed into South Vietnamese territorial waters, she was attacked by several of our gunboats assigned to the command. We later learned that the trawler had been destroyed and the crew decimated.

While in the northern gulf and abeam of the demilitarized zone (DMZ) after dark, we could see the headlights of North Vietnamese truck convoys rolling south along the coastal highway known as Highway One. When our aircraft were actively bombing the north and our ships were bombarding the coast, the headlights seemed to extinguish at the DMZ. But when Washington ordered a bombing halt in 1970 to advance prospects for peace, the stream of traffic from the north was visible well into South Vietnam. This underlined another of the peculiar ironies of this war.

Another situation provided more irony. Owing to the perceived risk of escalation involving the USSR or China, the Cold War rules of engagement (ROE) had a major impact on our efforts in Vietnam. This was the case where we allowed hundreds of Soviet and Chinese cargo ships transiting the Gulf of Tonkin to deliver support to North Vietnam through the principal port of Haiphong. I was not the only one who wondered why we allowed these ships laden with supplies, fuel, weapons, and ammunition to transit right under our noses. We all understood that those cargo ships were providing significant war support to the North Vietnamese and the Vietcong in the south. Much later, in the final days of the war, we finally mined the approaches to Haiphong Harbor and successfully turned back Soviet and

Chinese Communist shipping bound for North Vietnam.[17] It remains a mystery why we didn't take this preventive action much earlier in the war, when it might have made a difference.

* * *

After departing the combat zone in the early spring of 1971, we escorted the aircraft carrier USS *Ranger* (CVA-61) to the Sea of Japan. While there, we made a port call at the large Japanese naval base at Yokosuka. This city happened to be close to where my father had been stationed and my family had lived in the mid-'50s. The call afforded me an opportunity to visit my boyhood haunts. I took several days of leave to visit Yokohama American High School and the complex of shops and clubs I had frequented thirteen years before. I also took a taxi to Yamashita-Cho, where the American consulate and our residence had been located, only to discover, to my great disappointment, that the consulate had closed and the building—a quarter-size replica of the White House that the Japanese had built to thank us for our help following the Kanto Plains earthquake in 1923—had been razed!

* * *

We left Yokosuka in early April 1971 in company with the USS *Chicago* (CG-11), bound for our respective homeports. About

---

17 On the dubious rules of engagement bearing on shipping bound for Haiphong Harbor, see John Nichols and Barret Tillman, *On Yankee Station* (Annapolis, MD: Naval Institute Press, 1987), 19–21.

three days west of Pearl Harbor, *Knox* suffered a major calamity: a main space fire, a conflagration fed by fuel, which engulfed the ship's only fire room. The fire had ignited because the "oil king," a first-class boiler technician responsible for transferring fuel from a storage tank in the after part of the ship to a service tank in the fire room, had left a sounding tube open, not replacing the cap.

The circumstances that led to the fire deserve explanation.

Our transit commander, the admiral aboard *Chicago*, had ordered a speed of advance (SOA) of seventeen knots for the trip home. The chief engineer and I had calculated that transiting at that speed we could arrive in Pearl Harbor with 20 percent fuel. Seventeen knots was also the maximum speed that we could maintain on a single boiler; *Knox* was capable of speeds of up to twenty-eight knots, but fuel consumption surged exponentially if we brought the second boiler on line. While in transit, we noticed that in fact *Chicago* was making more than the ordered seventeen knots at times, and we routinely had to light off the second boiler to keep from falling out of our assigned station, which was within visual range of *Chicago*. Those speed excursions (known in the fleet as "going home turns") caused us to consume fuel much faster than in our original calculations.

Rather than request a slower speed and thus conserve fuel, the captain decided to augment the propulsion fuel with aviation fuel (JP-5) that we had in a storage tank in the after part of the ship. He reasoned that by doing this, we might not need to slow the group transit and at the same time we would have enough fuel to make our homeport. The transfer of fuel *was* theoretically feasible because according to our manuals, it was possible to adjust the fuel pumps and the burners on the boiler fronts to use JP-5 if necessary.

The problem with this approach was that the specific gravity of the black oil, the propulsion fuel normally used to fire the boilers, was significantly higher than that of the JP-5 fuel that we proposed to transfer to the service tank in the fire room. *But the gauges to monitor tank fill levels were calibrated for NSFO, not JP-5.*

Per the captain's instructions, the oil king began the process. While sounding, or measuring, the service tank as the lighter fuel was being transferred into it, the oil king left the cap off the tank's sounding tube while he went to the adjacent auxiliary room to read the gauges for the approximate fuel level in the tank.

The disaster occurred when the service tank became completely full with JP-5, but the gauges that the oil king was reading in the next room indicated that it was only half full. Before he could catch his error, the pressurized JP-5 shot out of the sounding tube onto a nest of hot steam valves, and the inevitable happened. The fire room was ablaze until the electrical system tripped off the line and the electric pumps were disabled following the loss of power.

General quarters were sounded, with the OOD announcing "Fire, fire, fire in the fire room!" over the ship's public address system. We scrambled to our battle stations as we all had been trained. Black smoke engulfed the entire ship as the intakes for our ventilation fans recirculated smoke spewing from the engine room throughout the ship. Miraculously, no one was seriously injured, although there were several smoke inhalation casualties in the repair party that fought the fire.

After that, *Knox* was dead in the water, unable to operate. After receiving our distress call, *Chicago* slowed, reversed course, and after several harrowing hours in heavy seas, we were taken in tow by the larger ship for two days. When we were one day out of Pearl Harbor, the tow was transferred to an ocean-going fleet tug and the *Chicago* left us, bound for her homeport in San Diego. To the credit of our chief engineer, Lieutenant (later Captain) John Heufelder, we restored the fire room sufficiently to operate undamaged equipment, just in time to cast off the ignominious tow and enter our homeport on our own steam in view of our welcoming families and a band celebrating our return! It had been quite a scare.

Several changes were directed as a result of our casualty. The navy removed all aluminum catwalks from engineering spaces in all ships because ours had been burned into powder. Strict instructions in the form of lessons learned were provided to other ships of the *Knox* class regarding procedures to be followed when transferring fuel. The number of oxygen-breathing apparatus in the class was doubled.

Owing to procedural oversights in the formal investigation process that followed, no punishments were administered. The fire had taken a toll on our ship, as the engineering spaces were dirty and damaged. We spent the next two months in the Pearl Harbor Naval Shipyard engaged in repairs to the engineering plant in readiness for our next deployment, which was only six months away.

* * *

The first half of my second and last deployment to the combat zone aboard *Knox* featured almost continuous operations in the Gulf of Tonkin: as a plane guard destroyer, and on the "gunline" in South Vietnam providing naval gunfire support (NGFS) to marine units fighting in the northern part of South Vietnam (the I Corps Tactical Zone) and to army units engaged with the enemy to the south (the II Corps Tactical Zone). We maintained a brisk operating pace of forty to sixty days in a combat zone, followed by rest and repair stints at the naval base in Subic Bay. Between combat missions, we were afforded short R&R visits to Kaohsiung, Taiwan and a memorable Christmas visit to Hong Kong.

One humorous incident that befell us while on the gunline illustrated the informality that characterized relations between ourselves and the army units we were supporting. One evening just before dusk, our fire mission completed for the day, we were steaming off the coast preparing to replenish gun ammunition from a supply ship during the night. I was the OOD when a call came from the after lookout reporting a helicopter inbound to our ship. I was incredulous. I called the lookout on the phone and said, "Wave him off!" The problems I faced were several: our flight deck was not certified to land manned helicopters, there was no fire party on station, and we did not have the requisite lights to guide the pilots. Never mind, the winds were acceptable and two intrepid army warrant officers who had been directing our gunfire attempted to land their Bell UH-1 *Iroquois* (Huey) helicopter on our deck!

When questioned, they declared they had an inflight emergency when a chip light indicated problems in the tail rotor transmission. Captain Hays, who had hurried to the bridge when I called to announce the attempted landing, was perplexed. He asked the pilots why they were attempting to land on an uncertified deck. Their reply was that after a check of the filters in the transmission oil and a helping of dinner in the wardroom, they would continue to their base, a few miles inland. The sun had set well before the Huey lifted off our deck. The captain decided not to report this incident, leaving matters for the army chain of command.

* * *

In the middle of that second deployment, we were diverted from the combat zone to make a protocol visit to Colombo, Ceylon (now Sri Lanka). It was a very long journey from the base in Subic Bay, through the Straits of Malacca, and across one-half the width of the Indian Ocean. The stated purpose of our visit was to show the flag there because there had not been a visit by an American warship to Colombo for many years. Apparently, the embassy in Ceylon and the State Department had pressed the navy to conduct a ship visit and to show the flag.

Colombo was an interesting port of call. The vestiges of the British colonial period are a prominent memory. While touring the city, a group of us stared in amazement at an enormous, oversized statue of Queen Victoria, in a garden overgrown with weeds, facing what had been the British governor general's palatial home. Sadly, the home and the statue had not been maintained by the government of Ceylon, whose appreciation for their history as a British colony was not apparent.

While in Colombo, a surprising development caused us to sortie quickly and to begin a fast transit to the Maldive Islands, five hundred miles away. It was not explained as to why we had embarked the deputy chief of mission (DCM) at the US embassy in Colombo or that his presence aboard was the reason for this sudden tasking. In addition to his duties in Ceylon, the DCM also served as the US diplomatic representative to the Republic of Maldives. We learned that whenever the DCM traveled to Male, the republic's capital, he had to go by sea because there were no suitable air services to the island at that time. Although a US warship was not his usual means of transportation, this mission was urgent and we were available.

Our transit was not without challenges. First, there was the question of fuel endurance, which limited the speed we could make on one boiler, much to the chagrin of the DCM. The second had to do with navigation. As we studied our charts and the navigable approaches to the island, we discovered that the soundings on the applicable chart were limited to a single set of depth observations that had been submitted to the Navy Hydrographic Office following a transit by the USS *Vincennes* (CA-44) in 1937.

Strictly speaking, the protocols in use at the time in the Pacific Fleet had the navigator, typically a junior officer, reporting to the XO responsible for safe navigation. As Captain Hays saw things, as the *Knox*'s operations officer, I shared responsibility with the navigator for the safe navigation of the ship.

After researching the sailing directions with the navigator, I became keenly interested in what aids to navigation existed so that we could plot and follow a safe course through a prominent reef a mile or so off the island. To our surprise, the sailing instructions described two landmarks that could be used for visual fixes. One was the "sultan's tomb" on the north side of the channel. The other was "a thirty-foot palm tree on the south side of the island." To our consternation, those observations from the 1937 visit were no longer useful; neither the tomb nor the palm tree was observable thirty-three years later. So we improvised. We put our small whaleboat in the water and used the "lead line" method to sound the depth, the ship proceeding slowly behind the boat through what looked like an opening in the reef. This was a laborious and time-consuming navigational method, but it worked, and we anchored unscathed in the harbor at Male.

The mission to the Maldives was classified "Top Secret." As the operations officer responsible for radio communications, I was privy to several FLASH-precedence messages from Secretary of State Henry Kissinger, addressed to the DCM. I learned that the reason for our trip had to do with a vote that was scheduled in the General Assembly of the United Nations (UN) to unseat the Republic of China (Taiwan) as the legitimate government of China. A second vote would seat the People's Republic of

China (PRC) in its place. Secretary Kissinger's message stated that the impending vote in the UN was expected to be very close and that the vote of the Republic of Maldives was critical to our efforts to block the seating of the PRC. A series of "Top Secret" messages containing negotiating points from the State Department was received in our communication center. At least as interesting were the cables we sent to the State Department from the DCM, reporting his progress.

By 1970, the Soviet Union had made significant inroads and exercised some influence with the Maldivians, and the DCM appeared to believe that the outcome of his mission was in doubt. During a reception on our ship, several particularly important members of the Maldives government who had been invited by the DCM turned out to be graduates of Lumumba University in Moscow. The university, named after the assassinated Congolese leader Patrice Lumumba, was established for the express purpose of indoctrinating third world leaders in the virtues of Marxism-Leninism. Others had been schooled in different technical and scientific centers of learning in the Soviet Union. Speaking Russian (as English was not useful), I engaged some of our guests in light conversation and learned that all seemed pleased with their experiences in the Soviet Union. They also seemed anxious to visit the United States, and they made that quite clear.

After extending conditional offers of development aid from our government, the leadership of the government of the Maldives voted with the United States to keep Taiwan seated in the UN and to block the PRC. Nevertheless, the bad news was that this one vote was not sufficient for us to muster the majority needed in the General Assembly. The PRC was seated.

You will appreciate that this experience was heady stuff for a junior naval officer who had specialized in Soviet East European Studies while in college.

* * *

Returning to waters off the coast of Vietnam, we had a change of command, and Captain Hays was relieved at sea by Commander Ned C. Roberts. We were fortunate that the new captain was also an experienced destroyer veteran who had served in the combat zone and was familiar with operations there.

The pace of events changed toward the end of our deployment. The process of "Vietnamization" announced by the Nixon administration in 1971 led to a rapid reduction in the number of US forces engaged in the war. The number of carriers on Yankee Station dropped from three to two. Although we continued to provide limited NGFS support to remaining US forces and to South Vietnamese units when ordered, it was evident that the end of our engagement in this poorly managed war was near. A short visit to the port at Da Nang by *Knox* confirmed our suspicions as we witnessed the withdrawal and embarkation of the South Korean Marine Division (the Tiger Division) onto transport ships taking them home to Korea. Touring the base, it was also clear that many of the patrol gunboats, once manned by US crews in Da Nang and later transferred to the South Vietnamese Navy, were no longer in operation. Owing to a lack of maintenance, they were in poor condition and inactive in the effort to interdict Vietcong traffic.

These developments were important to me because before Vietnamization began in earnest, I had received word from my BuPers detailer, Lieutenant John Todd, that my next assignment would be to a navy unit "in country"—that is, in Vietnam. I understood that it was my turn, and I was reconciled to that challenge. Not long after I received this notification, however, the navy began withdrawing in-country combat units, leaving only advisory personnel. My assignment prospects changed, and Lt. Todd informed me that my orders to Vietnam would not be forthcoming. My next assignment would not be defined until after our deployment.

CHAPTER 3

EDUCATION AND RESEARCH: FOUNDATION FOR STRATEGY AND POLICY

Harvard University and the Naval War College

In August 1972, I arrived in Cambridge, Massachusetts to enroll in the John F. Kennedy School of Government at Harvard University. How this unusual assignment was made possible is a story worth telling.

While still in *Knox* and deployed to the western Pacific, I had been selected early and below the normal promotion zone for promotion to lieutenant commander. This was great news, but for one thing: My detailer in the Bureau of Naval Personnel (BuPers), Lt. John Todd, had corresponded with me again, shortly before the end of deployment, to further discuss my next assignment. He had informed me that with an assignment in Vietnam no longer a prospect, I had been selected for a command at sea in the grade of lieutenant, probably to command a patrol gunboat (PG). At the time, several of those ships were homeported at the naval base in Guam and still active in the coastal waters of

Vietnam. Several others were assigned to the Sixth Fleet, where they shadowed Soviet naval units in the Mediterranean. In either case, I had been genuinely excited by the prospect of a command at sea as a lieutenant.

The excitement was in vain, however, because it turned out that once I was selected for promotion to lieutenant commander, I was no longer eligible for an assignment reserved for lieutenants. Todd informed me that my next assignment would be made by the Lieutenant Commander Desk at the bureau. I dutifully called my new assignment officer, who informed me that my orders were the least of his concerns: he had hundreds of "frocked" (interim promotion but not being paid at the higher level) lieutenant commanders who were coming out of Vietnam and he needed to assign them as a matter of higher urgency. He instructed me to "sit tight" and provide him my preferences for the next assignment, admonishing me that I could expect to remain in my current assignment aboard *Knox* for several more months.

Thus, realizing that I did not have any other attractive options at sea in the realm of possible assignments, I went about requesting an assignment to a graduate education program at a civilian university where I might pursue the PhD degree that I had always wanted. The best approach was to apply for "duty under instruction as a scholarship recipient," the same program I had used to complete a master's degree at Notre Dame six years earlier.

I applied to five universities whose programs seemed interesting, including Harvard, where my father had received his undergraduate degrees and his PhD. Harvard at the time was a hotbed of student and faculty opposition to the war in Vietnam from which I had just returned. Following a vote in the faculty senate, Harvard had dismissed all the ROTC units on campus, including the navy. In retaliation, the Chairman of the House

Armed Services Committee, Congressman Edwin Hebert, D-LA, had put a rider on the 1970 Defense Authorization Bill proscribing the use of appropriated funds for the education of military personnel at any institution that had dismissed an ROTC unit. The upshot was that I could not expect an assignment to Harvard if the government had to pay for the education. But if Harvard were to provide me a scholarship, it might be possible to work around Congressman Hebert's restrictions.

As it happened, when Harvard accepted me, it was as a master's of public administration (MPA) student at the Kennedy School; the dean, Dr. Don Price, explained that my admission to a Harvard PhD program would await consideration of the record I established in my MPA coursework. At the same time, he extended to me the offer of a Littauer Fellowship to cover the cost of tuition. I accepted immediately, knowing that I would have my navy salary and benefits to support myself and my family while enrolled and confident that I would prove myself worthy of admission to the PhD program when the time came.

We moved our household to Acton, Massachusetts, a suburb just north of historic Concord, and I began my studies in the fall of 1972. I selected my courses with a view to applying next for admission to the Graduate School of Arts and Sciences and to the PhD program in political economy and government. This degree had been created to combine study in the disciplines of political science and economics.

Hard work paid off, and I was accepted to the PhD program in the spring of 1973. The navy, with the strong support of my early mentor, Commander (later Admiral) Mike Boorda, agreed to extend my assignment at Harvard by one year so that I might complete coursework and the candidacy exams for the doctorate.

I should add parenthetically that securing this extension was no easy task because the navy had been asked to shut down its presence at Harvard. The resentment about the exception that I had used to circumvent the "Hebert rule" was apparent in BuPers. Some in the bureau feared a reaction from Congressman Hebert were he to learn of the exception. Strangely, I did eventually hear directly from the congressman's chief of staff, who called me at home to ask how I had managed to attend Harvard on active duty. He had learned of my status after reading a biography attached to an article I had written for the *Naval Institute Proceedings*.[18] I explained about the fellowship that I had been granted by Harvard, and he seemed satisfied.

Critics of the military itself and of the military-industrial complex abounded at Harvard in 1973.[19] The attitude of students and faculty at Harvard during the Vietnam War had a significant impact on the political science and economics departments. Noted academic experts on military strategy and national security policy such as Professors Ernest May, Samuel P. Huntington, and Thomas C. Schelling, among others, were pressured to change course offerings and the direction of their research away from their established interest in national security policy. Instead, the professors in question had shifted the focus of their work to satisfy critics of national security studies. Huntington took to theorizing about "green revolutions," and Schelling drew examples from ice hockey to refine some of the game theory principles he had once applied to competition and conflict between great powers.

I note all of this because I selected Harvard—noted for national security studies—determined to pursue advanced degrees

---

18 My article, "The US Sixth Fleet, Quest for Consensus," appeared in *Naval Institute Proceedings*, June 1974, 18–23. It won first honorable mention in the prize essay contest.

19 For a detailed description of the trend among academicians drifting away from participating in the making of national security policy, see Michael C. Desch, *Cult of the Irrelevant: The Waning Influence of Social Science on National Security* (Princeton, NJ: Princeton University Press, 2019).

as a serving and career naval officer. By the time of my arrival, the choice of fields had become severely limited. In the past, the university had been a close collaborator with the government in national security studies. All of that had changed by the early '70s, but I persevered. I decided that after completing the requisite courses in political theory and economics, I would focus on comparative foreign policies; communism as practiced in the Soviet Union, communist China, and Eastern Europe; and on the economics of national security.

I completed the requisite coursework during my two years of residency, amounting to sixty semester hours in 1972–1974, and took the written candidacy exams in political theory and public finance in the late spring of 1974. In June of that year, I sat for my oral examinations with four noted professors: Thomas Schelling (economics of national security), William Kaufman (defense strategy), Robert Bowie (comparative foreign policy) and Adam Ulam (Soviet foreign policy). Success in these exams was a prerequisite in my pursuit of the doctorate in political economy and government.

While I was at Harvard, there were several incidents that were as startling as they were disappointing. On arrival, I discovered, almost by accident, that there were several mid-career army officers also enrolled in the MPA program. The army had somehow avoided the wrath of Congressman Hebert and had continued to send three officers to Harvard at government expense to prepare them for duties as career faculty in the social sciences department at the US Military Academy.

I was surprised to learn that these officers were not as interested as I was in focusing on courses and subjects bearing on national security and foreign policy. Furthermore, in their dress and grooming, they had gone to ground to meld into the larger graduate student population. (The mature reader will recall what the accepted dress and grooming standards were on Ivy League campuses in the early 1970s.)

I happened to meet an army colonel at a lecture presented at Harvard's Center for International Affairs. After learning that I was a naval officer enrolled at the Kennedy School, the colonel asked me if I knew the three army officers enrolled in my program. He was clearly disappointed that they had not been in touch with him and he asked me to inform them of his interest in speaking to them. I dutifully complied, and to my amazement, not long after, the long hair and rather cultish appearance of my counterparts improved markedly.

The inclination to merge into a student body openly hostile to the military and to the presence of officers on campus was, sad to say, understandable. Here we were, veterans of the Vietnam conflict, having to work our way around and through repeated anti-war demonstrations. One winter morning as I went to class, there was a group of students outside an academic building collecting money for the relief of the Bach Mai Hospital in Hanoi, which had received collateral damage during a B-52 bombing raid earlier that week. I was disappointed by this display of sympathy for an enemy but went in without expressing my sentiments.

At another point, I received word from my immediate superior while at Harvard that Admiral Elmo Zumwalt, Chief of Naval Operations (CNO), who had commanded naval forces in Vietnam and was recently returned from the war, would be addressing the Harvard Law Forum. I was invited (expected) to attend in uniform. That evening, I walked across the Harvard Yard to the law school and ran a gauntlet of demonstrators gathered to protest the admiral's presence on campus. It is difficult to exaggerate the anger I felt as I was cursed and even spit on on my way to the law school auditorium.

Notwithstanding these challenges, my two years in residence at Harvard were as valuable as they were interesting. The rigor of the coursework, the stimulating lectures and seminars, and the privilege to learn from the most remarkable collection of intellectuals assembled at this university made all the unpleasantness bearable. Imagine: lectures on bureaucracy and organization theory in seminars led by the noted James Q. Wilson. In one sobering encounter after a lecture, Professor Wilson made clear that he was not supportive of students in the military pursuing doctorates in the social sciences at Harvard. He had served in the navy as a supply officer during the Korean War, and his own experience in uniform had led him to conclude that the military had "no need" for PhDs beyond those engaged in academic research or teaching. To make his point, I had to retake the required written candidacy exam in administrative science. After my first attempt, he noted that I had failed to discuss "conflicts" in the application of certain principles to large bureaucratic organizations. I did not repeat that mistake in the subsequent exam. Several months after and following my success in the final oral examinations, I was gratified when Professor Wilson wished me luck in my future career.

Soviet policy seminars with Dr. Adam Ulam were especially stimulating. Professor Ulam was a leading expert on the foreign policies of the Soviet Union, and his biographical treatment of Stalin provided among the best analyses of the foundations for Soviet foreign policy in the postwar period. Public finance cases taught by Samuel Musgrave made the case for progressive taxation and redistributive fiscal policies. European political institutions analyzed by Professor Stanley Hoffman provided useful contrasts with our own. US foreign policy seminars led by Robert Bowie, a former State Department policy planning chief under John Foster Dulles, provided insight into the foreign policy imperatives of the Eisenhower administration. Finally, there was macroeconomic theory, team taught by Drs. Martin Feldstein (Reagan's chairman of the Council of Economic Advisers) and Janet Yellen (the current secretary of the Treasury.)

A unique experience for this career military officer while at Harvard came via an invitation to participate in periodic "briefings" for a noted gadfly and defense critic, Congressman Les Aspin (D-WI). At the time, Aspin was a severe critic of defense spending levels for what he asserted were "bloated, gold-plated programs." As a guest of the Institute of Politics at the Kennedy School, Aspin would appear in Cambridge, typically on a Saturday morning. The stated purpose of his visits was to expand his critique and to "bounce ideas" off like-minded faculty at Harvard. I remember that Graham Allison, Sam Bowles, Joseph Nye, and many graduate students in political science and economics attended these sessions.

One of the graduate students who attended was Robert Pastor, who was a mentee of Professor Joseph Nye, a prominent member of the political science faculty. Pastor was a friend with whom I shared several classes, and from our many conversations, it was obvious that Pastor was an avowed and unapologetic Marxist. A fierce adherent to the revisionist school of American foreign policy (unbridled "imperialism" was the watchword used by critics of US foreign policy), he would expound polemically on this theme in a foreign policy seminar we attended together.

Several years after we had both received our PhDs, I had lunch with Bob in Washington. He was by this time on the staff of the National Security Council (NSC) and serving as President Carter's special assistant on the Panama Canal treaty (where he led negotiations that culminated in our relinquishing control of the canal). I was on the navy staff where we had argued strongly but in vain against the administration's policy. There was no doubt in my mind regarding Pastor's motivation in and his commitment to ceding a strategic waterway that he regarded as a vestige of our "imperial" past.

I went by invitation to several of these Institute of Politics meetings. A member of the institute who was a moderate conservative on the political science faculty thought I could be persuaded to engage Aspin. I participated quietly for the most part in the "enlightenment" of the congressman, but my intent was to understand and, to the extent that I disagreed, ultimately challenge the line of criticism the group espoused. At one of these sessions, the topic under discussion was strategic nuclear forces. Aspen asked the group "how many expensive *Ohio*-class ballistic missile submarines (SSBNs) was 'right,'" given the number of nuclear weapons available in the other legs of the strategic TRIAD. The discussion turned to the comparative costs of the missiles to be carried by the SSBNs and the fact that the missiles had improved greatly in yield and accuracy. The group coalesced around the idea that the number of subs could be sharply reduced. I disagreed, noting the stark differences in the vulnerability of the submarines when compared to the other legs of the Strategic Nuclear TRIAD. Aspin was not impressed. I can honestly say that when attending these sessions, I was the only exception to the consensus view that the military and the military-industrial complex were too large, too expensive, and as the war in Vietnam had proved, much too eager to engage in wars that ran counter to the liberal credo of the period.

As I reflect on the experience, I cannot avoid noting what a dramatic change this was from the activities at the Institute of Politics that had prevailed in another period. Led by the likes of McGeorge Bundy, Walt Rostow, Henry Kissinger, and Thomas Schelling, that institute helped shape national security policy during much of the Cold War. It is also interesting to note that while all of this took place in the early and mid-1970s, coinciding with the anti-war movement at the time, liberal critics such as Graham Allison and Joseph Nye reappeared a few years later at the center of defense policy making under President Jimmy Carter. Most remarkable, perhaps, was Les Aspin's ultimate accession to the helm of the Defense Department under President Clinton!

The challenge of having to finish all my required coursework and exams in the two short years allotted to me was exhausting. I can truthfully say in retrospect that my two years at Harvard University were probably the busiest of my career. When I left Cambridge in the summer of 1974, there remained a doctoral dissertation to be written. I had already completed an outline for my dissertation director, Robert Bowie, and my principal readers, Professors Kaufman and Schelling. All had accepted my thesis, which was to explain how the "posture" of the Sixth Fleet in the Mediterranean had changed in the twenty years of its existence. Specifically, I proposed to explain why the force structure and force levels in this particular case had remained rather constant, notwithstanding significant changes in US defense strategy and the improved capabilities of the ships and aircraft that comprised the fleet. The project would be of value to me as a serving officer, and it would enable me to perform at an informed level in positions I hoped to hold in the future in political-military affairs and defense strategy.

In August 1974, I transferred to the command and staff course at the Naval War College in Newport, Rhode Island. This assignment was made for two reasons. As discussed, the navy had agreed to extend my tenure at Harvard for one year, but the bureau was not about to extend these orders for a third year so that I could complete my dissertation. Because I was a relatively new and junior lieutenant commander, I needed at least one more year ashore before I could return to sea duty as the executive officer (XO) of a destroyer. All of this was explained to me by my assignment officer, Cmdr. Boorda. I fully intended to attempt completion of the dissertation within the year allotted at the War College before returning to sea duty. To that end, I took advantage of an opportunity that came up when Vice Admiral Stansfield Turner, then the president of the War College, was invited to be a guest speaker at the Institute of Politics while still attending classes at Cambridge.

When I met with Admiral Turner, he suggested that I should write my doctoral dissertation while attending the command and staff course at the War College. I was provided a quiet office in the old War College building, Mahan Hall. There, I would spend a large part of the year in splendid solitude, working on the dissertation.

I was also pleased to receive funding from the War College for travel in the fall of 1974 to Europe. I was able to visit Belgium, the United Kingdom, France, and Italy. It also gave me the opportunity to interview several former Allied commanders in the Mediterranean, including Admiral Sir Derick Holland-Martin, one of the last commanders of the British Mediterranean Fleet. I was also able to access the archives of the NATO Military Committee in Brussels and specialized libraries in Rome, London, and Paris. Upon my return, I continued researching the navy's archives in Washington as well as conducting interviews with a dozen former Sixth Fleet commanders.

After compiling literally thousands of three-by-five-inch note cards with relevant facts and transcribed reminiscences, I began writing in earnest. I trekked back to Cambridge regularly to submit draft chapters of the dissertation and to receive comments and occasional criticism from Drs. Bowie and Kaufman. The dilemma I faced was straightforward: Bowie and Kaufman wanted me to write a piece that was critical of the navy and of the logic the navy used to validate its force levels. Before reading anything that I had written, they had independently concluded that the size of the Sixth Fleet, and especially the number of aircraft carriers required, were levels that reflected bureaucratic inertia and budgetary politics.

My navy readers, on the other hand, were uniformly interested in a dissertation that validated the strategic arguments made in defense of navy budgets. Vice Admiral Julien Le Bourgeois, who had succeeded Admiral Turner as president of the War College, and his chief of staff, Captain Hugh Knott, made that point to me repeatedly. As Captain Knott put it, "Remember who is paying your salary!" In fact, my task was made easier because my research confirmed that bureaucratic imperatives were not the only drivers. National strategies, diplomatic exigencies, and Allied insistence on tangible demonstrations of US guarantees under NATO all had important bearing on the size and configuration of the Sixth Fleet during the Cold War.

While working on my dissertation, other interests also occupied my time at the War College. I attended several lectures that generated considerable discussion and even heated debate. One such lecture, in the spring of 1975, was by General Russell Daugherty, USAF, Commander of the Strategic Air Command (SAC). Describing the general tenets and objectives underlying US nuclear strategy, the general asked for a show of hands in response to the following question: "How many of you think that nuclear weapons are just another type of munition to be employed in war?"

The audience's response revealed that very few of us thought of nuclear weapons in those terms. He then asked how many of us thought nuclear weapons were in a "special category" and primarily useful to deter war. Amazingly, almost the entire room raised their hands in response. The general was not happy with our views regarding the utility of nuclear weapons. He criticized us for not accepting his arguments about the "conventionality" of nuclear weapons. As I reflected on the subject, and as we continued to debate in our naval warfare classes, it was clear that by the mid-'70s, the logic behind the strategy of "massive retaliation" and dependence on nuclear weapons for "war fighting," driving principles in US military doctrine during the '40s and '50s, was not widely shared among the mid-career officers in attendance. Clearly, the arguments for "flexible response" and reliance on "conventional" military weapons that had characterized the shift in military doctrine in some circles beginning in the '60s now seemed pervasive. I found myself in complete agreement with the majority of my classmates.

Another issue of importance to me and my colleagues at the War College had to do with the relative importance and value of the navy's three categories of warfare weapons systems: aviation, submarines, and surface forces, which had been relabeled surface warfare. Until the early '70s, the surface forces within the navy had been further divided into three communities: cruiser-destroyer, amphibious, and the service forces. Promotion opportunities in each of those communities differed, and some felt there was a bias in the surface forces community favoring destroyermen for career progression. Undeniably, officers in the cruiser-destroyer specialty had historically enjoyed a clear advantage in both prestige and promotions. Statistically, officers in the amphibious and service forces had not competed equitably for promotions to the highest ranks.

But distinctions of this type were not limited to the surface forces. In naval aviation, the fighter and attack specialties were seen as elite. In the submarine community, there had been a clear distinction between officers who had served in nuclear submarines and those who had served on diesel boats.

In any case, by 1974, navy leadership had decided that by integrating the surface communities into a single surface warfare specialty, the talent might be shared more equitably across all the surface communities. Another stated objective was to require surface officers to qualify for designation as a surface warfare officer by completing a set of requirements as the prerequisite to wearing a distinctive pin or device on their uniforms. The device was meant to instill pride in the surface warfare community.

All this change came into force while I was at the War College, and it resulted in considerable disquiet and cynical commentary from hard-core destroyermen. Most of the surface officers in attendance at the War College were proud cruiser men and destroyermen, me included. We were not happy to be bundled with the amphibious and service force communities. After all, we had cut our teeth standing rapid maneuvering watches while assigned to ships with "real" combat missions and had specialized in a body of tactics meant to destroy enemy ships and aircraft. Although we recognized that officers who served in other types of ships also possessed critical skills and deep knowledge, cruiser-destroyermen fancied themselves "combatants," as distinct from "support" forces. We were graduates of the Naval Destroyer School (DesTech) and proud of our community. We compared ourselves favorably to the elites in the other warfare specialties and saw ourselves as heirs to a gallant tradition.

The president of the War College at the time was an officer who had served at sea exclusively in destroyers and cruisers. Yet, to encourage our acceptance of the new specialty, Vice Admiral Julien Le Bourgeois took the opportunity to lecture us. His approach to rationalizing the need for a surface warfare specialty was to criticize all of us "black shoes" for lacking "professionalism," compared to our counterparts. The means he chose and the audience he targeted for criticism in front of all our classmates did little to reassure us that the move was a positive development.

The disgruntlement of many surface officers in our class at the War College was evident during our graduation ceremony. As we were assembled in Colbert Plaza for the graduation ceremony, a chartered airplane flew overhead towing a banner that read "SURFACE LINE IS MIGHTY FINE!" The college president was not pleased with this display of what he thought was misplaced pride.

Another event of special note during my year at the War College involved an unprecedented visit to the United States by two destroyers of the Soviet Navy. The port call to Boston in May 1975 marked the first visit by Soviet warships since the end of World War II. As a designated intelligence subspecialist, I was included in a group of six War College students allowed to tour the Soviet destroyers *Boykiy* and *Zhouchy*, which were moored at a commercial pier in South Boston.

The ships provided a remarkable contrast to ours. The habitability of the crew was dismal in comparison to quarters in our modern destroyers: the bunks were stacked three and four high, the storage space allotted to sailors was extremely limited, and the head facilities were cramped and malodorous. Our tour guide, an English-speaking chief petty officer, tried mightily to move us along and away from the crew's quarters.

The bridge and pilot house of both ships appeared very basic in their design and primitive in relation to our ships in terms of equipment to support the conning officer. Visibility from the conning station was poor, and the electronics available to the bridge watch teams were limited to a single radar repeater and several radios.

The ships were, however, heavily armed. They sported medium- and light-caliber guns and first-generation surface-to-air missile systems. Large anti-surface torpedo tubes were installed amidships. The air and surface search radars and the electronic warfare (EW) equipment were bulky in comparison to US systems. It was quite clear that even though there were multiple weapons installed, the volume in the ships limited the magazine space to support so many weapons. We concluded that there must have been a limited number of reloads. As one of my classmates remarked, "These ships appeared to be one-round warships."

One operational deficit that we all noted was the lack of effective damage control in a combatant. There were very few fire main stations, and the "knife edges" and rubber gaskets around watertight doors and hatches were badly compromised by large dents, cuts, and deteriorating rubber. Moreover, the wave guides on the face of the ship's masts running to the radars and EW antennas were exposed and not armored. This would have made the sensors extremely vulnerable to fragmentation weapons.

This visit confirmed in my mind that Soviet designers of these vessels planned for a short naval campaign and overwhelming firepower at the onset of hostilities. The tour revealed that there were real flaws in the surface navy of our putative enemy. We were reassured that our ship designs and maintenance standards were clearly superior to those of the Soviet Navy. How to deal with the Soviet challenge at sea was of importance to my generation, and our visit suggested that our foe saw their challenge as dealing a massive—if short-lived—blow to our carrier task groups. It appeared that they almost expected that after all the ammunition was expended, the ships mounting the weapons would be expendable!

I finished my studies at the War College, earning a Distinguished Graduate certificate at the graduation exercises in July 1975. I then drove the family across the country to San Diego, California to join the USS *Waddell* (DDG-24), where I had been ordered as the XO. I was delighted to be able to return to sea in what was at the time the most desirable destroyer type, a guided missile destroyer (DDG). In fact, *Waddell* was the newest ship of the *Charles F. Adams* class.

One task that remained after I arrived in San Diego was the final revision of the conclusions chapter of my dissertation. A month into my XO tour, I bought an airline ticket and flew back to Cambridge to defend the dissertation.[20] I was awarded the PhD in political economy and government at commencement exercises in June 1976.

20 Philip Dur, "The Sixth Fleet: A Case Study of Institutionalized Naval Presence, 1948–1968" (PhD diss., Harvard University, 1975).

CHAPTER 4

PRELUDE TO COMMAND: "WARSHIP *WADDELL*"

Executive Officer, USS *Waddell* (DDG-24)

The tour as executive officer (XO) of the USS *Waddell* (DDG-24) qualified as my most demanding operational assignment to date. I served over time under two different commanding officers (COs) who were virtually opposites in terms of leadership style and command manner. As the second ranking officer in the destroyer wardroom, the XO must be the captain's alter ego. The contrasting leadership styles of Commander Donald G. Anderson and Commander William S. Manning made this assignment challenging.

Commander Anderson was among the first African American officers to have commanded a warship in the navy and, I believe, the first to have commanded a guided missile destroyer (DDG). At the time, the *Adams*-class DDG was the most desirable at-sea command for a surface warfare officer in the grade of commander. A native Philadelphian and a graduate of Villanova, Anderson tended to delegate many of the prerogatives of command to the XO except ship handling—particularly the training of junior officers—and nonjudicial punishment.

Developing a comprehensive training program for the crew and mentoring the department heads fell almost entirely to me. Initially, I welcomed the latitude for decisions and the breadth of responsibilities, recognizing that this was indeed perfect preparation for the day that I might assume command. The challenge was to run the ship in a manner that satisfied the captain. I assumed he wanted to be assured that I had attended to the myriad details of operating a complex warship manned by 350 officers, chief petty officers, and sailors.

The timing of my tour as XO coincided with one of the most troubled periods in our navy's modern history. The post-Vietnam period was marked by poor retention, lower quality recruits, and many instances of racial and other forms of dissent. As one measure of the times, in 1976, I could count eighteen convicted felons in *Waddell's* crew. Judges had given these misfits the choice of the navy or jail. They had chosen accordingly. We were left to deal with people who had virtually no interest in serving their country or serving in the navy.

Early in my tour, I struggled with Captain Anderson's expectations of me. I had never been known as an introvert or passive player in the wardrooms I had served in, but I was more than a little uncomfortable taking on responsibilities that I had always understood belonged to the captain. A further source of my discomfort was Anderson's reluctance to guide me on how I should decide before, coupled with the tendency to critique some of my decisions, after the fact. Over the first few months, I became so frustrated with this situation that I telephoned my old friend and mentor Commander Rudy Daus, who was at the time on shore duty in Washington. Rudy was someone I greatly admired, and he gave me some good advice: whenever possible, I should brief the captain before I took a decision or issued an order to gauge his support. Rudy's sense was that the captain would soon tire of second-guessing my decisions. He noted, "If he doesn't like your decisions often enough, he'll fire you. Otherwise, press on!" Following Rudy's advice improved my relationship with the captain markedly.

I also did what I could to extend the CO's relationship with the chiefs' mess, and this improved the climate in the command. Getting the chiefs' confidence impacted the entire crew. I recall that Anderson's wit and keen sense of humor were particularly welcome at a dinner in the mess in celebration of the promotion of petty officers to chief petty officers.

Wardroom meetings chaired by the captain were rather infrequent but productive. In short, although his leadership style was somewhat reserved, mine was fundamentally complementary, and I came to appreciate the confidence he placed in me. Preparing for operations at sea and our underway periods provide an example of the complex relationship between a captain and his first mate. When it came time to get underway, on many occasions the captain boarded the ship after boilers were on the line and steam was at the guarding valves. It was often just after we had adjusted our mooring lines to prepare for our departure from our berth at the pier and long after the navigation and sea details had been set.

An expert shiphandler from whom I learned a great deal about handling a destroyer, Capt. Anderson had an uncanny knack for recognizing what our seniors expected of him and for getting it done. A shining example of his understanding the priorities established by the chain of command was our success in the difficult operational propulsion plant examination (OPPE) in the spring of 1976. These inspections by an exacting team of senior engineers had been instituted almost three years before. Failure of an OPPE had often resulted in the relief of COs, and the "pucker factor" was commensurately high. As the date for the inspection approached, Anderson would review our progress and preparations with me and the chief engineer on a daily basis. If we needed more budget, extra hands, or outside assistance, he would arrange them. These measures paid off and *Waddell* was the first DDG in San Diego to pass the OPPE with the unconditional grade of satisfactory. Anderson went on to major command of a guided missile cruiser as a captain.

Waddell was the most capably armed destroyer in the navy's inventory during the mid-'70s. Her main battery was the TARTAR guided missile system. She also carried two 5"/54- gun mounts, an ASROC launcher (with rocket-thrown torpedoes and nuclear depth charges), and MARK 32 surface-launched torpedo tubes. Her sensor suite included a three-dimensional air search radar as well as a long-range air search radar and surface search radars. *Waddell* also featured an improved or "trammed" SQS-23 sonar and a modern EW suite. The ship was propelled by four high-pressure boilers and geared steam turbines. The latter means of propulsion were notoriously difficult to operate and maintain.

The details described above are important in understanding the challenge of keeping this machinery and these various combat systems in prime condition and the teams operating and maintaining them combat-ready. During my time with Captain Anderson, *Waddell* completed a major overhaul at the Long Beach Naval Shipyard, followed by extensive weapons systems tests and trials and a series of propulsion and machinery examinations, including the OPPE. To add to the tension, after completing overhaul and a number of tests and trials, we were examined by a number of weapons specialists and underwent a nuclear technical proficiency inspection (NTPI).

After almost two years in overhaul, a novice crew had to be trained, as we had experienced a 60 percent turnover in personnel during the overhaul. We entered refresher training shortly after returning to our homeport in San Diego. There, we forged the teams we would need to steam and fight the "warship, *Waddell*," as we knew her.

As to steaming the ship, one event demonstrated the prowess of our new engineering team and provided a lasting memory to all who served in *Waddell* at the time. Leaving Long Beach, we sailed for San Diego, our homeport, with the plan to conduct a required four-hour full-power run during the transit. Full power required us to operate all four boilers at a steaming rate of 100 percent. The seawater injection temperature during our trial was less than 60°F, which was ideal for a full-power trial. Without elaborating on the thermodynamics, the efficiency of a steam plant improves proportionally with the increasing difference between the temperature of the saturated steam expelled from the steam turbines and the temperature of the seawater in the tubes of the main condenser. In short, the conditions were ideal for our full-power trial. During the four-hour trial, the ship's navigation plot showed an average speed over the ground of 40.2 knots. This was a remarkable attainment for a *Charles F. Adams* class DDG.

Waddell engineers were so proud of their accomplishment that they made up a huge banner and unfurled it as we approached our berth in Coronado, with friends, dependents, and superiors on the pier. The banner read, "WARSHIP *Waddell*, FORTY KNOTS, NO SMOKE!" Coincidentally, we were moored outboard of the nuclear-powered cruiser USS *Bainbridge* (CGN-25). To my surprise, the engineers crafted another banner which they hung on a handrail and which read, "…and we did it with fossil fuel!" Our nuclear brethren did not share the humor. Subsequently, I recognized an opportunity to build morale throughout the crew. I had certificates and small cards printed for every sailor documenting this remarkable moment.

The accomplishments of every department in the ship while preparing to deploy to the western Pacific in the year following overhaul were simply outstanding. At the end of a yearlong competition, we won the Battle Efficiency "E", marking us as the best DDG in the six-ship destroyer squadron (DESRON) 7. In addition, every department earned an excellence award "E" in 1976.

One month before departure for a scheduled deployment to the western Pacific, we held a change of command at which Commander Anderson was relieved by Commander William Squires Manning. On his departure, Commander Anderson wrote a fitness report for me that was among the best I ever received. The hiccups early in my tour as his XO were clearly forgotten by June 1976.

As previously mentioned and as I could never have anticipated, the leadership style and command manner of these two skippers were starkly different. Commander Manning, who had excelled as a varsity tennis player at the Naval Academy, was very engaged in the business of commanding a warship. A former submariner, Manning had transitioned to the surface navy as a relatively senior lieutenant commander. Like many submariners of his generation, those not selected for nuclear power training by the notoriously hard-nosed Admiral Hyman Rickover were obliged to reestablish their credentials by service in the surface fleet. The best among these were given opportunities in cruisers and destroyers. Commander Manning earned his spurs as combat systems officer in a guided missile cruiser, followed immediately by an XO assignment in a guided missile destroyer. These back-to-back sea tours had earned Manning a place in command of his own DDG.

He was an affable and understanding mentor. Unlike Anderson, he wanted to be informed of virtually every detail before personally deciding on a course of action. Because I had previously assumed many of the captain's responsibilities, I had to surrender some of my former prerogatives and otherwise adjust my role in discharging the duties of an XO.

All told, the transition in leadership styles was a challenging one for me and the wardroom, but we gradually came to terms with the changed environment. I will readily admit that Captain Manning was a superb leader and an expert mariner in his own right. He had developed excellent ship-handling skills in both submarines and surface ships, and he imparted his experience brilliantly to me and the department heads. His presence and approach to command were models to emulate.

Our deployment to the western Pacific began with an extended transit to Australia. In the company of two of our squadron mates, the USS *Hoel* (DDG-13) and the USS *Decatur* (DDG-31), we were escorting an amphibious ready group made up of a number of warships, and a marine amphibious unit (MAU)[21] landing force. The goal for this transit to Australian waters was to participate in Exercise "Kangaroo II," which included an amphibious landing in Shoalwater Bay and an exercise for the marines of our task group training with an Australian Army group.

The transit to Australia was a long one, but I remember one particular day as if it were yesterday. As the XO of *Waddell*, I was responsible for the safe navigation of our ship. And because our new CO, Capt. Manning, was the junior skipper in the task group, *Waddell* was designated as the lead ship for the entire formation of eight ships transiting a narrow channel on the backside of the Great Barrier Reef and into Shoalwater Bay. We proceeded with extreme caution, and I was more challenged in navigation and piloting than I had been since my days in *Knox*. The column of ships, in a tight formation, was quite a sight. I remember that as

21 Renamed sometime in the 1980s as a Marine Expeditionary Unit (MEU).

I pored over the chart and the plots laid down by the quartermasters, the captain remarking to me that the seven ships astern of us were counting on us to see them through several tight turns in the channels leading into the bay. I also remember that I did not feel any less anxious after hearing the captain's remark.

While the marines were ashore conducting exercises, I recommended to the captain that we obtain permission from our commodore, John Addams, and from the Royal Australian Navy to conduct our required naval gunfire support (NGFS) qualification on an Australian gunnery range on nearby Green Island. After much discussion, the commodore authorized the exercise. We left our anchorage and proceeded to fire the prescribed day and night live firing exercises. Happily, we renewed our NGFS qualification with high marks. I note this accomplishment because *Waddell* was the first and quite possibly the last US ship to obtain such a difficult qualification on a foreign range.

After completing the Kangaroo II exercise, all the ships proceeded to Sydney for a well-deserved five-day port visit. Now, Sydney was, and probably still is, the most desired port visit available to ships in the US Pacific Fleet. The Australian public receiving us was overwhelmingly pro-American, and the World War II generation had not forgotten the Battle of the Coral Sea; as they saw it, our victory there foiled a Japanese invasion of Australia. One of my most challenging tasks in Sydney was filling all the invitations for our crew and wardroom from Australians anxious to host American sailors. But because we had been at sea for almost fifty days before arriving in Sydney, filling the many invitations was difficult because our crews were quite anxious to get on liberty—shore leave, to be on their own and to enjoy the sights and attractions. We all came away with wonderful memories of the best port visit in our seven-month deployment.

During the Sydney visit, we uncovered a forgotten moment in our naval history. While conducting raids on Union commerce in the Pacific, the Confederate Navy raider, CSS *Shenandoah*, which was under the commanded of one Captain James Iredell Waddell, CSN, had stopped in Melbourne, Australia in January 1865. The ship's visit there was intended to replenish stores and to undertake voyage repairs. The *Shenandoah* apparently ran up quite a tab, which was settled with a check drawn on a southern bank in Confederate dollars. But unbeknownst to both Captain Waddell and the Australians, the war was effectively over when the checks were presented to the bank. As a result, the accounts had been left unpaid. When we in the USS *Waddell*, Captain Waddell's namesake, arrived in Sydney, the Royal Australian Navy turned the tables: they jokingly presented us with a formal invoice and a letter demanding payment of the *Shenandoah*'s account in US dollars, with interest. I do not recall the sum precisely, but it was astronomical![22]

The irony that this bit of history involved a vessel of the Confederacy was not lost on me or my shipmates, recalling that only a few months before, *Waddell* had been under the command of an African American naval officer. Today, that irony would seem even more pronounced. During the mid-1960s, the navy had named five newly commissioned destroyers after Confederate naval heroes: *Waddell*, *Buchanan*, *Semmes*, *Tatnall*, and *Page*. Perhaps more remarkably in retrospect, in the early '60s, two strategic missile submarines had been named for Confederate generals, the *Robert E. Lee* and the *Stonewall Jackson*. Without arguing the logic behind the naming of these ships, it seems clear that in today's charged political climate and the popular

---

22 For a detailed account of the CSS *Shenandoah*'s cruise to Pacific waters, see Dwight Sturdevant Hughes, *A Confederate Biography: The Cruise of the* CSS Shenandoah (Annapolis, MD: Naval Institute Press, 2015).

denial of some of our troubled national heritage, it would be inconceivable for a secretary of the navy (SECNAV) to name ships after Confederate leaders.

Leaving Australia, the task group transited on a northerly course to the Philippines. The track took us through the Solomon Islands chain and through "the Slot" (New Georgia Sound) and "Iron Bottom Sound" at its southern end, made famous in World War II. It was there that so many destroyers and cruisers had been sunk by Imperial Japanese naval forces during the Guadalcanal campaign. Sensing a historical opportunity, the wardroom and I made a recommendation to Captain Manning and he to the DESRON commander, Commodore Addams (now embarked on our ship), that the three destroyers leave the amphibious ships that were planning to lay wreaths in the waters off Guadalcanal and instead proceed at flank speed through the Slot. There, we could throw our own wreaths in a salute to the destroyermen who had gone down in the seven ships that were sunk there in 1943 in a single engagement. The commodore agreed and ordered our column formation of three destroyers to proceed through the Slot at thirty knots!

The remainder of our deployment to the western Pacific seemed rather routine, the war in Vietnam having ended more than three years before. *Waddell* was tasked to join an exercise off the coast of Korea, Team Spirit 77, which concluded with a port visit to Pusan, Korea.

Then, just before departing for San Diego in June 1977, we participated in what was to be the last exercise in the Shark Hunt series with the Republic of China (Taiwanese) Navy (ROCN) in the Taiwan Straits. Our participation in this exercise coincided with a reevaluation of US foreign policy. The Shark Hunt series were anti-submarine warfare (ASW) exercises, and countering PRC submarines was the mission for which we trained. Following

US recognition of the PRC as the legitimate government of China, the series was terminated. The visit to Kaohsiung that followed the exercise was also one of the last by US warships. I was saddened by the effect of the "one China" policy. The ROC had been a solid ally and the Taiwanese had been gracious hosts to our navy in difficult times.

A curfew in Kaohsiung after midnight, first imposed in 1970 following a spate of subversive incidents, remained in effect during our visit. We were warned that any of our crew not off the streets by midnight would be detained in outdoor military police facilities until dawn the following day. This effort to control unwanted activity in the streets took its toll on our crew. I was informed each day of how many sailors had been detained by the Taiwanese. Multiple offenders were subsequently denied further liberty ashore while in Kaohsiung.

Another remarkable moment during our visit was observing the ROCN drawing anti-swimmer nets across the harbor entrance at dusk each day and removing them the morning after. The nets were intended to block PRC swimmers (saboteurs) from entering the harbor surreptitiously. Apparently, swimmers from the mainland had been apprehended by the Taiwanese several times in the months preceding our visit.

The homeward transit to San Diego was a bittersweet passage for me. My relief as XO, Lieutenant Commander (later Captain) Conrad Vandershroeff, joined us for the voyage home, and we conducted a turnover of my responsibilities and duties while en route. I say bittersweet because even though the assignment had been demanding and often quite challenging, I genuinely enjoyed my turn as the first mate. I had learned more than I could ever have imagined about how to command and what pitfalls to avoid. Stepping off the brow onto the pier in San Diego, I glanced up at the bridge wing and all the "Es" painted thereon and took great pride in the part I had played in making "Warship *Waddell*" the top DDG in San Diego. My mates and I felt that we were arguably the best DDG in the Pacific Fleet. Few could have won an argument to the contrary.

CHAPTER 5

CRAFTING NAVAL AND ALLIANCE STRATEGY

Office of the Chief of Naval Operations, OP-60

Within the Office of the Chief of Naval Operations (OPNAV) and under the Plans, Policies and Operations directorate (OP-06), the Strategy and Plans Division (OP-60) had been a pivot and center of power in the navy following World War II. Two Chiefs of Naval Operations (CNOs), Admirals David McDonald and George Anderson, were former directors of the division. Following the Defense Reorganization Act of 1958, and especially the McNamara reforms in the early '60s, OP-60 and its parent directorate were eclipsed, in both stature and relative influence within OPNAV, by the Directorate for Navy Program Planning (OP-090) and its subordinate Systems Analysis Division (OP-96).

The shift in the OPNAV center of gravity accelerated during Admiral Zumwalt's tenure as CNO during 1970–1974.[23] As a rear admiral, Zumwalt had served as the head of OP-96, and

---

23 See Larry Berman, *Zumwalt, the Life and Times of Admiral Elmo Russell "Bud" Zumwalt, Jr.* (Annapolis, MD: Naval Institute Press, 2012), 231–234.

upon ascending to the CNO position, he empowered the OP-090 directorate to reform what he saw as the cumbersome and contentious OPNAV organization. Project SIXTY, a plan to drastically reduce excess ships in the fleet within sixty days, was an example of how the "analysts" and "net assessors" became dominant in determining navy policies and program objectives.

I arrived for my assignment in OP-60 (more precisely OP-605) in August 1975, following my tour as executive officer (XO) of **Waddell**, during which my time had been occupied with the fast pace of deployed operations and leadership of a 350-sailor crew. The XO job, second in command, was well defined in navy tradition, and I found it comparatively easy to get along with those with whom I was serving. The world of OPNAV, I was about to discover, was much more complicated. Bureaucratic politics were endemic, and branch heads, division directors, and even Deputy Chiefs of Naval Operations competed for influence and favor within the navy hierarchy.

My first experience in this headquarters atmosphere preceded my arrival in Washington. I had originally been ordered by the Bureau of Naval Personnel (BuPers) to a slot in OP-965, the Long-Range Planning branch of OP-96. Because OP-96 and virtually all the divisions of OP-090 were the most sought-after assignments in OPNAV, I was both pleased with and honored by my orders.

One month before I left San Diego, however, I was notified that my orders had been modified and that I was now going to report to OP-605 in the OP-60 organization. The scuttlebutt in the navy was that OP-60 was no longer regarded as a top-shelf assignment for officers in OPNAV. After some detective work, I discovered that a peer who was also an acquaintance had interceded and recommended another officer to the branch head, then-Commander (later Captain) Norm Mosher. (I learned later that the intercessor was a close friend of the branch head.) I was surprised to learn that a branch head could apparently reject what BuPers proposed. And so, I reported to OP-605, determined to make the best of my situation.

As I was arriving in OP-605, Vice Admiral William J. Crowe had just checked aboard as the ultimate boss, deputy CNO for Plans, Policy and Operations. Admiral Crowe came to OPNAV following a tour as Commander of the Middle East Force. He subsequently attained the highest rank in the uniformed military hierarchy, Chairman of the Joint Chiefs of Staff (CJCS). I came to know Admiral Crowe very well and think that he was among the most intelligent and gifted flag officers with whom I served in my career. His background is something of an inspiration.

A diesel submariner in his early career, when a lieutenant commander he had earned Admiral Hyman Rickover's wrath by choosing not to transfer to the nuclear submarine force via Nuclear Power School. He had opted instead to finish a PhD in political science at Princeton's Woodrow Wilson School. His dissertation, which I read, was about the long decline of the Royal Navy (RN) following the Suez crisis of 1956.

Admiral Crowe explained to me that upon leaving Princeton, he had accepted command of a diesel submarine, fully recogniz-ing that the nuclear power club (the "nukes") were ascendant in the submarine community. He knew that there would likely be a price to be paid for having declined to join the nuclear navy. Crowe could instead have requested a transfer to the surface community, as many of his contemporary diesel submariners had, but he opted instead to take command of a diesel boat and take his chances. The bet paid off. After a series of ascend-ing career milestones—promotion to Captain, command of a submarine squadron, and a tour as a senior advisor to the Vietnamese Riverine Force during which he achieved a stellar combat record—he was selected for promotion to rear admiral. In recognition of his keen intellect, one of Crowe's first assignment as a flag officer was as Deputy Assistant Secretary of Defense (ASD) for International Security Affairs (ISA) for East Asia Pacific. Subsequently, he went on to command the Middle East Force, where he was acclaimed for his skills and brilliance in diplomacy, and for his strategic negotiations with Iran and the countries around the Persian Gulf, especially Bahrain and Saudi Arabia.

Notwithstanding his many accomplishments, the folklore in OPNAV preceding Crowe's arrival there was that he was a "political" admiral. That label probably derived from his tours in the Office of the Secretary of Defense (OSD) as a political-military specialist. Additionally, because he was not a member of a "real" warfare specialty (diesel submarines didn't count) and because he had not commanded a numbered fleet, detractors argued that he would be outclassed in the competition for four stars by other vice admirals coming from the principal warfare specialties. Admiral Crowe ultimately proved the contrary: he was promoted to four stars not long after leaving OPNAV and, as noted above, eventually ascended to the vaunted position of CJCS under President Reagan. I greatly admired Admiral Crowe, and I maintained a close relationship with him until his passing.

Following the annual navy-to-navy staff talks in 1976, the RN approached their US counterpart with a proposal to develop a joint concept of operations for the US and British navies in the Atlantic Command area. This proposal was formulated by the RN in anticipation of the decommissioning of the RN's last classic aircraft carrier, HMS *Hermes* (a ship equipped with catapults and arresting gear), and with her passing, the demise of Britain's historical role in NATO's Striking Fleet Atlantic (STRIKFLT). Without a "proper" carrier and carrier-based fixed-wing aircraft, the RN was now in a determined search for a comparably important role—and a command—in the STRIKFLT.

The new capital ships in the RN were the "through deck" cruisers or helicopter carriers of the *Invincible* class, which was designed primarily to support anti-submarine warfare (ASW) operations, and the embarked aviation elements were limited to helicopters and a relatively small number of vertical/short takeoff and landing (V/STOL) aircraft. The British proposed to commit two of these ships and their accompanying surface ship escorts to the STRIKFLT. In fact, even before discussions on the necessary revisions to allied contingency plans and to the STRIKFLT command structure, the RN had already renamed their prospective contribution Anti-Submarine Warfare Group Two (ASWGRU 2; replacing STRIKEGRU 2 in NATO parlance).

Determined to maintain a flag officer billet in the STRKFLT, they had proposed a task force designator to their contribution even before discussions on how to employ the British assets in the event of war had been completed. The rub was that the mission and role of this new force had not been well defined in their own national force justifications, and pressure was mounting in the Ministry of Defence (MOD) for more clarity. A formal and joint concept of operations to be developed with the US Navy was deemed essential for planning and for legitimization in parliamentary debates.

This was happening the fall of 1977, only a few months after my arrival at OPNAV, and it presented a welcome escape from my duties as the Western Hemisphere and Polar Regions staff officer in OP-605. I was off to London to start developing this joint concept. I say escape because the politics of the OP-60 staff required that the NATO plans officer, a captain in a different branch, should represent the US side in this bilateral effort. Captain Bill Shaughnessy, a wise and gracious diesel submariner and the leader of our branch OP-605, had read my dissertation on the Sixth Fleet. He decided that I instead should represent OP-60 in this project. The opposition to my participation came from Captain (later Rear Admiral) T. J. Johnson, who wanted the project for himself. Johnson argued that since I was only a lieutenant commander, I was much too junior to work with more senior British counterparts. (I had in fact been selected for promotion to commander but had not been formally promoted.) Shaughnessy took matters to OP-60 Rear Admiral Jim Stockdale, who was persuaded that I should be given the task. To get around the problem of relative seniority, Admiral Stockdale promoted me (without pay) as a commander, and I flew to London.

Captain Mike Livesay, of the Plans Directorate in the MOD, was the lead British member of our bilateral team. His assistant was Commander John Coward, a nuclear submariner. We went to work in London, drawing on a template that I had brought with me. It began with the assumption that in a period of "warning" of war with the Warsaw Pact, the STRIKFLT commander would build a strong force around three or four US aircraft carriers and upward of fifty cruisers and destroyers. The STRIKFLT would transit the North Atlantic and enter the Norwegian Sea through the Greenland-Ireland-United Kingdom (GIUK) gap. This template was at the heart of a new maritime strategy that was just now being advanced by the US Navy. It was intended to be an offensive strategy and a clear refutation of the position that the navy's principal role in the event of war was the defense of sea lines of communication (SLOC) across the Atlantic.

It was fortunate, and somewhat fortuitous, that I in my new assignment had been working closely with then-Commander (later Admiral) Hank Mauz, the NATO plans officer in another branch of OP-60. Mauz was the principal officer working to recast Allied strategy for the North Atlantic, away from sea lane defense and toward offensive operations against the Soviet Navy. This proposed strategy contrasted sharply with a much more limited and defensive role that was advanced by the OSD. That mission prescribed for the navy had been incorporated in the famous review of defense posture by the Carter administration, Presidential Review Memorandum/NSC-10 (PRM-10), which was hotly debated in the Joint Staff and stridently challenged by the navy and Marine Corps and their allies in Congress.

The disagreement on the navy's role in what we called a NATO war can be fairly described as a veritable strategic chasm. NATO plans during this period were predicated on the "swing" of three carriers and support ships from the Pacific Fleet to the Atlantic as augmentation forces to be assigned to the Allied Command Europe. The plan that had been prepared in the early years of the alliance had been designed to increase the conventional strike capability of NATO's European command, which was led by a Supreme Allied Commander Europe (SACEUR), historically an American. It had persisted precisely because our European allies took the commitment of augmenting Atlantic naval forces from the Pacific as an important measure of our capability to defend Allied territory.

The leadership of the Carter administration did not accept the historical commitment, for either programming or budgetary purposes, that carriers would engage in offensive strikes. For defense intellectuals, the "swing" concept was atavistic and irrelevant because it was premised on an outdated strategic plan.

To complicate matters, the Commander of the Pacific Fleet (CINCPACFLT), Admiral Thomas Hayward, was strongly opposed to the idea of swinging his carriers to the Atlantic in the event of war with the Warsaw Pact. His staff, led by Captain Jim Patton, one of Hayward's strategic planners, had prepared a study called, Project Sea Strike, which had the Pacific Fleet carriers launching strikes against Soviet forces and bases in the Far East at the onset of hostilities. Several of us on the navy staff in Washington, wrestling with strategic concepts and planning for a major war with the Soviet Union, concentrated on the Atlantic and European campaigns. To my mind at the time, the plan to put the Pacific Fleet into conflict with the Warsaw Pact was a distraction because a NATO war was the force-pacing scenario, and our immediate battle with OSD was the navy's contribution to NATO and the defense of our European allies.

Everything changed in July 1978 with the appointment of Admiral Hayward as the CNO. The NATO allies (and SACEUR) were soon informed that the "swing" strategy was a dead letter. The doubters among us were persuaded that in the event of war with the Soviets, the entire navy would go on the offensive in the Atlantic and in the Pacific. I became a committed convert.

The new NATO strategy, which came to be known as the Maritime Strategy,[24] was elaborated and codified in a study called Sea Plan 2000. Planning for war in the North Atlantic would feature a large carrier battle force that would be preceded by an advance ASW group tasked to "sanitize" the path of advance in anticipation of a contested transit into the Norwegian Sea. The advance group would counter Soviet naval forces, especially submarines positioned to block entry into what were termed Soviet bastions, which protected their nuclear-powered, ballistic-missile-carrying submarines (SSBNs). Importantly, the strategy included prompt offensive operations to seek out and destroy Soviet SSBNs. Once in the Norwegian

---

24 Many of the underlying assumptions and details regarding these operations remain classified. A definitive account of the evolution of the Maritime Strategy can be found in Peter M. Swartz and Karin Duggan, *US Navy Capstone Strategies and Concepts: (1981–1990): Strategy, Policy, Concept, and Vision Documents* (D0026415.A1) (Arlington, VA: CNA, 2011). The author, a retired captain, is an acclaimed expert on the origins and development of the strategy and its impact on US national security.

Sea, the striking battle force was to attack and destroy Soviet units at sea. That task completed, the STRIKFLT would then destroy the bases from which the enemy operated. That phase of the plan envisaged operating carriers in Norwegian fjords, enclosed by mountainous terrain, to complicate Soviet air and missile attacks on the carriers.

Initially, this concept of operations, and the strategy from which it derived, were rather controversial in NATO circles and the Joint Staff, and they were simply anathema in OSD. Simply put, critics were not supportive of the navy planning for offensive operations in the event of conflict with the Soviet Union and the Warsaw Pact. Among the arguments mustered against the new strategy were concerns that the proposed naval campaign would jeopardize the transatlantic resupply of ground and air forces in Europe. The most provocative criticism was that the navy's actions would immediately trigger nuclear responses from the Soviets.

Nor were British admirals wildly enthusiastic about offensive missions they felt were extremely dangerous in the waters north of the United Kingdom. In my early discussions with Livesay and Coward, they would frequently draw on past Allied intelligence estimates that predicted a major effort by Soviet air, submarine, and surface forces to oppose and defeat the STRIKFLT's entry into the Norwegian Sea. Their concern was palpable. If the British ASWGRU 2 was to "lead" the carrier striking force, conducting ASW along the plan of intended movement (PIM), they might bear the brunt of Soviet opposition. For our part, we felt that the advanced capabilities of US attack submarines and ASW aircraft, the anti-air and anti-missile defense potential of our anti-air warfare (AAW) platforms (especially the F-14 *Tomcat* and E-2C *Hawkeye* aircraft embarked in our carriers), and the imminent arrival of the very capable Aegis guided missile cruisers, combined to make our estimates of the risks manageable.[25]

After numerous meetings in Whitehall and at the Pentagon over the course of a year, we finished our work and produced the report "Joint Concept of USN-RN Operations in the Atlantic (1980s)."[26] The concept of operations comprised two scenarios. One scenario assumed a sudden "short warning" conflict with the Soviets. The other was predicated on the assumption of advance warning in a period of rising tensions. The timelines were especially important to the British side. Alliance strategy was defensive, but in the "sudden" scenario, proximity to Soviet and Warsaw Pact bases might require the European NATO navies to "integrate into effective military formations" at the very onset of hostilities; the British were mindful of how the feasibility of this plan could impact a timely defense of the British Isles. In contrast, the RN agreed that if the alliance forces were given ample warning, operations in the "early stages" could be "aggressive" and "concentrated," seeking to destroy enemy forces while they were still deploying.

We briefed the paper to senior officers on both sides of the Atlantic and generally received high marks from our bosses. Two years later, while in command of USS *Comte de Grasse* (DD-974) and while en route to participate in exercise OCEAN VENTURE, I learned from Captain Livesay, then transiting the Atlantic with our task group while in command of HMS *Invincible* (CAH-1), that the RN had adopted the concept and its tasking "for

---

25 For a fictional account of how NATO maritime forces might have fared against the Soviet opposition in the North Atlantic, see John Clancy, *Red Storm Rising* (New York: Putnam, 1986). Clancy's own appreciation for the capabilities of Aegis cruisers was formed while embarked with us in *Yorktown* in 1986. Clancy wrote in my copy, "To Capt. Phil Dur, CO, USS Yorktown: This ship must survive."

26 Captain M. H. Livesay, RN and CDR P. A. Dur, USN, "Joint Concept of USN-RN Operations in the Atlantic (1980s)," September 1978.

training and planning purposes." Livesay subsequently went on to flag rank and ended his career as the Second Sea Lord (Chief of Naval Personnel) with four stars. His colleague on the study, Commander (later Vice Admiral) John Coward, went on to senior commands in the RN, including in a destroyer that established a brilliant record in the Falkland Islands War with Argentina. He finished his career as Flag Officer, Submarines, the senior British submariner.

My work with the RN on the joint concept was an entry into the next opportunity in OP-60. In the summer of 1978, Admiral Crowe and the new leader of OP-60, Admiral Bob Hilton, decided to reorganize the entire organization and to establish a long-range planning branch, to be named Strategy and Concepts (OP-603). Crowe was thereby directly challenging the notion then prevalent in the navy staff that OP-96 was primarily responsible for long-range planning in the navy. Crowe argued instead that strategy had to drive programming and budgeting. To staff this new organization, several officers were pulled out of OP-605, OP-601, and other branches of OP-60.

I was fortunate to be in this new group along with Commander (later Admiral) Hank Mauz, Commander (later Rear Admiral) John Bittoff, Commander Bill West, and Lieutenant Commander (later Captain) Peter Swartz. The story was that Admirals Crowe and Hilton had chosen us to man this new branch because we were "thinkers." I should note that the branch was manned by truly outstanding naval officers who were as ambitious as they were talented. Interestingly, the cooperation and teamwork within our organization was astoundingly good. This led one former member to reflect on how surprising this was, given what he characterized as a "kennel of alpha dogs."

Admiral Mauz was the most illustrious veteran in 603. His task was to detail and refine the strategic objectives of NATO navies in the North Atlantic and Norwegian Sea. (Mauz went on to four stars and command of the Atlantic Fleet before retiring.)

Coincidentally, my responsibilities in this new branch included energy security, the Mediterranean, and the Middle East. This assignment was up my alley, given my work at Harvard and at the War College. My focus was offensive operations against Soviet forces in the Mediterranean and Black Seas. To that end, I was assigned to lead a study describing options for the Sixth Fleet and Allied navies in the early stages of war with the Warsaw Pact. I was later gratified that the responsible Allied commander for the southern region of NATO, Admiral H. E. Shear (CINCSOUTH), agreed with its findings.

Not long after we had formed OP-603, a study directive dated August 19, 1977 from National Security Advisor Zbigniew Brzezinski to the Secretary of Defense et alia charged the Pentagon with conducting a study of the vulnerability of oil supplies in the Persian Gulf. The directive, which came to be known as the "Petroleum Vulnerability Assessment," directed conduct of a study, but it was clearly designed to force interagency recognition of the fact that in 1977, we were not capable of defending our access to Persian Gulf oil. Indeed, the Joint Chiefs of Staff (JCS) did not have a strategy, never mind a workable current plan, to mount a defense of Iran and Saudi Arabia if the Soviet Union were to attack across the Zagros Mountains or gain passage through Iraq to the Arabian Peninsula. When the National Security Council (NSC) "tasker" arrived in OPNAV, I was assigned as the navy's action officer. I jumped at the chance, and it was, in retrospect, a defining moment in my navy career.

Admiral Crowe, remarkably familiar with the Middle East, was vitally interested in this NSC initiative. I met with him almost daily as all the services and the Joint Staff prepared the JCS response to the Brzezinski directive. When we finished the draft study for the secretary of defense's signature, the same interservice group went to work on a complementary military strategy for the Middle East and Persian Gulf. That project was a three-month-long effort with daily meetings and weekends of debate, discussion, and drafting. I was pleased that the navy's interests and imperatives were well represented in the strategy's recommendations. My air force counterpart in the strategy working group, Colonel John Warden, became famous for his advocacy of an offensive air strategy, targeting "centers of gravity." It became a blueprint for the eventual air offensive in Operation Desert Storm.

I welcomed the opportunity, arranged by Admiral Crowe, to brief the Persian Gulf strategy to the CNO, Admiral Hayward. It was our strong recommendation that he should vote in the affirmative to approve it at a forthcoming meeting of the JCS. The interactions with Admiral Crowe and Admiral Hayward during this project had important bearing on the future of my career as a political-military strategic planner.

It is common knowledge among officers aspiring to extraordinarily successful careers in the navy that an assignment as personal aide to a senior admiral can be an important stepping-stone. A position as aide to the CNO is a veritable career catapult. My chance came that fall, when Captain John Nyquist, the executive assistant (EA) to Vice Admiral Jim Doyle, the "dean" of the surface warfare community, informed me that I had been nominated to compete (with an aviator and submariner) for assignment as the personal aide to the CNO (OP-001).

I was interviewed by Admiral Hayward for almost forty minutes, and we discussed his expectations and the qualifications for the job as he saw them. (I recall one disquieting moment during the interview when Admiral Hayward described how disappointed he had been with one aide in his previous assignment as CINCPACFLT. The poor fellow had gotten the admiral to a speaking engagement in Chicago one day early.)

I did not get the personal aide job, but my disappointment was eased somewhat by communication from the CNO's EA. He explained that it was felt that I was "overqualified" but that I would be a candidate for assignment as the CNO's administrative assistant. A selection to that post would be made soon thereafter.

To my chagrin at the time, Admiral Crowe subsequently persuaded the CNO that I would be better suited and could "do more for the navy" by taking a job that had just opened in the OSD. I know of the intervention because Admiral Crowe called me about it one gray afternoon. It was with some reluctance and disappointment that in October 1978, I reported to the undersecretary of defense for policy and joined a branch called Planning and Requirements.

Time and events, however, would demonstrate that the assignment would lead to some rather positive results.

CHAPTER 6

"MARITIME SUPERIORITY" AND DEFENSE OF THE PERSIAN GULF

Office of the Secretary of Defense (Policy)

The Planning and Requirements branch had been established shortly before my arriving for duty there in October 1978. Led by an accomplished army officer, Colonel John Sewall (a future major general), the branch reported to the undersecretary of defense for policy (USD/P) and the deputy undersecretary of defense for policy review (DUSD/PR), new positions established by Secretary of Defense Harold Brown. Receiving congressional approval for an undersecretary for policy had been a signal accomplishment for Secretary Brown.

In the early '60s during the Robert McNamara era, the notion of a strategy providing guidance for budgeting had been regarded as nostalgic by hard-nosed system analysts. In the mid-'70s, the Program Analysis and Evaluation (PA&E) branch, led by an assistant secretary, had succeeded the Systems Analysis branch and was the "heavy" in the Office of the Secretary of Defense

(OSD). This was the case because that organization alone was responsible for both providing program guidance to the services and evaluating their Program Organization Memoranda (POM) and budgets as part of the Five-Year Plan. Following McNamara's logic, the view from OSD amounted to "if it's not programmed and not budgeted, it's not planned." The navy, in particular, had long chafed under the strictures imposed by PA&E and its predecessor, System Analysis, since McNamara. The 1980–1985 Five-Year Defense Plan (FYDP) was no exception.

Approved by Congress in 1975, the position of undersecretary for policy was filled the following year by a kindly and somewhat passive gentleman, a former secretary of the army, named Stan Resor. Resor's tenure in the position was short-lived, and with the position gapped, DUSD/PR Admiral (ret.) Daniel J. Murphy, the only nominal deputy, maneuvered adroitly to assume some of the responsibilities left unattended.

But Murphy's initiatives were challenged on several fronts. One was by Assistant Secretary of Defense for International Security Affaris (ISA) David McGiffert, who was for all intents and purposes the State Department's man in the Department of Defense (DOD). Absent an undersecretary, McGiffert saw himself as the "senior" member of the policy team. Another challenger was Robert W. Komer, the influential advisor to the secretary of defense on NATO affairs. Because he was not exactly in the policy "cluster" and because he reported directly to the secretary of defense, Komer was to prove a formidable competitor.

The issue that occupied most of my time and energy was the drafting of the first Defense Policy Guidance (DPG). To answer long-standing criticisms by Congress and the Services of Defense budgets and programs for lacking underlying strategies or policies, Brown decided to publish the DPG, which would guide and inform the Consolidated Guidance (CG) issued by PA&E.

Heretofore, the CG had been the only source of guidance to the services as they prepared their budgets and POMs. Brown's decision proved most helpful for the navy, which had been locked in a frustrating and acute struggle with the author of earlier CGs, Russell Murray, the assistant secretary of defense (PA&E).

The debates with Murray went to the very heart of the navy's mission and raison d'être. The navy saw its primary mission during the Cold War in two parts, one subsuming the other. The first was "sea control," which was defined as the ability to penetrate and operate in those maritime areas vital to the United States and its allies while denying our putative enemies the same latitude. But the navy's most vocal opponents and critics, especially in PA&E, tried to limit the navy's mission to "defend the sea lanes" and to protect shipping in narrowly defined waters across the Atlantic, the western Pacific, and the Mediterranean. This struggle over limiting sea control to sea lane defense was not just a semantic exercise—it had clear program and budget implications.

The second, and central, part of the navy's Maritime Strategy was to leverage "control" of vital ocean areas to promptly launch offensive operations against the Soviet Navy (especially the ballistic missile submarines [SSBN]), even in its home waters, and to attack the ports and bases that serviced the Soviet fleet and Soviet Naval Aviation (SNA). This, in other words, expanded the existing concept to "*offensive* sea control," a term that captured both missions. Under the navy's strategy, the prerequisite for success in war was maintaining a margin of maritime superiority in peacetime sufficient to ensure we had the means necessary to prevail in the event of war. Critics in OSD, especially Assistant Secretary of Defense Russell Murray (who had spent years at the navy's think tank, the Center for Naval Analyses) saw this— correctly, I might add—as the navy attempting to build a case for more and better armed aircraft carriers, strike aircraft, fighters and supporting cruisers, destroyers, and submarines—in short, the means necessary to enable the conduct of simultaneous offensive sea control operations against the Soviet Union in the Atlantic, Pacific, and Mediterranean.

As it happened, while working in OSD to promote the navy's Maritime Strategy and the case for *Nimitz*-class carriers, I was a member of a small group of mid-grade colleagues who met to informally discuss strategic issues and alternate futures for the navy and its large carrier task forces (as they were called then). Our group of between six and eight commanders and captains was chaired by a captain working in the office of Undersecretary of the navy James Woolsey. Captain Mosher's expertise was operations analysis. He and several others in the group argued the need for smaller carriers in dispersed formations as the alternatives to forces that were too vulnerable to Soviet submarine, air, and missile attacks.

The tenor of our meetings, and the heated conversations we were having, had come to the attention of the Chief of Naval Operations' (CNO) office, then embroiled in controversies regarding the case for more *Nimitz*-class carriers. Rear Admiral Bill Cockell, the executive assistant (EA) to the CNO, characterized our group as a new *Jeune École*, recalling a rebellious group of naval officers famous in the history of the Marine Nationale. Concern in the CNO's office was manifest by a visit to one of our meetings from a flag officer, none other than a future four-star admiral, Charles (Chuck) Larson. He probed our intentions and cautioned us not to get too far afield from official positions in our discussions.

The cancellation of a *Nimitz*-class aircraft carrier in the fiscal 1978 budget cycle had demonstrated that the Carter administration and the DOD were determined to limit navy force structure to "sea lane defense." By implication, Murray and Komer seemed intent on discrediting the navy's case for maintaining a margin of maritime superiority.[27]

The challenge of writing and framing a case for maritime superiority and ensuring that governing defense policy which translated to making a case for means adequate to execute the navy's mission in war soon became my first preoccupation in OSD, as it had been during my tour in the Office of the Chief of Naval Operations (OPNAV). Adm. Murphy tasked me and another member of the team to provide him with "tightly reasoned" statements on the need for an offensive navy that could be included in the draft of the DPG.

Because I had arrived in the Planning and Requirements group after the other navy member of the team, I had to work fast. Murphy was clearly dissatisfied with the drafts that had been prepared before my arrival. He told me that he had called "the navy" (presumably Adm. Crowe), requesting that an officer familiar with the navy's case for an offensive maritime strategy be transferred to his staff in OSD to work on this problem.

I felt that an earlier attempt crafted an argument that was rather stilted and overly conditional. Having just left the navy staff, it was clear to me as well as to Adm. Murphy that the early draft would certainly not be welcomed by the navy.

But the representatives of the army and air force in our group were not enamored with my proposed approach to promoting the capabilities necessary to ensure our superiority at sea, lest it draw resources and attention away from their own service budgets. The army and air force were clearly preoccupied with ensuring their own resources to reinforce and defend NATO's central region.

27 For a detailed account of the effect and application of an offensive maritime strategy, see John Lehman, *Oceans Ventured: Winning the Cold War at Sea* (New York: Norton, 2018).

The lone civilian in our Planning and Requirements group, Dr. Richard Haass, did not participate actively in our debates about the navy's missions. In retrospect, I am intrigued by what his view might have been, after discovering that the subject of his doctoral dissertation at Oxford University was a normative piece arguing for the establishment of a "zone of peace" in the Indian Ocean, free of the naval forces of both superpowers. That viewpoint was clearly not consistent with how we, the navy, saw our future. Richard, who is president of the prestigious Council on Foreign Relations at this writing, is an acclaimed author of several best-selling books on foreign policy. He had a most impressive career as a strategist and diplomat.

Having persuaded Admiral Murphy that we now had a potentially effective argument, we pressed on with the draft DPG, inserting treatment of maritime superiority that was consistent with the Maritime Strategy for the navy that we had crafted while in OP-603.

When circulated within OSD, the draft was roundly criticized in stinging comments from the assistant secretary of defense, PA&E, the special advisor to the secretary for NATO affairs (Ambassador Komer), and even the Joint Staff. At that time, the Joint Staff was dominated by army and air force officers, and the prevailing view prioritized requirements for the defense of the central region of NATO, even at the expense of the navy. As one example, the army, with help from the Joint Staff, was advocating trading an aircraft carrier in the FYDP for another installment of prepositioned overseas matériel configured in unit sets (POMCUS) to equip one heavy army division in case of its rapid deployment by air to Europe on warning of a Warsaw Pact attack.

The logic for creating the DPG is that its contents were to inform the preparation of the CG, which mandated priorities for service programs and budgets. But in that first year, the preparation of both documents almost coincided. Murray and Komer were simply not going to remain silent regarding the logic we presented in the draft DPG where the navy was concerned. An offensively equipped, three-ocean navy to take the fight into the home waters and littorals of the Soviet Union was simply not in their playbook.

A development that suggested the tide might be turning in our favor occurred when the secretary of defense offered what could only be termed a criticism of Murray's draft CG for fiscal years 1981–1985.

In a memorandum to the secretary of defense, PA&E had disputed the definition of "maritime superiority" that we had advanced in the draft DPG for that year. Because of the marked differences between the two guidance documents for that year regarding the missions of the navy in a NATO-Warsaw Pact War, Admiral Murphy had signed a memorandum (which I prepared) to the deputy secretary of defense, summarizing the essence of the problem we had with the limited role that PA&E had advanced to justify the navy's force programs. Murphy had argued that we should "improve the readiness and effectiveness of these forces to conduct offensive operations and then test their adequacy to attack Soviet bases and facilities."

Regarding our statement that the US Navy should be able to "threaten Soviet forces and facilities, even in their coastal waters," Murray had warned against "carrier strikes against the USSR, owing to high risk." His draft CG had averred that carrier forces were to be "sized and configured principally based on meeting contingencies outside of Europe and on peace time presence needs." He had gone on to direct that the capabilities that the navy needed to operate on the European flanks (Norwegian and Mediterranean Seas) and that sea lines of communication

(SLOC) protection during a NATO conflict "should be checked for adequacy." Finally, with regard to maritime "superiority," he argued that "sufficiency" be substituted instead. Murray's concluding recommendation to Secretary Brown had been that our initiative in the draft DPG be disallowed and that his views regarding the navy's programs priorities should prevail.

To our surprise, Secretary Brown disagreed with Murray. I recorded the comment he made in the margins of Murray's memorandum:

> I disagree [with Murray's logic]. The CG needs rewriting to say that we want to be able to attack Soviet land facilities later in the war, if we are able early in the war to seal off the GIUK line and corresponding Pacific straits, destroy Soviet Navy outside them and gain sea control. Then have options to **move to attack...land facilities.** (Emphasis added)

After a classic and protracted debate in meetings and memoranda circulating all around the Pentagon, we in OSD policy and the navy had won a major struggle against critics who thought superiority at sea was both too expensive and too dangerous a charter. The evening we received Secretary Brown's comment on Murray's memo, I was invited up to Admiral Murphy's office on the E-ring of the Pentagon's first deck, where he poured us both a celebratory drink.

Shortly thereafter, on learning that the air force was delaying the assignment of a colonel as his military assistant, the admiral asked me to serve as the "interim" military assistant. I moved up to his office in November 1979 and remained there until April of 1980.

***

While serving in that role, I had a ringside seat to the uncertainty and confusion in the national security community that accompanied events leading to the Iranian revolution and the abdication of the shah. The revolution spelled the collapse of the "Twin Pillars" strategy, devised during the Nixon era. Hardly a strategy, the policy had entrusted the security of our interests in the Persian Gulf to the Iranians on the one hand and Saudi Arabia on the other. It collapsed with the revolution in Iran. The Planning and Requirements directorate now became heavily engaged in preparing recommendations and comments on an assortment of policy statements and decision memoranda. We also helped prepare briefing books for meetings of senior DOD officials with key allies in Europe and the Middle East as they struggled to coordinate a "Western" response to the events in Iran.

There were clear signs at the time of a raging debate within the National Security Council (NSC) in the arguments put forth by Admiral Murphy, Assistant Secretary for ISA McGiffert, and the Joint Staff. A hard line was championed by National Security Advisor Brzezinski, who was determined to respond to what he saw as a "crescent of crisis" (the nations that stretched across the southern flank of the Soviet Union from the Indian subcontinent to Turkey, and southward through the Arabian Peninsula to the Horn of Africa) that was emerging following Khomeini's accession to power. A more passive group (in DOD, it included McGiffert) was led by Secretary of State Cyrus Vance.

While DOD Secretary Brown's direct reports Murphy, Komer, and McGiffert debated the options, the secretary himself, in contrast, seemed rather quiet and equivocal in the wake of the shah's fall. I remember reading materials prepared by ISA for the secretary's weekly breakfast meetings with Secretary Vance and National Security Advisor Brzezinski; they left me wondering whether Brown, the cabinet official with the gravest responsibility in this crisis, should not be taking a more determined stand. Although Iran was a vexed problem that worsened over the spring and summer of 1979, the takeover of the American embassy in Tehran in November and the Soviet invasion of Afghanistan in December of that year provided the exclamation points to the regional crises brewing before us.

In Planning and Requirements, our interest with regard to those developments in and around the Persian Gulf was their impact on our defense posture. Because there were not many options for deployment of ground forces or land-based tactical air, I was specifically focused on developing options for naval deployments to the Persian Gulf and the Indian Ocean, should circumstances require this. As described previously, prior to my assignment to OSD, I had participated in two Joint Chiefs of Staff (JCS) actions that had virtually anticipated the developments that were now at hand. The first was my work on the JCS response to Brzezinski's request of DOD for a petroleum supply vulnerability assessment. Our contribution was an assessment of the defensibility of the critical oil-producing areas on the Arabian Peninsula. The second, for which I had been the navy action officer, was the JCS strategy for the Middle East and Persian Gulf.

As we developed contingency plans for the defense of our vital interests in the region, the conclusions were stark. Notwithstanding the importance of US and allied access to the petroleum resources in the Gulf, we had already concluded in the earlier JCS work that the United States was woefully unprepared to secure our interests if they were attacked. Because the shah appeared stable on his throne at the time, we had not examined our ability to defend Iranian oil-producing areas in southern Iran and in the northern reaches of the Gulf. Nixon's "Twin Pillars" strategy had been deemed adequate to contain any threats to the "moderate" Arab oil producers from the only likely threat, Iraq. The novel specter of a Soviet attack on Gulf oil-producing areas, driving across the Zagros Mountains of Iran, became a scenario of concern. In that case, we would be clearly outmatched and certainly outdistanced.

What followed in late 1979 and throughout 1980 was an accelerated effort to redress these glaring deficiencies in long-term strategy for the region—in particular, the lack of base access there. Beyond the small facility the navy used in Bahrain that hosted the Middle East Force (three to four ships), and a strategic air base and anchorage at the former British station on Diego Garcia in the Indian Ocean, we did not have access to the necessary infrastructure to either base or stage large forces in the event of hostilities. The Soviet invasion of Afghanistan rang a loud alarm.

Admiral Murphy took the lead in OSD, arguing for an accelerated DOD-led effort to bolster our presence and increase our activities in the Indian Ocean area. In May 1979, Murphy transmitted a memorandum to the secretary of defense outlining the case for an enhanced naval presence in the Indian Ocean. He asserted that critics in the State Department and in ISA were wrong to allege that Murphy's recommendations were "escalatory" measures disproportionate to the threat. He elaborated:

> Too often...we couch our assessments in terms of relative Naval capabilities in the area...ignoring the fact that the opposition is there on the ground and in some numbers...the most telling comparison is that the Soviets can stage TU-95's and IL-38's out of Aden almost at will.

We negotiate for monthly P-3 flights out of Dharan or weekly operations from Djibouti.[28]

In a speech I helped write to the National Security Industrial Association on May 24, Murphy had summarized the consensus view in the policy group and the Joint Staff:

In the first place, we have longstanding commitments to several states in the region, and since the signing of the Camp David Accords, an even greater stake in them… Secondly, we have all grown increasingly dependent on the oil resources of the region. Thirdly, the withdrawal of British power, which culminated almost a decade ago, left a vacuum, which the Soviets, their clients, and their surrogates have hastened to fill…in the Horn of Africa, the Yemens and Afghanistan for starters. Fourthly, the sudden collapse of the Iranian monarchy and the resulting disorder have eliminated Iran as the regional counterweight to threats from unfriendly powers [Iraq]. Events in Iran have underlined the risk for other traditional regimes attempting to cope with the pressures of modernization and development. Taken together, these factors underline the need for a strategy of deeper involvement in the area by…the US and its allies.

It was the Soviet invasion of Afghanistan that forced a consensus in the NSC that much more had to be done to secure our interests. Even the State Department following Secretary Vance's resignation and its allies in DOD, the timid staff elements (ISA and PA&E) stiffened, abandoning the cautious line taken earlier in response to the Iranian revolution. Secretary Brown and

28 Daniel J. Murphy, Memorandum to Secretary of Defense, May 30, 1979.

National Security Advisor Brzezinski now led the charge to begin expanding our access to bases in the Middle East. Following a flurry of activity led by the DOD, agreements were negotiated with Egypt, Oman, and Saudi Arabia to support extensive surveillance and presence operations by land-based assets. At the same time, Brown commissioned the JCS to develop recommendations and measures that could be taken should the United States need to deploy significant forces to the region on short notice.

Having assumed duties as undersecretary of defense for policy (a position vacant since Resor's departure some two years before), Robert Komer, the former NATO advisor, took the lead in OSD for initiating the actions ordered by Brown. His deputy, the newly named deputy undersecretary for policy, was Walter Slocombe, a brilliant lawyer who had earned high praise for his work in the arms control arena. Parenthetically, Komer's famous bravado style (hence the nickname Blowtorch Bob) forced Admiral Murphy into a supporting but less influential role, and by the end of 1979, crisis response in the DOD was dominated by Komer and Slocombe. The other weighty players were Deputy Director for Plans and Policy Major General Richard (Dick) Boverie, USAF, and Paul Wolfowitz, an accomplished academician and deputy assistant secretary for regional programs in PA&E.

The task at hand was monumental because we were starting from a zero base. Wolfowitz undertook an analytical study of force requirements and alternative means to block a Soviet invasion from the north; we now had an ally in PA&E. The team I worked with in Planning and Requirements became the responsible staff element in the policy group, and we reported to Boverie, thence to Slocombe, and finally to Komer.

For his part, Komer, who in the past had downplayed any initiative that had the potential to detract from his almost myopic focus on Europe, and specifically the central front of NATO, was by this time a zealous convert to the cause following the Soviet invasion of Afghanistan. He became the leading advocate of the Rapid Deployment Joint Task Force (RDJTF) concept and the resources required to organize, train, and ready the deployment of three to four divisions to the Persian Gulf within thirty days. Although all of the policy group in OSD was still distrustful of "the navy" (to use FDR's oft-quoted critique), the emergence of a veritable crisis in the Persian Gulf area led to a change in perspective. Given the long distances to the theater from bases in the United States and Europe and the paucity of land bases from which we could operate, Ambassador Komer became more interested in sea-based and prepositioned forces, and the demands for sea control in that theater. In view of my work on "maritime superiority," however, the former champion of the army's overriding needs to defend in Europe reminded me regularly that he did not yet trust me personally to think "jointly." Nevertheless, Komer was impressed with our work on the RDJTF.

Within the services, bureaucratic battles raged. Responsibilities for the Middle East area had bounced among several chains of command since the end of World War II. The Unified Command Plan (UCP) in effect in 1979 had the region divided between the army-led European Command and the navy-led Pacific Command. The line dividing the two theaters was the western border of Pakistan. To confuse matters even further, the Indian Ocean was in the Pacific Command area of responsibility (AOR), but the Persian Gulf and the Red Sea were the responsibility of the European commander. The effort to take the lead in organizing and planning in support of the new Persian Gulf strategy was centered on the army staff. As discussions in the Joint Staff and OSD progressed, the ambitious and inspired army specified commander (CINCUSREDCOM), General Volmey Warner, overplayed his hand. When his campaign to command the RDJTF was not accepted, he resigned in protest.

Following negotiations in the Joint Staff and in meetings of the chiefs with Secretary Brown, an interim solution was agreed upon. The command of the RDJTF would be entrusted to Lieutenant General P. X. Kelley, a thoughtful marine and future commandant. He established his headquarters at MacDill Air Force Base (adjacent to the USREDCOM headquarters) to begin the detailed contingency planning and to begin plans for the training of forces assigned. The forces designated for the RDJTF were one Marine Expeditionary Force (MEF), the 18th Airborne Corps (comprising the 82nd Air Assault Division and the 101st Air Mobile Division), the 6th Armored Cavalry Regiment, and the 24th Mechanized Division. The commander of the RDJTF would report directly to the secretary of defense through the JCS, pending a review of the UCP and the establishment of a new unified command for the Persian Gulf region.

The single most demanding requirement was to develop workable plans and time-phased logistics to deploy and stage a large combat force closing on the Arabian Peninsula. I shifted my focus to defining the improvements necessary to Ras Banas, a former Soviet facility on the Red Sea coast of Egypt, which had been offered by the Egyptian government and was one of the key bases required to support the RDJTF. Planning the work on this base and the concept of operations for its use became my full-time job between late April 1980 and my departure from OSD in June.

The inspiration for this project came in the form of a memorandum from National Security Advisor Brzezinski to Secretary Brown, dated April 29, 1980, following a meeting of the NSC regarding our base access problem. President Carter had apparently requested an estimate of what it would cost to improve the base at Ras Banas. Brzezinski asked for a response by May 2, 1980, only three days later. Thankfully, we had identified what was available at Ras Banas and what had to be done to improve it. Our work included a notional time-phased force deployment plan for the units to be staged there and supported. Finally, we developed a concept of operations to move forces across the Red Sea and to protect them once on the Arabian Peninsula.

This was heady work, and it entailed long days and nights and endless meetings on three floors of the Pentagon with PA&E, the Joint Staff, the services, and with our bosses Komer, Slocombe, and Boverie. After we had answered Brzezinski, I could look back with satisfaction at the work we had already completed: improving our strategy, developing our plans, and defining programs, all performed in rapid response to the grave turn of events in the Middle East.[29]

When I took my leave from OSD, I was invited to don my uniform (we normally wore civilian attire to work in the Pentagon in those days) and to appear at an award ceremony in the office of Deputy Undersecretary Walt Slocombe. He presented me with the Defense Superior Service Medal. The citation that accompanied the award read in part:

> He was instrumental in developing a definition of United States Maritime superiority and formulating planning guidance for...Maritime forces in the FY81–85 and FY82–86 Defense Policy Guidance. He also played a key role in developing policy for the staging and deployment of the United States...forces to protect vital interests in the region of the Persian Gulf and Indian Ocean.

29 I was later gratified to learn on the eve of Desert Storm in 1991, while Paul Wolfowitz was serving as the undersecretary of defense (policy) in the George H. W. Bush administration and I was assigned as the defense attaché in Paris, he was heard by a former colleague to remark, "Where is Dur and his base at Ras Banas?"

CHAPTER 7

THE MARITIME STRATEGY" IN ACTION

Commanding USS *Comte de Grasse* (DD-974)

Having detached from Office of the Secretary of Defense (OSD) in May 1980, I began a four-month basic training and indoctrination course for prospective commanding officers (COs). I was delighted with my orders to command USS *Comte de Grasse* (DD-974). She was a ship in the latest *Spruance* class of destroyers equipped with gas turbine propulsion, which had replaced the problematic high-pressure steam engineering plants of the ships I had served in before. In addition, the ship's name was unique. Unlike the other *Spruance*-class ships which were named for flag officers who had distinguished themselves in World War II, she was named for the French admiral who had defeated a British fleet at the entrance of Chesapeake Bay in 1781. As I will note later, his contribution to our independence led to the defeat of the British during the siege of Yorktown. My grandfather, whose mother came from Lorraine, had immigrated to the United States in 1890, and we had a strong abiding pride in the Dur family's French heritage. As mentioned earlier, I had lived in France for three years as a boy in conjunction with my father's diplomatic assignment in Lyon. In short, I was excited to command "the Count," as we knew her.

The first task I faced was getting underway from a berth on the Molo Santangelo, a pier in the inner harbor of Naples, Italy. The ship was "Med moored," which meant that two anchors had been set at angles to position and hold the bow, while the stern was moored with crossed lines to bollards on the pier. Now, when breaking that moor, the trick was to recover the two anchors while creeping ahead, keeping the stern from swinging as a result of wind and current. The night before we were to get underway for exercises with the *Saratoga* task group (TG60.2), I quietly walked the pier and then sat in my chair on the darkened bridge. I was pondering the sequence of events to clear the harbor safely the next morning with my crew straining to observe how the new captain would manage this evolution without a pilot. Planning paid off—and my confidence grew—as I used the engines and rudders to hold the ship in a proper orientation despite a cross wind. We recovered the two anchors cleanly and made our way through the breakwater into the Tyrrhenian Sea.

Among the most difficult challenges early in my tour were while we were deployed in the Mediterranean, transiting in company with USS *Briscoe* (DD-977) to our final port call, the port of Gibraltar. In the mid-afternoon, when we were less than fifty miles from port, we received a distress call on the very-high-frequency (VHF) radio from an Indian merchantman. The captain of the Indian merchant ship announced that he had a man overboard. The currents in that part of the Mediterranean are strongly affected by the narrow passage known as the Strait of Gibraltar, and with that in mind, both *Briscoe* and *De Grasse* began an expanding search pattern east of the man's reported position. After several fruitless hours and with dusk approaching,

Commander Geoff Chesbrough in *Briscoe* announced that he was continuing to Gibraltar. He directed that I, the junior captain, stay and continue searching until dark. I dutifully remained until informed that the missing Indian sailor was accounted for.

I would be making my first landing on a pier, in a new ship type, in an unfamiliar port, and in darkness. I cannot exaggerate the anxiety that I felt. To make things even more exciting, there was a north wind gusting to about thirty knots across the narrow channel entrance into Gibraltar. About two miles west of the channel entrance, I embarked the Gibraltarian harbor pilot who was to assist me with passage through the harbor to a berth alongside *Briscoe*, now comfortably moored.

Approaching the channel entrance, I ordered a two-thirds bell (about ten knots of headway) at the pilot's suggestion. I kept the conn, but I was inclined to accept the experienced pilot's recommendation given the challenges. However, the closer we got to the buoys marking the channel, I could tell that our attempts to steer into the middle of the channel were not working. The wind and current were driving us upon the southern-most buoys. The pilot kept asking for more left rudder, but I soon sensed that rudder alone would not do the trick.

With only twenty to thirty yards of clearance on the southern line of buoys, I ordered first a "standard bell" (15 knots) and then a "full bell" (20 knots) to clear the last buoys. The pilot became excited, yelling at me to stop the engines, lest we prove unable to kill our way before hitting two ships moored just inside the harbor. I ignored his excited advice, and upon entering the breakwater I ordered a "back full" (astern) bell, which slowed the ship immediately. I turned to the shocked pilot and explained that this was a characteristic response of controllable-reversible pitch propellers. (The effect was dramatic as the ship could stop in a little more than one ship length regardless of the speed ahead.) We proceeded into the harbor and moored, unassisted by tugboats, alongside *Briscoe*. I was as relieved as I was gratified that we had succeeded in this tough test.

Shortly after taking command, "the Count" participated in a challenge to Libya's closure of the Gulf of Sidra to US warships. As part of Task Group 60.2, we were assigned duties escorting the USS *Saratoga* (CV-60) into the Gulf of Sidra. The reason for our entry was to conduct missile exercises that had been announced earlier in a notice to mariners (NOTAM).

Following our return from the Mediterranean to our homeport in Norfolk, Virginia, the interdeployment period, which was intended to be for crew rest and ship maintenance, was anything but. We spent two months in the spring of 1981 in the Caribbean, undertaking refresher training (REFTRA) at the Guantánamo Naval Base, conducting anti-submarine warfare (ASW) in the Virgin Islands Operating Area, and gunnery exercises in the Puerto Rican Operating Areas.

During our six-week stay in Gitmo, I got a good look at one of the Cold War's points of confrontation: there were a number of instances of refugees taking serious risks to gain political asylum on the base. Several swam through dangerous shark-infested waters trying to gain entry, and one asylum seeker actually entered the base by ditching a Cuban patrol boat on a sandbar near the entrance to the harbor. In yet another incident, two uniformed Cuban Army soldiers attempted to cross into the base over land, but the would-be defectors were wounded and captured by Cuban forces before they could reach the US perimeter.

I wrote my mother to tell her of my experiences in Guantánamo, and she replied by admonishing me to avoid any contact with Cuban officials because their intelligence services surely had my name on file. She did not realize how difficult it would have been for me to encounter any official Cubans on our corner of the island.

The ship having completed refresher training in August 1981, we were assigned to escort the USS *Eisenhower* (CVN-69) during a major fleet exercise in the North Atlantic and the Norwegian Sea. It was a major test of strategy in a realistic setting: the offensive Maritime Strategy we in the navy had been advocating since the late 1970s would now be demonstrated to our allies and putative enemies alike. OCEAN VENTURE, as the exercise was dubbed, has since been made famous in a book recently published by former Secretary of the Navy (SECNAV) John Lehman.[30]

Our participation began with the transit across the Atlantic at a high speed of advance. While in the mid-Atlantic and in a rescue destroyer station astern of *Eisenhower*, we rode up onto a rogue swell about twenty feet high from crest to trough. We had been trying to maintain a speed of about thirty knots to match the carrier's ordered speed and to remain in our assigned station. As the large swell approached, we were in the process of recovering our SH-2D Light Airborne Multipurpose System (LAMPS) helicopter which was in the "short final" phase of approach. The bow of our ship rose at a sharp angle onto the rogue wave, and I waved the helicopter off. When the bow descended on the backside of the swell, it submerged as far as the forward gun mount, or about thirty feet. Immediately after recovering our composure and settling back into more moderate seas of eight to ten feet, I was notified that an alarm had sounded, signaling a loss of pressure in the bow-mounted sonar dome's pressurization system.

After recovering our helicopter, we slowed the ship with the permission of the *Eisenhower*, and I climbed down into the sonar

30 John Lehman, *Oceans Ventured: Winning the Cold War at Sea* (New York: Norton, 2018). See especially pp. 65–68.

trunk with my weapons officer, Lieutenant (later Captain) Brent Gooding, to investigate the casualty. We confirmed later that the fifty-foot horizontal excursion of the bow, rising and falling on the swell, had resulted in an overpressure in the interior of the dome and caused a rupture or split in the rubber window installed on the dome's face.[31]

When I reported the casualty to the task group commander in *Eisenhower*, Rear Admiral Jerry Tuttle, I expected the worst. Had Admiral Tuttle followed established procedures for this type of casualty (there having been several instances of split rubber windows before our accident), we might have been ordered to turn around and return to our homeport across the Atlantic at a slow speed to minimize damage to the sonar transducer.

Wanting to remain in the exercise and therefore determined to avoid the fate of a premature return to Norfolk, I asserted (accurately, as experience then demonstrated) that we could maintain the prescribed pressure at speeds of twelve knots or greater. We reasoned that this should be possible because the tear was on a seam in the window; therefore, at those speeds, the tear should close and reseal itself because of the pressure generated on the face of the dome by the oncoming sea. Admiral Tuttle agreed, and he and the Commander of Second Fleet (COMSECONDFLT) interceded with our type commander in Norfolk. We were permitted to continue the transit, thereby able to remain in what was the most realistic warfare exercise in my naval career.

OCEAN VENTURE 81, an offensive sea control exercise, was designed by Vice Admiral James Aloysius "Ace" Lyons while he was both serving as the US Navy's COMSECONDFLT and wearing an additional hat in the NATO organization as Commander of the Striking Fleet (COMSTRIKFLT). "Ace" Lyons

---

31 A rubber window installed in the forward portion of the dome is acoustically transparent, thereby improving the performance of the sonar.

was a vocal and forceful proponent of training the fleet as it would fight. I knew the admiral well, having worked for him as the responsible action officer on several Joints Chiefs of Staff (JCS) papers. Lyons was known for his demanding leadership, combative style, and strident efforts to advance navy interests and positions in the Joint arena. Following promotion to flag rank and an assignment in the strategy division of the Joint Staff, he earned the admiration of many for his intellect and bureaucratic skills. Although often challenged, he rarely lost an argument to his counterparts in the other services. His later appointment as COMSECONDFLT in 1981 gave him the opportunity and the resources to direct an exercise that would demonstrate the change in our maritime strategy both to our NATO allies and to our putative enemy, the Soviets.

This was, after all, the height of the Cold War. The threat to our navy, and to all the NATO navies in the North Atlantic, was the Soviet Northern Fleet and Soviet Naval Aviation (SNA) based in the Kola Peninsula. Lyons redesigned the annual major NATO exercise, moving a two-carrier strike fleet (which included the British Anti-Submarine Warfare Group Two [ASWGRU 2]) and almost forty combatant ships through the Greenland-Iceland-United Kingdom (GIUK) gap into the Norwegian Sea within striking range of the Soviet Union.

Soviet reactions were predictable, and they obliged by presenting challenging opposition. As we transited waters between Iceland and the United Kingdom with the *Eisenhower,* we did so at a high speed of advance, mindful that our current intelligence reports estimated that several Soviet diesel submarines were lying in wait to intercept and simulate attacks on our forces. If they followed our practice, "simulations" would entail gaining correct attack positions relative to their targets, and workable fire control solutions for the weapons appropriate to the task. We maneuvered to avoid. During the transit, our helicopter gained contact with active sonobuoys on one of the Soviet submarines in the gap, positioned to intercept our group. The helicopter simulated a torpedo attack, and we kept moving at thirty-plus knots!

In the Norwegian Sea, we were regularly overflown by many Soviet aircraft, including cruise missile-armed bombers, TU-16 *Badgers*, and TU-22 *Backfires*, mainstays of Soviet anti-carrier weapons systems. The STRIKFLT was continuously shadowed by several Soviet surface combatants and trailed by nuclear attack submarines.

The Soviet reaction, as measured by the number of aircraft and ships shadowing, grew especially acute when one of the task groups, of which we were part, rounded the North Cape of Norway. The exercise objective established by Admiral Lyons included conducting simulated air strikes against Soviet bases in the Kola Peninsula. To simulate this part of the strategy, carrier aircraft conducted "mirror-image strikes" against mock targets in southern Norway. Even the meteorological environment added to the realism, featuring very heavy seas, rainy weather, and the bitter cold so typical of the Norwegian Sea.

As a participant, I will attest to the invaluable training the fleet received in all warfare disciplines. Destroyers, designed to conduct ASW, EW, anti-air warfare (AAW), and anti-cruise missile (ACM) defense while providing escort and cover for aircraft carriers, were no exception. We covered all our primary missions. All in all, OCEAN VENTURE 81 was an exhilarating test for destroyermen.

Leaving the exercise while it was still in progress in the Norwegian Sea, "the Count" transited south to Scapa Flow, an isolated, windblown bay formed by three of the Orkney Islands, where a destroyer tender, USS *Yellowstone* (AD-41), had been prepositioned to service any surface combatants or submarines experiencing a casualty and needing repair. This too was a realistic addition to the exercise as an essential requirement in wartime. The tenders have long since been decommissioned, which, in my mind, was a serious mistake. World War II showed us the importance of afloat repair capability in an extended conflict.

After a few days in Scapa Flow, we moored alongside the anchored *Yellowstone*, and the tender's divers inspected our sonar dome. They confirmed that the dome required repair once we returned to the United States.

From there, we were directed to Milford Haven in the English Channel to pick up some supplies for other ships in the exercise. The entry into Milford Haven, which is used extensively in simulators to train ship handlers in the art of navigation and piloting, was long and tortuous. We entered the channel in the dark in order to be at our assigned berth by 8:00 a.m. as directed; our passage was without incident.

Reentering the English Channel, we proceeded to rendezvous with the Royal Navy (RN) destroyer HMS *Antrim* (Dl8) and formed a two-ship surface action group (SAG) tasked to participate in OCEAN SAFARI, the second phase of OCEAN VENTURE. We were tasked as an "Orange" force; our mission in the exercise was to simulate a Soviet group and to oppose, of all things, a carrier task group formed around the French carrier FS *Clemenceau* (R98). This was a curious assignment, as our namesake was Admiral François Joseph Paul, Comte de Grasse, the victor in a battle with a British fleet off the Virginia Capes in 1781. Here we were teamed with *Antrim* to fight the Marine Nationale two hundred years later. I suspected mischief on the part of the staff of COMSECONDFLT who had made the ship assignments for this phase of the exercise. Quite obviously, history and namesakes were not a concern.

After three days of searching in the Bay of Biscay, we located and successfully targeted the *Clemenceau*. *Comte de Grasse* simulated a Soviet *Kynda*-class cruiser, and we simulated firing a salvo of four cruise missiles over the horizon, reporting this to the exercise umpire embarked in *Clemenceau*. He judged our attack a success, and we approached the French task group at best speed. When we visually encountered the first French ship, the DDG FS *Cassard* (D614), we simulated taking her under fire with our guns by rapidly flashing our search light.

We then sent *Cassard* and *Clemenceau* a flashing light message, "*Souviens les Jacobins*" (Remember the Jacobins). My attempt at humor, avenging the French revolutionaries who had not dealt kindly with the family of the nobleman De Grasse, amused Vice Admiral Claude Gagliardi, the French commander aboard *Clemenceau*. When we met shortly thereafter, Adm. Gagliardi explained that he had "no appropriate response" and that he was in any event a "servant of the French Republic."

Later, following the final phase of OCEAN SAFARI, we made a port visit to Brest, France, as the prelude to what would be a year of close collaboration with the Marine Nationale and specifically with the French destroyer FS *De Grasse* (D612). Plans had already been made for the two ships to celebrate the two hundredth anniversary of the battle of the Virginia Capes and the surrender of the British to a Franco-American force after the Battle of Yorktown. After we moored at the French naval base on September 19, the Marine Nationale provided me helicopter transport to Lorient, where the French destroyer, *De Grasse*, was undergoing a scheduled overhaul. I went aboard the ship and met with Captain (*Capitaine de vaisseau*) Jean Brunet to begin planning for his forthcoming visit to Norfolk and our participation in this grand celebration of our alliance.

Upon my return to Brest, we hosted a cocktail party in honor of Admiral Paul de Bigault de Cazanove, the French commander of the French Atlantic Fleet (CECLANT), who had also been aboard *Clemenceau* during OCEAN SAFARI. This occasion marked the first cocktail party allowed on a US ship visiting a foreign port since Prohibition days. The strict rule imposed in 1914 by then-SECNAV Josephus Daniels forbade the use of alcohol aboard commissioned ships of the US Navy. A relaxation of the long-standing prohibition was announced just before our visit to France. It was fitting that *Comte de Grasse* was the first US ship to serve her guests good French champagne and wine while in a French port. Since we were only weeks away from celebrating Admiral De Grasse's victory, I also took a small delegation with me to Paris and, together with the mayor of Paris, we laid a wreath at the monument to the admiral in the Trocadero Gardens. It was the first of several memorial celebration of the nobleman's contributions during 1981 and 1982.

In the interest of balance while dealing with close allies, we left Brest and made a visit to Plymouth, England, a principal base and dockyard for the RN. Following that visit we returned to Norfolk in late October, where we entered a repair availability for routine preventive maintenance and minor repairs before we would be taking a significant role in the celebration of the bicentennial of the Battle of Yorktown. "The Battle of the Chesapeake," as the French know it, was fought on September 5, 1781 and preceded the victory at Yorktown. De Grasse and his fleet of twenty-four ships of the line won what George Washington termed "a pivotal victory" at the Virginia Capes. A British fleet under the command of Rear Admiral Thomas Graves, comprising nineteen ships of the line, was attempting to deliver reinforcements and supplies to the British Army in Yorktown, which was under the command of General Lord Cornwallis. The British fleet was defeated at the entrance to the Chesapeake and forced to disengage and retreat. By defeating Graves and forcing the retreat of the British fleet, De Grasse effectively sealed Cornwallis's fate at Yorktown. He surrendered soon thereafter.[32]

During the bicentennial celebration, our *Comte de Grasse* and the French *De Grasse* were assigned the most prominent and the best anchorages in front of the Yorktown monument, which stood on a hill above the York River. The monument, which had been erected for the centennial of the victory, celebrates the American and French forces who fought and died there during the siege.

Both of our ships were honored with visits by VIPs. Aboard the French ship, President Mitterrand hosted a luncheon for President Reagan. We in *Comte de Grasse* hosted a breakfast and tour of our ship for Vice President George H. W. Bush, who graciously addressed our crew on the mess decks.

The vice president's visit to our ship was arranged by my former boss, Admiral Dan Murphy, USN (Ret.), now serving as the vice president's chief of staff. The occasion was a huge honor for me and my crew. As protocol would dictate, the navy ensured that many of my superiors in the chain of command would be present during the visit. Vice President Bush arrived in Marine Two, a specially configured *Sea King* helicopter, which made a perfect landing on our flight deck (as one would expect). Before the helicopter's arrival, SECNAV John Lehman and Admiral Harry D. Train II, Commander in Chief of the Atlantic Fleet (CINCLANTFLT), landed in a navy helicopter. They were joined by the commander of the Second Fleet and other lesser dignitaries in my chain of command. As a result, there was room for only three of my officers at the breakfast table.

---

32 For a detailed account of Comte de Grasse's contribution to our independence, see Charles Lee Lewis, *Admiral De Grasse and American Independence* (Annapolis, MD: United States Naval Institute, 1945).

While at breakfast, the vice president mentioned to me and anyone else listening that it had been almost forty years since a navy ship had visited the bucolic port city of Kennebunkport, Maine. By coincidence, the Bush summer home, Walker's Point, is in Kennebunkport. Secretary Lehman turned to Admiral Train and suggested that a ship visit to Kennebunkport might be arranged soon enough.

I watched how the chain of command worked with keen interest as the idea was literally passed down the line. The requested visit did not materialize, however, until I took the initiative while in command of the USS *Yorktown* (CG-48) some four years later.

On our departure from Yorktown, *De Grasse* and *Comte de Grasse* transited down the York River in a line abreast. Entering the Chesapeake Bay, we increased speed and made high-speed turns and a sweeping pass in front of the lighthouse at Cape Henry to honor our common namesake. The maneuvers were filmed by our helicopter, and a photo of the event hung for many years in the Marine Nationale's headquarters on the Place de la Concorde.

The next few weeks were given over to a long-deferred dry-docking period at the Norfolk Naval Shipyard to repair the damaged sonar dome. We spent the Thanksgiving holiday in drydock in Portsmouth, Virginia. Leaving the shipyard, we sailed up the York River, reloaded all our ammunition at Yorktown Weapon Station, and then began a transit to the Mediterranean for what would ultimately be another seven-month deployment to the Sixth Fleet and Northern Europe. While deployed, we participated as part of a carrier task group in several fleet exercises and bilateral exercises with allied navies.

We also made memorable visits to Malta, Tunisia, Morocco, Spain, Italy, and of course, France. Our stop in Sfax, Tunisia included an awkward moment wherein I was asked to join the

American consul in laying a wreath at a cemetery dedicated to Tunisian "martyrs" who had died in a rebellion against French rule. In France, "the Count" was always a celebrated guest.

One visit was particularly special. Anchored just off the breakwater in Cannes, we were joined by our colleagues in the French *De Grasse*, in full view of hundreds of people walking along the famous La Croisette Boulevard. Many of our crew traveled by car to the city of Grasse, the birthplace of the count. There, our soccer team played a team from the French ship in the municipal stadium for what we named after Admiral De Grasse's flagship "the *Ville de Paris* Cup," with at least a thousand people in attendance. We lost the soccer match badly and offered to follow that match with a game of softball. The French politely declined.

That evening, Captain Brunet and I were guests of the mayor of Grasse at a reception for the city's notables. The mayor was a proud member of the French Communist Party, and I undertook my visit to the Hôtel de Ville with a little trepidation. As Brunet and I presented ourselves and the plaques of our ships to the mayor, he asked which one of us commanded the *De Grasse*. Brunet explained that he commanded the French *citoyen* (citizen) ship *De Grasse*. I could not resist turning to the mayor and noting that I commanded the *vaisseau noble* (the noble ship), USS *Comte de Grasse*. He replied that it was his understanding that America did not recognize titles of nobility. I countered that in this case we had made an exception in view of the role this nobleman had played in our revolution. The mayor smiled and turned to other subjects.

There followed a series of small exercises: naval gunfire support (NGFS) training on an Italian range in Sardinia and ASW training in the Gulf of Lyon with two other destroyers, a French frigate, and a maritime patrol aircraft flying from Sigonella, Sicily.

We were then scheduled for a visit to Villefranche-sur-Mer, the former homeport of the Sixth Fleet flagship. I welcomed that visit because, as I mentioned earlier, my first assignment in the navy had assigned me to the *Little Rock*, which was originally to have been homeported in Villefranche. This was to be a working visit to conduct a repair and maintenance availability with the USS *Puget Sound* (AD-38), which was at the time the flagship of the Commander of US Sixth Fleet (COMSIXTHFLT), Vice Admiral William Rowden.

Now, there are two large mooring buoys maintained by the Marine Nationale in the deep harbor of Villefranche. One of these is well inside the harbor and relatively close to the quai wall. The other is in more open water and somewhat farther from the shore. The harbor itself is a spectacular setting. To the immediate north are the foothills of the Alps, ascending to a height of more than six thousand feet. To the west is a set of hills that separate Villefranche from the city of Nice. To the east is Cap Ferrat, arguably one of the most beautiful peninsulas in Europe. On the waterfront in Villefranche there is a famous luxury hotel named Welcome, in English. It dates to the early twentieth century when the town attracted many prominent visitors from the United States and Great Britain. Villefranche was and remains a welcome sanctuary for many visiting ships of the US Navy.

In maneuvering into the harbor the rainy, windy day when we arrived, my ability to handle this 9,000-ton destroyer was severely tested. The complicated evolution took almost an hour and a half. It would not seem so remarkable but for the fact that the stages in mooring to the buoy were done in a wind with a speed of twenty-five knots, gusting to thirty-five knots. In fact, the wind was so strong that while holding the ship steady and in position near the buoy while the chain was being shackled, the ship's screws were turning ahead at a two-thirds bell, the equivalent power necessary to make twelve knots in a becalmed setting.

The ship safely moored, we set the normal in-port watch and announced liberty for the crew. After cleaning up and shifting into our "civvies," ten of my officers in my gig and I proceeded to what became our favorite restaurant in Villefranche, the storied La Mère Germaine, or "Mom Germaine," as our forebearers in the Sixth Fleet had named it. After we were settled, we noticed that Admiral Rowden and his lovely wife, Sally, were also seated in the restaurant and enjoying dinner. I was very pleased and honored when the admiral came to our table and extended his congratulations to us on the job we had done to safely moor our ship under such arduous conditions. During that visit, I also met and befriended the mayor of Villefranche, Joseph Calderoni, and his wife, Jeanine. The mayor, a highly decorated hero of the French Resistance, spoke no English, but his love of America and for the American Navy knew no bounds.

Near the end of our deployment to the Sixth Fleet and while in another tender availability, this time in Gaeta, Italy, I was summoned to Admiral Rowden's cabin in *Puget Sound*. There, the admiral informed me that our deployment would be extended by almost six weeks so that we could provide a suitable platform and a flagship for the Supreme Allied Commander Atlantic (SACLANT), none other than Admiral Harry D. Train, whom we had met in Yorktown. The plan was for SACLANT to host the NATO Secretary General, Joseph Luns, and the other major NATO military commanders for a luncheon meeting aboard our ship, which was to be moored in Antwerp, Belgium. Rowden explained that we had been selected for this high honor as a result of our demonstrated prowess in hosting VIPs.

The explanation proved the adage that success brings more challenge. The reaction from my crew when I announced the delay in our return to homeport was mixed. The bachelors were generally pleased because we were promised three more port visits in Northern Europe. Most of the married men, especially the junior officers, chief petty officers, and senior enlisted, were not so thrilled.

Leaving the Mediterranean, we transited to an operating area in the eastern Atlantic for some individual ship exercises on a British training range. We then entered a narrow channel to the Irish port city of Cobh, where we were hosted by the Irish Naval Service at what had been a former base of the RN, Queenstown.

In a ceremony in the city of Cork honoring my wardroom, an amusing moment occurred that still brings a smile. The Lord Mayor took me aside and asked me to explain how we had come to name an American warship after a French nobleman. I explained the reason for the name and some of the related history. The mayor nodded approvingly and suddenly clanged his champagne glass with a spoon, calling for a toast. "Ladies and gentlemen," he exclaimed in a loud and thick brogue, "I want to raise my glass to the Comte de Grasse! You may be wondering, as I was, how this French gentleman came to be the namesake of an American warship. Let me tell you how this happened. This French admiral and his mighty fleet beat the English and secured America's independence, a country, as you will recall, that became a refuge for a million Irishmen."

"Hear, hear!" the assemblage roared in approval.

From Ireland, we went on to Amsterdam, our second port visit in advance of the occasion planned in Antwerp for Admiral Train, then transited down the Schelde River, entering it at Flushing on the high tide at around 8:00 p.m. The current was swift, and as the tide began to ebb, it grew even stronger. We did have a river pilot aboard to help with the navigation, but the transit lasted all night, and we encountered significant turns in the river bends and odd currents. It made for an exhausting night's work.

We arrived at the entrance to a lock, which permits entry into the port of Antwerp but would not open for another thirty minutes. We had to drop anchor in the river to hold our position until the crew arrived to open the lock. I remember how hard we had to work to turn the ship against that river current to stem its effect. It took all the power we had to twist the ship against the current before anchoring. A long thirty minutes later, we reversed the procedure and carefully entered the lock as the first ship through that morning.

Once through the lock, we transited a reach into one of the world's busiest commercial ports and moored an hour and a half later at one of the terminal piers. The crew immediately began cleaning and polishing the ship in anticipation of the luncheon to be hosted by the admiral, which was scheduled for later that day. We had been moored no more than thirty minutes, and having been up all night, I was hardly prepared for visitors, when, to my amazement, Admiral Train himself arrived on the pier with his chief of staff to discuss plans and review our preparations. We hurriedly rendered the appropriate honors, and I escorted Admiral Train to the wardroom.

We learned that the admiral's invited guests were NATO Secretary General Joseph Luns; the Commander in Chief of the European Command (USCINCEUR), General Bernard Rogers; and the Commander in Chief Channel (CINCCHAN), Admiral of the Fleet Sir John Fieldhouse. I dare say that although we had hosted VIPs on my watch, this was the most august group to visit at the same time, save the visit by Vice President Bush the year before. In any event, honors were executed with precision, the ship shone, and with the help of our mess attendants, Admiral Train's stewards put on an impressive luncheon in our wardroom.

Before leaving Antwerp, we embarked thirty "tigers": sons, fathers, and brothers of the crew, who had been invited to transit home on the ship. This was a concession to our married men, arranged by our bosses back home. I was especially pleased that my son Philip, who was nine years old at the time, was able to fly to Antwerp on his own and experience a weeklong sea voyage with me.

While planning our transatlantic passage, we discovered that at the prescribed transit speed of sixteen knots, we would arrive in our home port on a Sunday morning. This was not permissible under local navy regulations. While we were still in the eastern Atlantic, I sent a message to the operational commander, COMSECONDFLT, requesting permission to increase speed to eighteen knots in order to make a Saturday arrival possible. With a crew ready to get home after an extended deployment, I felt that ours was a reasonable request.

It was approved, but although I had copied my Norfolk chain of command on the request, I came to understand that I had committed a breach of protocol. On the Friday before our arrival in Norfolk, I received a short message from the group commander, Rear Admiral William F. ("Scot") McCauley, requesting my presence in his office at 0800 in the morning on the Monday following our return. Although I had planned shore leave and a reunion with my family, I postponed those plans. The message from the admiral did not specify a subject, and my commodore, Captain Howard, who met us on arrival, did not inform me of the reason for my summons.

After waiting two hours outside the admiral's office, I was shown in and greeted with a stern "Sit down, Commander." The admiral informed me of his displeasure that I had gone directly to the operational commander, COMSECONDFLT, for permission to increase speed instead of working through him. As he put it, and not gently, "Commander, I am the admiral in your life, do you understand?" I responded meekly, "Aye, aye, sir," and took my leave.

After our arrival in Norfolk, we began an extended maintenance period, which included another gripping nuclear technical proficiency inspection (NTPI) and an operation propulsion plan examination (OPPE)—two of the most exacting inspections a destroyer can undergo. Then the opportunity to conduct intensive warfare training in the Puerto Rican Operating Area in company with the USS *America* (CVA-66). We proceeded independently to the navy's Atlantic Undersea Test and Evaluation Center (AUTEC) Range, situated in deep water east of Andros Island in the Bahamas. There, we began a round of very realistic ASW training on the instrumented range in what is known as the tongue of the ocean.

This set of ASW exercises would afford us a special opportunity. Earlier, while undergoing training in the Caribbean in late 1980, we had been sent to the AUTEC Range off Andros Island to serve as a surface ship target for the training of prospective submarine COs embarked in an attack submarine. In these exercises we were able to track the attacking submarine, but we couldn't shoot back. The submarine would fire MK-48 torpedoes at us. These were programmed not to hit, of course, but the sight of a torpedo the size of a small submarine passing ten feet under your ship at forty knots is sobering, to say the least.

For this next round of exercises, our type commander (COMNAVSURFLANT), Vice Admiral J. D. Johnson, approved a request that I made to enhance our training—namely, whether I might embark prospective destroyer COs and modify the training syllabus to allow our ship to conduct weapons firing exercises using the submarine as a target, just as they were targeting us. Surprisingly, the submariners agreed, and so this phase of training included a set known as free play. The opportunity was appreciated by embarked guests, our ASW teams, and by our LAMPS helicopter detachment, which was allotted several exercise torpedoes.

By way of background, *Spruance*-class destroyers were the first surface combatants to incorporate many of the quieting technologies originally developed for modem US submarines. These included isolation mountings for rotating and reciprocating machinery and the noise-reducing Prairie-Masker System. Simply described, the latter draws bleed air from the compressor stages of the installed gas turbine engines to produce large volumes of air, which are routed to belts attached externally to the hull around the main machinery spaces. These belts then emit blankets of air bubbles to shield the noisiest spaces in the ship. In addition, bleed air is also routed to the tips of the ship's propellers, thereby masking the noisy cavitation they generate. When "quiet ship" is ordered in the destroyer, all unnecessary machinery, such as oil purifiers, air compressors, and hydraulic pumps, is secured. The crew is admonished to quiet the ship. This meant stocking feet and no loud noises such as slamming doors and hatches, and so forth.

Through these free play exercises, we learned that our ship, when operating at moderate speed, was indeed a very quiet platform. It was *so* quiet, in fact, that the submarine "attacking" us was hard-pressed to detect and classify us as a destroyer. In the post-exercise debriefing from the AUTEC Range Authority, we were told that the exercise submarine had experienced considerable difficulty detecting and classifying *Comte de Grasse*. The problem had to do with refining their firing criteria; apparently, there were several times that our ship was misclassified by them as a "rain squall." In the past, submarines had enjoyed a large acoustic advantage over destroyers, but the improvements made to quiet the *Spruance*-class ships had altered the game.

During the three-day exercise on the AUTEC Range, we were able to get our torpedo shots off first in at least three of the nine times that free play was scheduled, despite a requirement to notify the submarine by underwater telephone and wait for permission from the range authority before releasing our exercise weapon. That communication was deemed necessary so that the submarine could confirm that it was impact rigged (a configuration taken to minimize any damage that might result were one of our torpedoes to malfunction and inadvertently hit the submarine). For some reason, we were never warned before the submarine launched a much bigger torpedo at us.

On leaving AUTEC, we went to Nassau for a well-deserved visit.

The timing of this visit coincided with the discovery of significant drug trafficking activity through the Bahamas.

During my call on the American chargé d'affaires in the Bahamas, George Antipas, he described to me in harrowing detail how a cartel led by the Colombian drug lord Carlos Lehder had overrun an island in the Bahamas called Norman's Cay. After occupying the airstrip, Lehder had forced American owners on the island at gunpoint to sell and depart their property. The Colombian apparently was being provided cover by the Bahamian prime minister at the time, Lynden Pindling.

Lehder's cartel was bringing large quantities of cocaine by air from the Guajira region of Colombia to Norman's Cay. There, it was repackaged into smaller parcels, which were delivered to Florida in either small aircraft or fast boats. After listening intently, I suggested to Antipas that the US Navy might be of help in detecting and monitoring this illicit traffic by air and sea and that he should request that help. The acting ambassador seemed very interested. On my way home, I sent a message alerting the chain of command to the embassy's interest and I added my own ideas about what we, the navy, might be able to do by way of surveillance. With one exception, my seniors were unimpressed with the recommendations. The exception was Vice Admiral James A. Lyons (COMSECONDFLT).

Parenthetically, the problem of drug trafficking through the Bahamas was also of keen interest to another former boss, Admiral Dan Murphy. By the time I left command of *Comte de Grasse* in August 1982, Admiral Murphy was chief of staff to the vice president of the United States, George H. W. Bush. When I arrived to take up my new assignment on the staff of the National Security Council (NSC), Admiral Murphy asked the national security advisor, Judge William Clark, to detail me "temporarily" to work on the South Florida Task Force. That task force, established by the vice president, was created to coordinate the disparate efforts of federal, state, and local agencies engaged in the interdiction of narcotics flowing into South Florida. The task force succeeded in bringing under one roof, albeit grudgingly, the Coast Guard, Customs Bureau, FBI, and Drug Enforcement Administration (DEA).

My specific tasking was to develop a plan to utilize DOD assets in assisting the drug interdiction effort. The enthusiasm for this tasking was sorely lacking in the Pentagon. Drawing on my visit to Nassau and my conversation with the ambassador, I went to work crafting formal requests (i.e., directives) from the vice president to the secretary of defense requesting the cooperation of certain of DOD's component services in the detection and interdiction of narcotics. The Joint Staff and the services resisted with vigor, protesting the drain on assets that would result from covering the task of surveillance and the absence of budgets. Their resistance notwithstanding, the vice president prevailed, and we obtained significant commitments to the surveillance of the air space by air force AWACS aircraft and navy E-2C *Hawkeye* aircraft.[33]

The first few orbits that were established in the fall of 1982 confirmed that indeed there was a very high level of covert and furtive air activity originating in the Bahamas and landing at small Florida airports. The offending aircraft would typically fly at low altitude having turned off their identifying transponders. As planned, the "tracks" of the suspect aircraft were passed to Customs Service air units, and many narcotics-laden aircraft were intercepted and their crews arrested.

I took the opportunity to witness these results firsthand. After detection of a suspicious aircraft, or "bogey," by a navy E-2C surveillance aircraft, an interceptor from the Customs Bureau Air Service division was launched in response. I joined the customs crew for the mission, and we intercepted the aircraft and followed him into a small airfield south of Fort Lauderdale. The armed customs officers forced the crew and passengers to exit. That intercept yielded two hundred pounds of cocaine and over one hundred thousand dollars. It also resulted in the arrest of the young pilot (a furloughed Eastern Airlines copilot) and three Colombian smugglers. I sat in on the interrogation of the pilot, keen to understand what prompted a university graduate to engage in such a crime. Sadly, he explained tearfully that he had a wife, two young children, and a mortgage. I left the room hoping the judge would be lenient in his case.

Shortly after our return to homeport, I was relieved of command of the *Comte de Grasse.* My relief was another experienced destroyerman, Commander Steve Hamilton who had completed

---

33 Letter from Vice President George H. W. Bush to Secretary of Defense Weinberger, September 29, 1982.

an important tour of duty in the Bureau of Naval Personnel (BuPers). The guest speaker at the ceremony was none other than my past and future boss, Vice Admiral Lyons. I had invited the admiral to my change of command; his aide subsequently called to accept and to inform me that the admiral would be the guest speaker at the ceremony. Now, the commodore (COMDESRON 10) was the usual guest speaker at ceremonies involving ships in his squadron. Sensing trouble, I called Commodore Howard to explain the circumstances. He was not pleased and wanted an explanation as to how the invitation to Admiral Lyons was tendered. I explained, and he seemed to understand that the responsibility in this case was not mine.

The ceremony came off without a hitch. Afterward, I reported my relief by Commander Hamilton to Commodore Howard, and he presented me with my first Meritorious Service Medal. I cannot exaggerate the sense of satisfaction I had, turning over a ready *Comte de Grasse* and a superbly trained crew to my successor. We had traveled more than thirty thousand nautical miles together, trained for all our missions in challenging and realistic exercises, passed all major inspections and readiness milestones, and visited eighteen ports in twelve countries. I could look back with pride because as a team, we had met the challenges and had had great fun in the process.

Alphonse Dur, my grandfather, who immigrated from France in 1890.

Me at two years with my mother and sister Elena. Destined for the navy!

Midshipman 4th Class,
University of Notre Dame,
1961

Admiral William I. Martin's sixtieth birthday aboard the *Little Rock.* Left to right:
Tex Treiber, Jack Kellerman, Rudy Daus, Bob Leivel, Jean Featzgeral, Jake Jacobsen, me

Saratoga in near collision with *Little Rock*

Little Rock Quarterdeck
I shake hands with VADM David Richardson, Commander Sixth Fleet, as I leave the ship July 27, 1968.

Receiving the Admiral Arleigh Burke Leadership Award from
VADM Thomas Weschler, Destroyer School, July 1970

Receiving the silver medal in the Naval Institute Prize Essay Contest from the
Chief of Naval Operations, Admiral Elmo Zumwalt, 1973

Taking a bearing while piloting *Waddell*, 1975

Conning *Waddell* alongside *Camden* in Gulf of Tonkin, November 1976

Celebrating winning the Battle Efficiency "E" in *Waddell*, July 1977

Award ceremony where I received Defense Superior Service Medal following my tour in the Office of the Secretary of Defense. Left to right: Deputy Undersecretary (policy review) Admiral Daniel J. Murphy, Deputy Undersecretary (policy) Walter Slocombe, me, my family, and Commander Michael Field

Photo as a commander en route to my first command

Comte de Grasse ("the Count") in drydock following repairs to ruptured rubber window in the sonar dome, October 1981

Comte de Grasse and Marine Nationale ship *De Grasse* underway
at the scene of the battle of the Virginia Capes

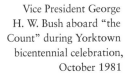

Vice President George
H. W. Bush aboard "the
Count" during Yorktown
bicentennial celebration,
October 1981

Sailors from "the Count" engaging sailors from FNS *De Grasse*, Ville de Paris Soccer Cup, Grasse, France, October 1981

Shaking hands with communist mayor of the city of Grasse, France, February 1982

Presentation of the De Grasse duo to French minister of defense,
Charles Hernu, Cannes, February 1982

Ceremony aboard *Comte de Grasse* honoring the French minister of defense, Charles
Hernu, February 1982. Left to right: Charles Hernu; US ambassador Evian Galbraith;
Marine Nationale chief of staff, Admiral Bernard Louzeau; Commander US Sixth Fleet,
Vice Admiral William Rowden; admiral commanding French Mediterranean Fleet,
Vice Admiral Jean-Paul Orosco; Commander Task Force 60 Rear Admiral James Service

Chief of Naval Operations
Admiral James Watkins,
presenting Navy Commendation
Medal to French lieutenant
Aimery Fustier, my Marine
Nationale exchange officer, April
1982

Briefing NATO Secretary General J. Luns aboard *Comte de Grasse*. To his left,
Admiral Harry Train, Supreme Allied Commander, Atlantic, April 1982

My wardroom and officers of the Irish Naval Service, Cork, Ireland, April 1982

Comte de Grasse in Villefranche-sur-Mer, our favorite liberty port

USS *Comte de Grasse* (DD-974)

My mother and father at my change of command prior to departing *Comte de Grasse*, July 1982

CHAPTER 8

SHAPING NATIONAL SECURITY POLICY AND STRATEGY FOR THE MIDDLE EAST

Director, Political Military Affairs NSC Staff and Military Assistant to President's Special Envoys

Before I begin recounting my experiences on the staff of the National Security Council (NSC), it is important that I explain how one navy commander got such an exciting opportunity. I should note that an assignment to the White House is not one that a military officer can request; the assignment is typically made under special circumstances, and mine was such an experience. As discussed in an earlier chapter, while assigned to the Department of Defense (DOD) in 1981, one of my superiors was now-retired General Richard T. Boverie. He figured prominently in my assignment to the Executive Office of the President as a member of the NSC staff.

The occasion that initiated the process was unusual. I was on the bridge of *Comte de Grasse*, about to get underway for a commodore's change-of-command ceremony at sea, when I was informed that I had received a call from the White House. The caller was none other than Major General Richard (Dick) Boverie, at that point retired and working on the NSC staff as an assistant to President Ronald Reagan. He was inquiring as to my availability to take a position at the White House on the NSC staff.

Surprised and somewhat taken aback, I explained that I was already under orders to the Strategic Studies Group (SSG) at the Naval War College in Newport, Rhode Island. I hastened to add how honored I was that he had thought of me for such an exciting opportunity. He explained that he had already asked Secretary of the Navy (SECNAV) John Lehman for permission to make me available for this assignment. My dilemma was that a former boss, Admiral Crowe, had nominated me for assignment to the SSG, a small group of "thinkers" who worked on future strategies for the navy and who reported directly to the Chief of Naval Operations (CNO). In short, it, too, was coveted assignment.

I explained all this and asked the general for a couple of days to consider my options. On our return to port, I called Admiral Crowe to explain the predicament. He told me the choice was mine to make but recommended that I stick with the orders I had in hand. In any event, he advised me to be certain that I had the NSC job before asking for a change in my orders.

With Boverie's help, interviews were arranged in Washington with Judge William C. Clark, the national security advisor to the president, and his deputy, Robert C. (Bud) McFarlane. The outcome was favorable. I sent a message to Admiral Crowe, and he replied by wishing me good luck. Following my change of command on *Comte de Grasse* a few weeks later, I reported for duty on the NSC staff in Washington.

My experiences on the NSC staff from August 1982 to November 1984 during the first Reagan administration afforded me a close and intense education in the workings of the national security community and the processes by which policy is made. "Sausage making" is not an inexact analogy. The process is often fitful and even chaotic, but from the outside, the results available to the public and analyzed by academicians often suggest unity and coherence.

There are many takeaways from and fond memories of this fascinating assignment. There were also keen disappointments for one who had idealized the business of national security. Among the latter is the challenge an officer detailed to duty on the NSC staff faces, taking care to balance the interests and the goals of the DOD with those of his superiors in the White House, especially those of the president of the United States. As Richard Neustadt, the noted theorist of presidential power, argued, the positions taken by Washington bureaucracies are often defiant of the agendas and objectives advanced by presidents: "The President's primary power is to persuade and bargain, not to command. The essence of a President's persuasive task is to convince such men that what the White House wants of them is what they ought to do for their sake on their authority."[34]

LEBANON, THE MULTINATIONAL FORCE, AND THE MCFARLANE MISSION

The Lebanon crisis (1981–1984) began with progressively more serious incursions by the Palestine Liberation Organization (PLO) against Israeli settlements in northern Israel in 1981–1982.[35] The Israel Defense Forces (IDF) responded in the summer of 1982

---

34 Richard E. Neustadt, *Presidential Power and the Modern Presidents* (New York: Simon & Schuster, 2001), 30.

35 An exhaustive account of the PLO in Lebanon may be found in Raphael Israeli, ed., *PLO in Lebanon: Selected Documents* (New York: St. Martin's, 1983).

by invading Lebanon in what was termed Peace for Galilee. In a massive armored assault, Israeli forces decimated PLO formations as well as Syrian armored forces and tactical air forces attempting to blunt their offensive. By early September, the IDF occupied much of the high ground around the capital of Beirut, and IDF artillery continued barrages against PLO forces in Beirut. The artillery action also caused significant collateral damage to noncombatant Lebanese.

The Reagan administration grew increasingly concerned about the violence visited on Lebanese (and Palestinian) civilians and the continuing Israeli attacks on Beirut. This eventually resulted in a serious effort by the administration to stop the Israeli offensive and at the same time pressure Syrian withdrawal from the beleaguered Lebanese nation. The US response, deploying a battalion of Marines, working together with comparably sized French and Italian forces, demonstrated anew the utility of forward-deployed navy and Marine Corps forces. The contributions of France and Italy reflected the grave concern of those governments for the situation in Lebanon and especially the plight of Palestinian civilians.

The deployment of Marines also resurrected historic tensions between senior army leaders and the navy establishment regarding appropriate military responses in crisis settings. While at the NSC, I had a ringside seat to the interservice controversy.

In addition, I witnessed serious disagreements between cabinet officers on Lebanon policy. The question was whether to use military presence, in conjunction with crisis diplomacy, to dislodge Israeli and Syrian forces from Lebanon and to restore peace to that troubled country. As several published memoirs have recounted, the president, National Security Advisor William Clark, and Secretary of State George Schultz were far more inclined to this than were Secretary of Defense Casper Weinberger,

Chairman of the Joint Chiefs of Staff (CJCS) General Jack Vessey, and Supreme Allied Commander Europe (SACEUR) General Bernard Rogers.[36]

Contributing a Marine Expeditionary Unit (MEU) embarked in amphibious shipping to the original mission of what became known as the multinational force (MNF)—thereby facilitating the withdrawal of PLO fighters from Beirut—seemed expedient to the administration and not overly controversial at that point. The navy and the Marine Corps had the forces on the scene, with organic support to sustain them, whereas the army did not have readily available a comparably sized unit sustainable with organic combat and combat service support.

The leadership in the DOD welcomed the withdrawal of the MNF after the PLO combatants were evacuated from Beirut; its reintroduction later at the president's insistence was strongly opposed by Pentagon leaders on the grounds that the mission was poorly defined.

The untold story is the Pentagon's determined opposition to a more clearly defined mission authorizing defensive measures in support of our forces in Beirut.

In brief, after Israel launched the Peace for Galilee campaign against the Palestinian Liberation Forces (PLF) in Lebanon in June 1982 and against the Syrian forces supporting them in the summer of 1982, the United States, joined by French and Italian allies, deployed battalion-sized units to Lebanon to form the MNF. The objective of the first MNF deployment was to stop Israeli shelling of PLO units driven into Beirut, which was devastating the Lebanese capital and inflicting untold casualties on civilians and Palestinian refugees in the Sabra and Shatila camps.

36 George P. Shultz, *Turmoil and Triumph* (New York: Scribner, 1993); see especially pp. 231–234. Caspar Weinberger, *Fighting for Peace: Seven Critical Years in the Pentagon* (New York: Grand Central, 1990), 164–174.

The first MNF accomplished the stated mission of covering and ensuring the evacuation of most, but not all, of the armed PLF from Beirut. After the tragic massacre of hundreds of noncombatants in the Palestinian camps in mid-September 1982, the MNF was reintroduced in Beirut. This time, the objective of the Reagan administration was facilitating the negotiated withdrawal of Israeli and Syrian forces then occupying two-thirds of Lebanon. In both instances, the US contribution to the MNF came in the form of a the reinforced 22nd MEU. This force, comprising a battalion landing team, a Marine medium helicopter squadron, and a service support group, was supported from ships of the Sixth Fleet.

In November 1982, two months after the MNF had been reintroduced, I was appointed assistant director for political military affairs on the NSC staff, responsible for the Middle East region. For most of that winter and well into the late spring, I spent my time working with staff colleagues Geoffrey Kemp and Howard Teicher. Kemp and Teicher were a two-man team in the staff's policy section responsible for the Middle East. I provided the military perspective on the team.

Progress in resolving a series of crises in Lebanon following the evacuation of the PLO in July 1982 was fitful. The mission of Ambassador Philip Habib to secure Syrian and Israeli withdrawal from Lebanon failed dramatically. Habib's usefulness as presidential envoy to the Middle East was finally compromised when President Hafez al-Assad refused to meet with him, alleging that Habib had lied to him in an earlier meeting regarding Israel's intentions for Lebanon. Coincidentally, the three nations contributing to the MNF missed an opportunity in the late summer of 1982 to pressure Syria's withdrawal from Lebanon when that country's position was weakest because the Israeli offensive that year had destroyed the Syrian Air Force and much of the Syrian armored force. Resupply from the Soviet Union began almost immediately, and ultimately, that closed a window of opportunity to restore Lebanese sovereignty.

From the start of our involvement, restoring Lebanon's sovereignty by removing the PLO fighters and the occupying Israeli and Syrian forces was clearly President Reagan's objective.[37] Contrary to arguments advanced by critics of the policy, the mission of the MNF was presence with *a purpose* and not benign *interposition*, as Secretary Weinberger described it.[38]

By the Pentagon's definition, a mission described as simple "presence" did not include rules of engagement (ROE) beyond elementary self-defense and then only if the threat could be precisely defined. Having deployed a combat unit into a veritable cauldron of hostilities, it seemed to many of us on the NSC staff almost inconceivable that a "peacekeeping" mission would not result in anonymous hostile acts against our forces by armed groups in Lebanon clearly antagonistic to the United States. It was abundantly clear from the beginning of our involvement that Syria and Iran were advising and otherwise actively supporting Lebanese factions opposed to the government and, by extension, the MNF. Sadly, the Pentagon did not approve a level of support for the Marines and ROEs appropriate to allow an effective defense. I will also posit that the two aircraft carrier battle groups, including a dozen surface combatants in the Sixth Fleet, might have provided effective support to the Marines had it been authorized from the start.

In the winter of 1982, while Ambassador Habib endeavored to negotiate the withdrawal of Israeli and Syrian forces, a serious confrontation between a Marine patrol and an Israeli tank

---

37 Ronald Reagan, *An American Life* (New York: Simon & Schuster, 1990), 442–446; Shultz, *Turmoil and Triumph,* 109. See also "Next Steps in Lebanon," National Security Decision Directive 64 (NSC-NSDD-64), October 28, 1982. The two objectives in Reagan's strategy were the prompt withdrawal of Israeli, Syrian, and Palestinian forces and strengthening the ability of the government of Lebanon to control, administer, and defend its sovereign territory.

38 Weinberger, *Fighting for Peace,* 152.

crew occurred just south of the Beirut airport, where US forces were billeted. Ordered to withdraw from the MEU's security perimeter, the Israeli tank crew refused, causing a lieutenant in charge of the patrol to brandish weapons as a warning. This incident created considerable excitement at the Pentagon and at the White House, and it led to additional intense discussion of additional measures that might be necessary to pressure an Israeli withdrawal from the region south of Beirut.

In an ensuing discussion with National Security Advisor Judge William C. Clark, he asked me for an opinion regarding what force deployments might serve to facilitate the withdrawal of Syrian forces from the high ground east of Beirut and promote security of the territories south of the Awali River, adjacent to Israel's northern border with Lebanon. I doubted that Israel would ever agree to rely on an international force (under the auspices of the UN, for example) to ensure the security of the border areas; Teicher and Kemp shared this view. Given the dependence of the government of Israel on our commitment to their security, however, I thought that it would be hard-pressed to refuse a US interposition force, if large enough and equipped sufficiently to provide reasonable assurance that it could surveil and respond to threats against Israel were it to be deployed at the request of the Lebanese government.

I offered that the 82nd Airborne Division might be one candidate for such a mission of limited duration because it was one of the few rapidly deployable army divisions with integral combat service support.[39] Judge Clark then shared the idea of deploying the 82nd with Secretary Weinberger in my presence.

---

39 In a thinly veiled critique of ambitious or "reckless" NSC staff, John Gans recounts my suggestion regarding the deployment of the 82nd Airborne Division to Lebanon as a case in point. He omits the context of my discussion with the judge and the conditions I thought were necessary for it to have been deployed for the stated purpose of securing Israel's northern border. John Gans, *White House Warriors: How the National Security Council Transformed the American Way of War* (New York: Liveright, 2019), 76.

Weinberger dismissed it out of hand. In his memoirs, Weinberger claimed that arguments for deploying larger units "advanced by McFarlane and the NSC Staff" were "wild adventures."[40] Yet, in earlier discussions about the size and configuration of the MNF, Weinberger had advanced a far more ambitious mission for US forces. According to Secretary of State Shultz, he had argued that "once all foreign forces had left Lebanon—to be negotiated diplomatically—US armed forces would form a giant cordon around the **entire perimeter of Lebanon's borders and coastline so that the Lebanese Army would be undisturbed as it retook control of internal security.**"[41] Given the history of Syrian intervention in Lebanese politics, Weinberger's offer of a perimeter defense was perhaps more "reckless" than an interposition force between Lebanon and Israel.

As to facilitating the withdrawal of Syrian forces from the areas east of the capital, I suggested that the considerations were the same as in the case for Israel: if the withdrawal of Syrian forces were formally requested by the Lebanese government, it might be open to comparably sized French and Italian forces beginning to replace the Israelis in the Shouf and then gradually extending their presence into areas that had been occupied by the Syrians since 1976.

I was not confused about the enormity of the challenges that would complicate any plan of that magnitude that was contingent on decisive action by the Lebanese government—a tall order—and the reactions of the Syrian and Israeli governments—even taller orders.

The winter of 1982 presented a window of opportunity to press the advantage of Syria's losses, but the odds were insurmountable.

40 Weinberger, *Fighting for Peace*, 159.

41 Shultz, *Turmoil and Triumph*, 108 [emphasis added].

In May 1983, Ambassador Habib resigned, and his responsibilities were subsequently assumed by the US secretary of state
himself. It fell to George Shultz to obtain Syrian agreement to one
he had personally negotiated with the governments of Lebanon
and Israel. The May 17 agreement, signed in May 1983 by Israel
and Lebanon, proved unworkable. The agreement required
the Lebanese to concede much of their sovereignty in southern
Lebanon. That concession was essential in order to secure Israeli
agreement, as that government would not trust any Lebanese
government to ensure the security of their northern border. In
that regard, the agreement seemed to me to be at cross purposes
with the president's stated desire to restore Lebanese sovereignty
over all its territory.

The May 17 agreement between Lebanon and Israel proved
unworkable because as was clear from the start, the Syrians would
never honor an agreement that limited their influence over the
Lebanese government. Syria and its Baathist leadership had never
recognized Lebanese sovereignty. Assad affirmed that Lebanon
was a Syrian sphere of influence, if not a colony, beholden to
Damascus. We in the NSC staff recognized the dim prospects for
this agreement from the beginning. I became increasingly pessi-
mistic as I watched the secretary invest so much time and effort
before the eventful meeting with Assad spelled its demise.

A renewed and intensified US effort to restore Lebanese sovereignty was launched on July 22, 1983, with the appointment
of Bud McFarlane, the deputy national security advisor, as the
president's special envoy to the Middle East. While participating
in a strategic war game at the Naval War College, I received a
call from Bud, asking me to join a small team and accompany
him on a mission to advance our cause in Lebanon and, more
broadly, the Middle East. I was honored, to say the least, and I
hurried home to pack, as we were to depart the following week.

When Bud asked me to join the mission as military assistant, I felt that a career goal was in the making. I took the invitation to mean that my thoughts and observations regarding the complicated and seemingly intractable problems facing the president in the Middle East were well regarded. I was not oblivious to the challenges that lay ahead, but a seat at the table was most satisfying.

The first mission undertaken by Ambassador McFarlane was launched at the beginning of August, and it took the team to London, Paris, Rome, and four Middle East capitals before arriving in Beirut. The visits to the European capitals were meant to coordinate US efforts with those of the other nations contributing to the MNF in Lebanon. I was fortunate to participate in meetings with foreign ministers and defense ministers of those countries. In Israel, we met with the defense minister Misha Arens and the chief of staff of the IDF General Moshe Levi.

Arriving in Lebanon, we met with President Amin Gemayel at his scenic ancestral home in Bikfaya. We also met several times with his foreign minister, Elie Salem, chief advisor to the president of Lebanon, Dr. Wadi D. Haddad, and chief of staff of the Lebanese Army, General Ibrahim Tannous. McFarlane also met with leaders of the Lebanese opposition: Walid Jumblatt, Druze chief and leader of the Progressive Socialist Party (PSP), and Nabih Berri, leader of the Amal, or Shia, Party. These meetings were meant to better understand the competing objectives of Israel, Lebanon, and the Lebanese factions. The purpose was also to convey the president's determination to help deliver a solution to the crisis launched by the Israeli invasion the year before.

McFarlane met discreetly with Jumblatt in Paris on August 27 in an apartment owned by François de Grossouvre, advisor to French president François Mitterrand. Howard Teicher and I were in a room adjacent to the one in which Jumblatt and McFarlane were meeting, taking notes. Suddenly, Jumblatt arose and opened the door to the room in which we were sitting on his way to use a bathroom. When he saw me and Teicher, he screamed in horror, apparently thinking we were there to assassinate him. Such was the state of Lebanese politics.[42] Jumblatt's reaction reflected an advanced paranoia fed by Syrian assassination of his father and multiple assassination attempts against him.

The meetings in Damascus between McFarlane and President Assad and Foreign Minister Haddam were intended to probe Syrian willingness to reach an agreement, and to determine the conditions for the withdrawal of Syrian forces from Lebanon. McFarlane's memoirs[43] describe these meetings in some detail. Suffice it to note here, we had no more success than Secretary Shultz in persuading the Syrians to accept a more conciliatory resolution of the Lebanese crisis.

Several experiences during this first mission illustrate the difficulties we encountered. Our working offices were in the American ambassador's residence in Yarze, on a hill overlooking downtown Beirut. (The embassy in Beirut had been bombed by terrorists four months before our arrival and was deemed too dangerous a setting for our meetings and communications facilities linking us to Washington.) I have a vivid recollection of the view. In the evening, we could observe the exchange of live fire between the Christian militia, the Lebanese Forces (LF), and the Sunni militia, the Al Murabitoun. The Lebanese Armed Forces (LAF) sat idly as the fighting in the city raged before their eyes. The Druze militia, high in the hills of the Shouf (a historically Druze district), would

42 For a corroborating account, see Howard and Gayle Teicher, *Twin Pillars to Desert Storm* (New York: William Morrow, 1993), 243–244.

43 Robert C. McFarlane and Zofia Smardz, *Special Trust* (New York: Caddell and Davies, 1994).

rain fire down on the army's positions near our residence with regularity. Army artillery units would respond by lofting shells over our heads into the Shouf. In addition, there was constant but sporadic artillery fire originating from the Syrian-controlled zone, the Metn, on both the LAF and the Christian militia.

Sporadically, shells landed all around the presidential palace in nearby Baabda and very close to the ambassador's residence. We regularly experienced the impact of shrapnel; on at least two occasions, pieces of incoming rounds impacted the room in which the ambassador and we were meeting, and on another, a guest bedroom in which we were staying.

Not long after our arrival in mid-August, the Marine battalion that was encamped at the Beirut airport began receiving fire from the same general direction as the artillery fire that was targeting the Defense Ministry, the presidential palace, and the US ambassador's residence. We discussed with Bud what could be done to enhance the safety of our Marines at the airport. The obvious solutions came to mind. One, we needed means to discover the origin of the fire more precisely. This need was met by the deployment of an army team from Europe with the requisite equipment.

Two, with Sixth Fleet destroyers and cruisers off the coast, we needed an adjustment to the ROE that would permit our ships to return fire when the Marines were under attack. While we were discussing navy support to the Marines, it occurred to me that four battleships were then being recommissioned. The first of them, the USS *New Jersey* (BB-62), was already operating in the Pacific. Therefore, might it be possible to redeploy *New Jersey*, that magnificent naval artillery platform, to the Mediterranean and the Sixth Fleet? I thought that the Syrians might not want to have an artillery duel with the *New Jersey*. Bud, a former active Marine, nodded in agreement and said he liked the idea. (The idea was finally put on the agenda on September 9 at a special meeting of the National Security Planning Group [NSPG]. It is telling in retrospect that the secretary of defense and the CJCS did not see the merit of our idea at the time.)

During this and subsequent visits to Lebanon, I came to know and admire the skill and persistence of our Israeli "allies." During our time there, we were engaged in trying to persuade and facilitate the orderly and phased withdrawal of the IDF from Lebanon and to leverage their withdrawal so as to gain agreement for a parallel retreat by Syrian occupying forces. The Israelis remained very resentful of the strong pressure that had been applied by President Reagan during their occupation of a large area just east and south of Beirut. The president had issued stinging criticism of their continued shelling of the city, well after the evacuation of the Palestinian fighters.

Responding to US pressure, Prime Minister Shamir had conditionally agreed in the stillborn May 17 agreement to withdraw Israeli forces from southern Lebanon. The condition was that the government of Lebanon formally recognize the State of Israel and agree to normal intercourse between the two countries, among other things. After President Assad refused to negotiate a Syrian withdrawal, citing the concessions Lebanon had made in the agreement with Israel, the Israelis began to plan a unilateral disengagement from their positions in the Shouf but not from Lebanese territory south of the Awali River.

While preparing for what culminated with the evacuation of the Northern Command from the high ground in the Shouf, General Amir Drory, the commander responsible for the Israeli occupying force in Lebanon, invited McFarlane to come into the occupied sector to see for himself the challenging mission facing the IDF. The Shouf was described by General Drory as a "blended" Christian-Druze community that had coexisted in peace for centuries but was now at war, instigated by the Syrians. He asserted that McFarlane's seeing the mission firsthand was essential in order for the United States to prepare to replace Israel as the "balancer" between hostile Druze forces, PSP, and the Christian militia, the LF.

After a discussion with the US ambassador to Lebanon, Robert Dillon, McFarlane accepted Dillon's admonition that the government of Lebanon would be gravely insulted if the presidential envoy was observed visiting the hated occupying Israeli force. Instead, Bud asked me to represent him, taking the tour of the Shouf that had been offered by General Drory.

I left a meeting in the Lebanese Foreign Ministry on August 24 and was driven in an unmarked car to a barricaded road in the lower Shouf. Mohammed, my Sunni driver, appeared anxious as we approached the area occupied by the IDF. Dropping me off, he made a hurried exit after assuring me he would pick me up at the same barricade in two hours' time. Still in the suit and tie that had been appropriate for my meeting with the foreign minister (which I had left prematurely), I walked on a dirt path for about two hundred yards before coming upon a camouflaged Israeli machine gun nest. The sergeant in charge of the position asked me to identify myself. He queried me to verify that I was the American visitor General Drory was expecting. I showed him my diplomatic passport and he led me to a waiting jeep, which took us to a villa that had clearly been someone's beautiful home and that the IDF now occupied as a forward headquarters.

In the thirty-minute briefing by General Drory that followed, he pointed out the various positions occupied by the Druze and Christian militias. Because the Christian militia was essentially friendly toward the IDF, his briefing concentrated on the challenges that might be posed by the Druze militia allied with Syria, which, curiously, was also very friendly to the occupying Israelis.

Drory explained that the Israeli relationship with the Druze in the Shouf was made easy by the number of "loyal" Israeli Druze inhabiting the Mount Carmel region of Israel. I remember thinking that this was one of the imponderable dimensions of Middle East politics. We then mounted the general's jeep and took a road tour around the Israeli zone. What I witnessed next was nothing short of remarkable.

Before us was a valley that at its lowest point featured an Israeli *Merkava* tank and its crew. The general handed me his binoculars and pointed out a sandbagged artillery position just outside a Christian village. Then he directed my gaze to the high ground to the west and across the valley, where a PSP artillery battery stood on the flank of a Druze village. I asked about the role of the tank. Drory explained that the only way the Israelis could quiet artillery exchanges between the rival Christian and Druze batteries was to have the Israeli tank fire one round at each; that somehow did the trick. I asked about the possibility of collateral damage and innocent casualties, to which Drory scolded, "Forget about that. This is Lebanon. This is the only way to control these factions."

We then boarded an IDF helicopter and flew above the high ground in the Shouf, directly over Druze and Syrian artillery positions. I asked the general why the Syrians did not engage the IDF—or the LF, for that matter. General Drory shrugged. "They know better."

Back at the headquarters, the general asked me, "Well, Commander, what do you think?" I thought a minute and then said that I could see what a formidable challenge the IDF faced in attempting to control the fighting between the Christians and the Druze (and their Syrian sponsors). Drory's reply still rings in my ears: "In one month, Commander, this will be your problem. Make sure Mr. McFarlane understands!"

Shortly thereafter, in a late-night meeting with Minister of Defense Misha Arens during a stopover in Israel, McFarlane referred to what General Drory had implied was the imminent withdrawal of the IDF from the Shouf. He stressed to Arens, the former Israeli ambassador to the United States, how important it was to get the Lebanese Army to do "a relief in place" of Israeli forces and to ensure that the state of order, currently being forcibly imposed on the Christians and the Druze, was maintained after the Israeli withdrawal. Arens seemed sympathetic and promised that he would explore the possibility but did not commit to it. He noted that the IDF had suffered numerous casualties along the extended logistical line from northern Israel into the Shouf; there had been several terrorist attacks against convoys en route to supply IDF units in the district. That attrition, as well as repeated US calls for Israeli withdrawals from Lebanon, had prompted the government of Israel to undertake a partial withdrawal from the Shouf.

Following our return to Beirut, I accompanied McFarlane to a meeting with General Tannous, in keeping with the agreement made with Arens. Its purpose was to assess whether we could organize a meeting with the Israeli and Lebanese military chiefs to arrange the relief of lines between Israeli and Lebanese units in the Shouf.

General Tannous, accompanied by Foreign Minister Salem and presidential advisor Haddad, greeted us warmly in the Defense Ministry at Yarze. Following a persuasive appeal by McFarlane, citing the logic we had discussed with the Israelis, General Tannous reluctantly agreed to meet his counterpart, General Moshe Levi, chief of the IDF, at a location just beyond Israeli lines in the lower Shouf. US Ambassador Dillon was adamantly opposed to our brokering a meeting between the Israelis and LAF; McFarlane overruled him. Parenthetically,

Major General Carl Stiner, at the time in Lebanon representing the CJCS, was very supportive of this meeting, which McFarlane himself planned to attend for all the right reasons.

On the appointed evening, we climbed into several armored cars for the transit from Yarze to the secret and somewhat distant setting for this unprecedented meeting between Israeli and Lebanese military chiefs. I was a little confused when McFarlane's state security protective detail (bodyguards) instructed me to get into McFarlane's car. They then proceeded to put McFarlane in one of the escort vehicles in which I usually rode. Simply put, if there were an ambush, yours truly would be the distinguished visitor.

The hospitality at the meeting itself included an array of Lebanese delicacies, good whiskey, and an assortment of imported beers. General Tannous opened the proceeding with a cautious welcome, recognizing what he termed "our difficult history with you." Tannous made specific reference to the Israelis having bribed a former LAF officer, Major Saad Haddad, and his Lebanese militia to provide some protection for the northern border of Israel. General Levi countered by reminding his Lebanese counterpart, "Your army could not limit the attacks on our northern settlements, and we had to employ Haddad to do your work."

The discussions were heated and lengthy as the parties tried to hammer out timelines and the locations of the fortified positions to be exchanged. During the meeting, there were many references to other incidents between the LAF and the IDF, which detracted from the friendly spirit we had tried to generate. Ultimately, however, the outcome seemed for the most part positive, and McFarlane, Stiner, and I left, hopeful that a successful relief of lines would be the outcome of the talks.

Unfortunately, our optimism was short lived. I returned to Washington on September 1 and resumed my duties at the NSC.

On September 4, the Israelis abruptly began to withdraw their forces from the Shouf after giving us and the Lebanese only hours of warning. The withdrawal, completed in less than two days, was so rapid that combined with the short notice, there could be no relief of lines.

This outcome confirmed our worst fears. Following the Israeli retreat, the LAF moved in to reoccupy the ridge lines abandoned by the Israelis. The best unit in the LAF, the 8th Brigade, which was commanded by a future president of Lebanon, General Michel Aoun, occupied a ridge known as Suq al-Gharb. On the night of September 10, a force comprised of Shia and Druze elements, as well as Palestinian and Iranian fighters, attacked the LAF and nearly pushed the brigade off the ridge.

McFarlane, still in Lebanon, described the fighting in an urgent cable to Washington as bloody and "hand to hand."[44] The casualties were significant enough to prompt him (and General Stiner) to urge immediate intervention by US forces to avert the defeat of the Lebanese Army. Secretary of Defense Weinberger, General Vessey (CJCS), and the European commander argued strongly against deeper involvement in what they insisted was a "Lebanese civil war," which it decidedly was not. Intelligence provided by the LAF confirmed that the attack was instigated and tactically directed by Syrian advisors. A connection between Shia combatants in the attacking forces and Iranian intelligence was also alleged by LAF intelligence. In short, but for the fact that the setting was in Lebanon, this was not a "civil war" in any strict sense. There were Palestinians, Syrians, and Iranians in the mix. The inspiration from the attack came from Syria and the leadership included Syrian and Iranian intelligence officials. The LAF ultimately held their ground and the crisis eased somewhat after Sixth Fleet destroyers opened fire on the Druze and

44 McFarlane and Smardz, *Special Trust*, 250–252.

Syrian batteries that had been hammering the LAF, the Ministry of Defense, and the ambassador's residence in Yarze.

There were several immediate US reactions to the near-disaster at Suq al-Gharb. First among these was a change in the ROE to allow support to the LAF were it to come under attack on its positions around the city of Beirut. On September 9, just before the attack on Suq al-Gharb, President Reagan convened a meeting of the NSPG to consider the deployment of the *New Jersey* to the Mediterranean to provide more firepower in support of the LAF as well as in defense of our MNF contingent. The matter of the deployment and its purpose was raised by Judge Clark, who recounted that it had been the recommendation of McFarlane, who was still in Lebanon.

Among the first to comment was Secretary Weinberger. He said that although he did not oppose the deployment, he was concerned that moving the *New Jersey* would be seen as an "escalatory action," which could draw us more deeply into what he tirelessly referred to as the "Lebanese civil war." He warned that an escalation of our presence and our activity in Lebanon would be seen in the Arab world as actions supportive of Israel's agenda.

I recall that Admiral John Poindexter, the deputy national security advisor at the time, had mentioned to me before the meeting while I was in his office that Lieutenant General Colin Powell, Weinberger's senior military assistant, had warned him of the secretary's uneasiness with a "navy initiative." Although it was not readily apparent at the time, General Powell, as the senior military assistant to Weinberger, may have played a decisive role in shaping his principal's views, and thus the reaction of the DOD, to the president's direction to move the battleship. Powell had clearly been chastened by his experience in the Vietnam War; he, like General Vessey, was a charter member of what we at the NSC called the "new never again club"—senior army officers who insisted on broad public support and congressional approval of all military operations that were likely to result in combat. According to a recent biography of Powell, the author affirms that "supported by Powell and the Joint Chiefs [*sic*], Weinberger counseled Reagan to reposition the Marines onto nearby warships. The President demurred."[45]

Weinberger's cautionary remarks were followed by General Jack Vessey's response to a question from the president regarding what the Joint Chiefs thought about the proposed deployment of *New Jersey*. Vessey dutifully reported that the Joint Chiefs of Staff (JCS) were not unanimous and that they were divided in their recommendation to the president regarding the movement of the *New Jersey* to the Mediterranean. Vessey replied that although he did not recommend the deployment personally, he was "required to disclose" that CNO Adm. James Watkins and Marine Corps Commandant General P. X. Kelley supported the move. The president thought for just a moment and then ended the discussion, saying that it would be "helpful" if we moved the *New Jersey* to the Mediterranean.

The ship arrived in the Mediterranean in late September. The brooding presence of the dreadnought off the Lebanese coast did not go unnoticed by our antagonists. We received word from our Lebanese Army sources that chatter on the radios used by the Druze militias and their Syrian mentors warned their gunners to carefully avoid direct attacks on the airport bivouac, lest the *New Jersey* "unleash hellfire" on their positions. The moratorium did not apply to the ambassador's residence in Yarze, however. It was in the line of fire between Syrian and Druze artillery and the presidential palace close by.

---

45 Jeffrey J. Matthews, *Colin Powell: Imperfect Patriot* (Notre Dame, IN: University of Notre Dame Press, 2019), 79.

This was certainly not the only instance that demonstrated how far apart the president and the DOD were in their view of US defense policy in Lebanon. Following another incident of Syrian and Druze shelling of the US and French MNF positions in Beirut, I had my first meeting with the president in the Oval Office.

On September 22, a flight of Dassault-Breguet Super Étendard aircraft from the French aircraft carrier FS *Foch* (R99), which was operating in support of the French Army contingent in Beirut, conducted a retaliatory strike against Druze (PSP) artillery batteries in the Shouf. These positions had been determined to have been the source of fire that had rained down on the French encampment two days before.

On the day following the French strike, Judge Clark had telephoned my office to ask if we had any intelligence or bomb damage assessment (BDA) on the results of the strikes. I'd gone to the White House Situation Room and put the question to the watch captain. He'd informed me that the CIA could provide imagery of the positions that had been attacked. I'd asked that they be obtained and magnified so that the artillery sites could be recognized. The pictures had arrived in short order. The quality of the imagery was excellent; one could discern that several D-30 artillery pieces had been dislodged from their revetments, and there were several craters in and around the sandbagged emplacements. Most interestingly, the pictures revealed the proximity of a Syrian Army D-30 battery, which shared a common ammunition bunker with the PSP battery. This had confirmed that the Syrians and the Druze were acting in close coordination. When I had informed the judge that I had imagery that showed the effect of the French strike, he had asked that I gather them up and that I meet him at the entrance to the Oval Office.

On being announced, we entered and approached President Reagan at his desk. He rose to examine the slides I was carrying, and the judge explained that they contained imagery of the damage to artillery sites after the French strike. Clark asked me to point out the highlights in the photographs that had been annotated with explanatory notes.

The president seemed very interested and asked several questions about the adjacent but undamaged Syrian battery. I pointed out that the Syrians shared an ammunition bunker with the Druze battery. The president turned to me and, without hesitating, instructed that if we were ever forced to retaliate against culprit PSP positions attacking our Marines, he expected that the common ammunition bunkers (serving PSP and Syrian artillery) would also be destroyed. He said that this should be done even if it meant risking damage to the Syrian position. Judge Clark turned to me and said, "You heard the president. Let's pass that on to the Pentagon."

After consulting with Vice Admiral Poindexter, I called Vice Admiral Art Moreau, the assistant to the CJCS, to convey what had transpired. His reaction was telling. Brushing off my account of the president's reaction, he admonished that the president "will have to issue these instructions in writing."

The reaction was startling but consistent with the stance the DOD had taken regarding responding to hostile fire from the Syrians and their Druze surrogates. For example, in response to a request from Poindexter for an analysis of the pros and cons of deploying a battleship off the Lebanese coast, Admiral Moreau had said that "naval gunfire behind Syrian lines directed at Syrian forces is not permitted by current ROE without a change of mission." Clearly the admiral was resisting the president's direction that attacks originating from behind Syrian lines should be countered with responsive fire.

Thereafter, as fighting escalated in October, I had primary responsibility for drafting more specific ROE instructions to the DOD in the form of a National Security Decision Directive

(NSDD-111) to be signed by the president. By design, that directive did not exclude strikes against Syrian batteries if they threatened Marine positions or the LAF.

When NSDD-111 was conveyed to the DOD, the language authorizing US forces to respond to fire emanating from the Syria-controlled zone was transmitted verbatim to the military chain of command. It read:

> The rules of engagement governing the use of US ground, naval and air support for the defense of the strategic high ground which controls the approaches to Beirut **will be modified.** The changes should allow support to the Lebanese Armed Forces (LAF), such as that currently authorized for Souq al-Gharb, when in the judgement of the US ground commander, LAF positions controlling strategic arteries to Beirut are in danger of being overrun by **hostile forces.** [Emphases added]

"Hostile forces" did not exclude the Syrians—to the contrary, they were whom we had in mind.

Very unhappy with the "modification" to the ROE, the CJCS transmitted an "interpretative" message to the responsible military commanders. Curiously, that message stressed that the change in ROE should not be construed as including options that would alter the "peacekeeping" mission of the US MNF.

The logic for this contrarian interpretation by DOD principals was clear. NSDD-111 had made specific reference to "hostile forces" and the secretary and chairman were determined to discourage any attacks against Syrian positions, even if they posed a direct threat to MNF forces in the city of Beirut. The communication may have been confusing to responsible subordinate commanders having to reconcile the demands of a "peacekeeping" mission with responding credibly to attacks from "hostile forces." It should be noted that the White House was not copied on the message that interpreted the president's directive for the military chain of command; I obtained a copy from my sources in the Pentagon. I knew that "peacekeeping" was not the mission the president had in mind. Supporting the Lebanese government and promoting the withdrawal of the foreign forces (Syrian) was.

At the same time, as our Marines came under fire during September and October, opponents of the president's objectives in other agencies of the government and in the White House itself were very active on Capitol Hill. We heard frequently from congressional critics of our engagement from both sides of the aisle. They appeared to be well informed, using many of the same arguments that emanated from opponents of the president's policy in the heated interagency discussions and debates. The "end runs" to Capitol Hill were typical practices of the people employed in the DOD and State Department (where policy for Latin America and support of the contras was concerned) who opposed the policies and objectives of the administration.

Lebanon was a clear example of organized opposition to clearly worded presidential direction. The secretary of defense and the CJCS decided to ignore guidance and to demur in the issuance of implementing directives to subordinates in the chain of command. The threat of a congressional resolution invoking the War Powers Act was the leverage flaunted by critics in the DOD and their allies in Congress.

Because of their failure to mount a deterrent and field credible defenses for our MNF contingent as directed in NSDD-111, on the morning of October 23, emboldened terrorists were able to drive through a security guard post and position a truck carrying an enormous truckload of enhanced explosives directly up against the large airport building used by our Marines as barracks. The detonation leveled the building, killing 242 and wounding many more. The terrorists struck the French MNF contingent almost simultaneously, inflicting eighty-seven casualties.

Following the bombing of US and French MNF positions, the most egregious example of what can only be described as direct disobedience of the president's orders was Secretary Weinberger's refusal to join the French in a combined strike on the Sheikh Abdullah barracks in the Bekaa Valley. NSDD-111, signed by the president on October 28 had *specifically* authorized attacks on those barracks. It read:

> Subject to reasonable confirmation of the locations of suitable targets used by elements responsible for the October 23 bombing, attack those targets decisively, **if possible, in coordination with the French.** [Emphasis added]

The Sheikh Abdullah barracks had been clearly identified by intelligence as the headquarters for the planners and as the rehearsal site for the Syrian-Iranian-sponsored attacks on the French and US positions. This story is well documented in both McFarlane's and Shultz's memoirs, but it bears repeating here since I was responsible for drafting the language in the NSDD and for the initial step toward coordination with the French.

After corresponding over a special communications channel with President Mitterrand's executive office, Admiral Poindexter dispatched me to Paris to meet with General Saulnier, his counterpart in the Élysée Palace and military advisor (*chef du cabinet particulier*) to the French president. I flew to Paris on an overnight flight and met first with our ambassador in Paris, Evian Galbraith, to brief him on my instructions and what I intended to discuss with the French general. Because both the

French and we had aircraft carrier battle groups on station in the eastern Mediterranean, our proposal was that we plan and conduct a joint strike against the Sheikh Abdullah barracks, which intelligence showed was the headquarters of the nascent Husayni Suicide Forces, led by Haydar Musawi.[46] We knew that the barracks had been used as a training area for the suicide teams that had attacked our Marines and the French Army positions. Intelligence had also confirmed the clear and explicit participation of Syrian intelligence operatives and their Iranian "advisors."

At the Élysée, I reviewed the intelligence with Saulnier, who had much of the same information. I told him that the NSC, with the approval of President Reagan, was examining the possibility of a retaliatory air strike on the barracks. We believed that a joint strike with the French, who had suffered eighty-seven casualties including fifty-five killed in a parallel attack on their position in Beirut, would be most desirable from both political and military points of view.

The general listened intently and then, to my surprise, asked me whether our military leaders were supportive of a strike. (Saulnier had probably been informed through French sources in Washington of the grudging support of the DOD for our position in Lebanon.) My answer was *bien sur*, that the military would obey the president's orders. Saulnier then asked exactly which military organization would be responsible for planning should the French president agree. I replied that at the time of our conversation, the Pentagon had not been formally tasked to plan a strike, but informal discussion with our navy staff had confirmed that our side would be led by Rear Admiral Jerry Tuttle, the commander of the *John F. Kennedy* battle group in the Sixth Fleet. The general told me that our idea "had merit" and that he would discuss the

46 This group was the precursor to the Hezbollah terrorist group.

matter with President Mitterrand and the French General Staff. I left that meeting optimistic that the French would join us.

I returned to Washington from Paris immediately after my meeting with Saulnier and reported the results to Admiral Poindexter and Bud McFarlane. I then visited with the navy Deputy Chief of Naval Operations (OP-06) (Plans, Policies and Operations), Vice Admiral Lyons, who was a strong proponent of decisive military responses to Syrian and surrogate elements in Lebanon following repeated attacks on our Marines. He confirmed that the navy would support a US-French air strike and that Rear Admiral Tuttle would be the responsible commander. Thereafter, Admiral Tuttle received "advanced planning parameters" from the navy staff, specifically from Admiral Lyons. Admiral Lyons assured me that the CNO had been briefed and was supportive of the concept. As the operations deputy (OPDEP) accredited to the Joint Staff, I assumed that the officers in J-3 (Operations) were informed of Admiral Lyons's initiative with Tuttle.

The concept was briefed to President Reagan on November 15 by Admiral Poindexter at one of the daily NSC briefings. The president gave his approval but asked that we ensure that there would be limited collateral damage. It is important to note for the record that his approval was given despite repeated objections to a "retaliatory strike" from both Weinberger and Vessey.

On November 17, Admiral Tuttle reported to his chain of command in Europe that he was ready to execute a plan that he had prepared with his French counterpart.[47] The French proposed to strike the following day. Tuttle's message was sent to the European headquarters in Stuttgart, Germany for General Bernard Rogers, USCINCEUR. Rogers was apparently personally unaware of the extensive planning that had already been done with the French commander in the Mediterranean. His staff

47 CTF SIXTY MESSAGE DTG 170714ZNOV83.

certainly was aware.[48] Admiral Tuttle waited in vain for approval from the chain of command, his message was being passed up the chain of command with a disapproving endorsement from General Rogers.[49]

Meanwhile, the French side was preparing to act. Having not received word of approval for US participation in the strike, French minister of defense Charles Hernu telephoned Weinberger before dawn in the United States to clarify US intentions. Weinberger alleged he knew nothing of the plan and had not had time to review it. It would not be approved. (As I learned in a subsequent tour as defense attaché in Paris some seven years later, Weinberger's response "shocked" the French military and President Mitterrand.)

I was despondent. On behalf of the commander in chief, I had broached the idea of a joint strike with French general Saulnier, President Reagan had approved a strike, and a detailed plan had been prepared by the forces in place to execute it. When it came time to execute, the secretary of defense walked away from it in stark disobedience of presidential direction. Replying to a query from Bud McFarlane on why he had blocked our participation in the strike, Weinberger's tendency to parry and sidestep was apparent. "He launched into a long series of obfuscations about misunderstandings with the French and all the things that could have gone wrong in the attack."[50]

This episode baffled the French, whose constitution (that of the Fifth Republic), drafted during the De Gaulle presidency, did not permit such flagrant disobedience. In France, only the president—and not the defense minister or even the prime minister—could authorize any preemptive hostile action. Alas,

48 SSO VAIHINGEN GERMANY MESSAGE DTG 162004Z NOV83.

49 USEUCOM MESSAGE DTG 170929Z NOV83.

50 McFarlane and Smardz, *Special Trust*, 270.

in our system, the articulated chain of command—four echelons between the president and the responsible commander who planned the strike—was able to foil a presidential decision.

Powell and Weinberger opposed the strike for contrarian reasons. As much as the president wanted to respond to those who had attacked our Marines, "the tragedy had scarred Powell and Weinberger and solidified their cautious approach to oversee military operations."[51] In the end, none of us at the NSC could have foreseen that Weinberger would not recognize the legitimizing advantage resulting from a joint Franco-American riposte against the perpetrators of the attacks against both MNF contingents. Informed of the outcome and of Weinberger's disobedience, the president told his national security advisor that it "was really disappointing... *We should have blown the daylights out of them. I just don't understand.*"[52]

In the weeks following the September 10 Suq al-Gharb attack, I had accompanied Judge Clark to the daily national security briefing for President Reagan. At these meetings, the judge would turn to me to update the president on recent events in Lebanon and specifically on the impact of Syrian and Israeli movements and their effect on our MNF. One of the more moving moments at several of the meetings was observing the president calling the next of kin of Marines killed by hostile fire in Beirut. The White House Military Office would research the identity of the deceased and the contact information for the survivors. The switchboard would place the call, and the president would thank the loved ones for the sacrifice of their Marine while conveying his own sorrow as well as the deep sorrow of the nation for their loss.

One morning in mid-October, shortly before the attack on our Marine barracks, we had finished briefing the president and

51 Matthews, *Colin Powell*, 79.

52 McFarlane and Smardz, *Special Trust*, 271.

Judge Clark and I were preparing to leave the Oval Office along with James Baker, Edwin Meese, and the vice president. Before the group got to the door, the judge asked me to stay behind with him, explaining that the president had a question for me. The president asked how many Marines President Eisenhower had deployed to Beirut in 1958 following the Chamoun crisis of that year. I explained that the initial cadre was the equivalent of the battalion landing team that we had in Beirut, but it had been quickly reinforced by another eight thousand Marine and army personnel who were moved to Lebanon in the weeks following the first deployment. To my amazement, the president took on a wistful look and he slowly walked to the window behind his desk, which looked out onto the Rose Garden. He said pointedly, "That pretty much ended that crisis…but then Ike didn't have to worry about being impeached for violating the War Powers Resolution."

In fact, the president's objectives were nearly identical to those proclaimed by President Eisenhower twenty-five years earlier. The latter justified the deployment of a much larger force by citing the "necessity to preserve the independence and integrity of Lebanon"; Eisenhower was responding to violence from the Al Mourabitoun militia then attempting to overthrow the presidency of Camille Chamoun, with the active support of the Egyptian and Syrian governments. His response was justifiable under the provisions of the "Middle East Resolution" passed by Congress in 1957, which authorized the use of military force to "block expansionary and forceful intervention by radical Arab socialists." The 1958 intervention was largely successful. Reagan, by contrast, had no such authority from Congress. He was instead constrained by the War Powers Act of 1973. His challenge was to pursue the stated objective of pressuring the withdrawal of Syrian and Israeli forces intervening in Lebanese affairs without invoking the threat of force, except in self-defense—a Sisyphean task, to be sure.

The exchange with President Reagan demonstrated to me how deeply he was committed to restoring sovereignty and peace to the Lebanese people for whom he cared very much. This may be one instance where the War Powers Resolution discouraged actions that might have prevented the cataclysmic chain of events that followed our failed mission in Lebanon. Inimical Arab powers and factions took careful note of our inaction following the assault on our Marines.

In October, following the departure of Judge Clark to become secretary of the interior and Bud McFarlane's appointment as his successor at the NSC, Donald Rumsfeld was named as the president's special envoy to the Middle East with the rank of ambassador. Rumsfeld was a close friend of Secretary of State George Shultz and his choice for the position. In his memoirs, Rumsfeld recounted that he was asked to continue our efforts of brokering an agreement with the Lebanese, the Syrians, and the Israelis to bring some stability to that tortured country.[53]

Rumsfeld went about putting together a team to assist in his efforts. I interviewed for a position on the Rumsfeld mission within a week of his appointment. During this interview, Rumsfeld explained that he understood that I had made quite a reputation for myself at the State Department (the incumbent ambassador in Beirut, Reginald Bartholomew, had labeled me a "dish breaker"). He implied that my activism was something that Secretary Shultz himself had pointed out as "forward leaning" activity in commenting on the NSC staff's role in policy making for Lebanon. Notwithstanding, Rumsfeld called me and asked me to join his team as his military assistant.

53 Donald Rumsfeld, *Known and Unknown* (New York: Penguin, 2011). See pp. 9–34.

This was to be a fascinating and extremely enjoyable assignment working for a master crisis manager possessed of keen intelligence. The assignment included two long trips to Lebanon, Israel, and Syria and later, a mission to Iraq, Kuwait, and Saudi Arabia.

Rumsfeld's approach to the mission of attempting to stabilize Lebanon was direct and characteristically unbureaucratic. As special envoy, Rumsfeld was responsible only to the president. He reported to the president via the national security advisor, his predecessor, Bud McFarlane. As mentioned, Rumsfeld had a special relationship with the secretary of state.

By contrast, he had from the beginning what can best be described as a complicated and often contentious relationship with Secretary of Defense Weinberger. This probably had to do with the fact that Weinberger disagreed with Shultz on virtually every initiative or proposal bearing on the mission and role of the MNF in Lebanon. It probably also derived from our close collaboration with Israel during his mission in the Middle East. In any case, the disagreement extended to virtually every dimension of US policy in the Middle East.

Resuming his mission, Rumsfeld set out with a dual track for progress in Lebanon. The first track was to pressure the Gemayel government to broaden and extend the dialogue with the Shia and Druze factions. This meant encouraging the Maronite Christian President Gemayel to make a major but necessary condition to both groups in return for a united front against continuing Syrian intervention in Lebanese affairs. The second track was to underline the determination of the United States and the other MNF contributors (France, Italy, and England) to assist in stabilizing the country by pressing for the withdrawal of Israeli forces from southern Lebanon to a line beyond the Awali River and by dislodging Syrian forces firmly entrenched in the Shouf and Allay districts.

Not long after his appointment and his first extended visit to the region, Rumsfeld came to understand the complexities he had inherited. Lengthy and repeated entreaties to Gemayel, his Greek Catholic foreign minister Elie Salem, and his Sunni national security advisor Dr. Wadi Haddad did not result in measurable progress toward compromise with either the Druze or Shia factions. Some progress was made in improving relations with the Sunni factions, as seen by the return from Saudi Arabia of the wealthy and powerful leader Rafic Al Harari. Al Harari had made his fortune in Saudi Arabia and returned to Lebanon with the expressed intent of assuming the prime minister role, as provided in the Lebanese constitution. Rumsfeld, a successful business leader in his own right, genuinely enjoyed his meetings and work with Al Harari.[54]

An attempt on Rumsfeld's life dramatically underlined the dangers attending his mission. One evening, Rumsfeld, Ambassador Reggie Bartholomew, and several of us on the staff stepped into the backyard of the residence to observe a murderous round of mortar and machine gun fire in the streets of Beirut below. Suddenly, a series of shots from small arms whistled around us, hitting trees on the edge of the garden. One of the state security officers shouted, "On the ground!" We all crawled through the lawn into the safety of the building. Later, and after the dispatch of several casually attired and ungroomed army special forces personnel protecting the residence, we learned that the fire had originated from a building still under construction not far away. We were also assured that the culprits responsible had been subdued.

---

54 In one meeting that I attended in late January 1983, Al Hariri, engulfed in clouds of smoke from a large Cuban cigar, posited that Syrian determination to "control" Lebanese politics would lead to shifting alliances between Damascus and the ethnoreligious factions competing for power. His assassination in 2005 following his resignation as prime minister the year prior was a tragic testament to his prescient description of Syrian intervention in Lebanese politics.

Another less positive development was the intensity of opposition from the pro-Syrian factions in Lebanon, which led to an escalation of the fighting between those factions and the Lebanese Army, and an increasing number of attacks on the president's palace, the Ministry of Defense, and the ambassador's residence. The attacks were originating from Syrian positions in the mountains around Beirut. These incidents led the Sixth Fleet commander to order surveillance flights over the Syrian positions by carrier-based aircraft. Some of those planes received hostile anti-aircraft fire from the Syrians.

The increasing number of attacks on those of our MNF based at the airport and on the residence in Beirut, as well as the attempted takedown of our reconnaissance aircraft, led to an air strike against Syrian positions in Lebanon on December 4. This retaliation was entirely consistent with the president's direction in NSDD-111 and was reaffirmed in NSDD-117 issued the day following the strike.

Whereas retaliatory actions may have been construed beforehand as a positive step toward curbing future attacks, the execution of the December 4 strike was a veritable disaster. At the insistence of Secretary Weinberger, who was concerned with the prospect of collateral damage, the European Command directed that attack be a daylight strike, with the added requirement that each target be first positively identified visually. The results of these directions were the choice of inconsequential targets, trivial weapons loads due to hurried preparation, and flight profiles that put the striking aircraft within range of Syrian batteries.[55]

After launching hurriedly following receipt of an untimely change in time over target, two of the striking aircraft were hit and damaged in the attack. Additionally, one American A-6E *Intruder* was downed by a Syrian missile, resulting in the capture

55 Lehman, *Winning the Cold War at Sea*, 328–332.

of the pilot and navigator by the Syrians. The crews were ultimately released by their captors to the custody of Reverend Jesse Jackson, who took up the mission to free the African American bombardier-navigator Lieutenant Robert O. Goodman. (The Syrians, playing an expert political hand, acceded to Jackson's request, thereby ingratiating themselves to the growing domestic opposition to our Lebanon policy.)

Rumsfeld came to understand that the strictures placed by the military chain of command on the execution of a punitive strike culminated in minimal damage to the Syrian positions and the humiliation of US forces supporting the MNF. Like McFarlane before him, he also came to understand that Secretary Weinberger and General Vessey were determined to limit military action in support of the Lebanese government and the Lebanese armed forces. As mentioned, their resistance was in spite of NSDD-111 and the president's desire to support the Lebanese.

One incident will illustrate the point. In mid-December 1983, the DOD suspended all reconnaissance flights by navy F-14s in Lebanese airspace. The objective of the reconnaissance had been to keep track of the Syrian artillery positions in the Metn that, with increasing frequency, were heavily firing upon the presidential palace, the Ministry of Defense, and the embassy residence in Yarze. The concern in the Pentagon was that if these photo missions drew Syrian fire, we would be obliged to respond with retaliatory air strikes, as we had once before. The prospect of having to continue air strikes led Secretary Weinberger to direct a halt to aerial surveillance of Syrian artillery positions in Lebanon. The decision, however, was not disclosed to either the State Department or to the White House.

On learning this, Rumsfeld was furious, as he had been attempting to leverage those same reconnaissance flights to gain concessions from the Syrian government. In January 1984, before Rumsfeld and I returned to Lebanon, Weinberger undertook to defend his decision during a meeting of the NSPG. As he laid out the tortured logic for suspending the flights, Rumsfeld interrupted him, exclaiming, "Cut the crap, Cap!"

The instructions issued by the DOD to subordinate commands were telling in that they resulted in little change in the ROE. Recognizing that the directions to the DOD in NSDD-111 had been ineffective, the president next signed NSDD-117 on December 5, 1983 to underline his concern. The following extracts from NSDD-117 are pertinent:

> The decisions directed in NSSD-111 bearing on diplomatic and military measures for Lebanon are **reaffirmed**. This explicitly includes measures to assure the **Rules of Engagement** provide for an effective self-defense against the range of foreseeable threats.
>
> The contingent of the MNF supported by naval surface and tactical air forces will pursue a policy of **vigorous self-defense against all attacks from any hostile quarter**. Responsive attacks will be used to **destroy targets** with minimal collateral damage
>
> In the event the above action cannot be carried out due to the risk of collateral damage or lack of precise information on the source of fire, **destructive fire will be directed against discrete military targets in unpopulated areas which are organizationally associated with the firing units**. [Emphases added]

I will posit in retrospect that the hesitant manner in which we supported our forces and the Lebanese Army ultimately led to the calamitous suicide attack on the Marine positions at the Beirut airport. To the contrary, had we responded earlier to pressure from Syria and its Lebanese surrogates, the tragedy that befell the MNF might have been averted. Sadly, the DOD had effectively signaled their opposition to the mission in Lebanon and revealed the divide within the US government, which was apparent from our military actions or, more to the point, inactions.

The issuance of NSDD-117 had been intended to stiffen responses to Syrian aggression. Sadly, it, too, failed to garner the support of Secretary Weinberger, the CJCS, and the military chain of command. The forces we had in the Mediterranean at the time were more than adequate to meet the president's guidance; it was the will within the military leadership to use those forces that was lacking.

The most telling account of why there was a failure to support our Marine contingent—and for that matter, for the government of Lebanon—was provided by Weinberger himself. In a memorandum to the national security advisor in February 1984, the secretary explained the condition he had put on retaliatory fire in guidance provided to General Rodgers: "In implementing this policy (NSDDs 111, 117, and 123), USCINCEUR has been told that…we have no wish to provoke an artillery duel or conflict with Syria." This condition led to what can best be described as ineffectual responses to literally hundreds of attacks. It was certainly not consistent with the president's direction that supporting forces would "pursue a policy of vigorous self-defense against all attacks from any hostile quarter."

During Rumsfeld's last trip to Beirut in January 1984, we continued our efforts to encourage President Gemayel to make major concessions to the Druze and Shia factions. Gemayel and his advisors were clearly reluctant, owing in part to fears in the Christian community that concessions would ultimately lead to increased Syrian domination of Lebanese politics and the continued persecution of the Christians who had sided with the Lebanese government.

Arriving in Beirut some three months after the attack on our barracks, we noticed dramatic changes in the activities and posture of our Marines at the airport. The battalion was now billeted literally underground in buried cargo containers to minimize their exposure to Syrian artillery. On a cold morning in early February, observing the airport bivouac area at a distance from the backyard of the ambassador's residence, the only visible evidence of a US presence at the airport that I could see was smoke coming out of dozens of small chimneys in the ground, spread over an acre or more. A single American flag flew in the middle of this subterranean encampment. Ambassador Rumsfeld and I were struck by the irony of the scene. What had happened to the mission of "stabilizing presence" by our proud Marines? I shared this thought with Rumsfeld, and he opined that if this was the best we could do, maybe we should pull out.

Later, during weeklong negotiations with the Gemayel administration, the presidential palace, Ministry of Defense, and the ambassador's residence once again came under bombardment. Our counter-battery radars confirmed that the source of fire included Syrian artillery and rocket battery placements in the Metn district. Ambassador Rumsfeld had me confirm the source of hostile fire on the radio with the Marine headquarters. Pursuant to the president's directive, he then asked that Colonel Timothy Geraghty, the commander of the 24th Marine Amphibious Unit, request that the *New Jersey* respond to the bombardment. I forwarded the request. After what seemed like an eternity, the battleship finally opened fire. The incoming fire from hostile batteries was quieted as the *New Jersey*'s rounds began impacting her targets.

This marked the first serious use of this formidable asset since the battleship's arrival in the Mediterranean some four months before. The widely reported inaccuracy of the rounds she fired on this occasion was the result of two problems. The first was the absence of effective spotting to adjust fire on the targets that were engaged. Apparently, the employment of air naval gunfire liaison company (ANGLICO) teams (ground spotters) or airborne spotters that were available had been deemed too provocative or dangerous by the chain of command. Second, we learned later that the bagged powder ammunition in the *New Jersey* was obsolete, and the "burn rate" of the propellants, which figures in the ballistic calculations by the fire control system, was incorrect. One problem led to inaccurate fire, the other to an inability to adjust that fire. The results were impediments to the mission of the *New Jersey* and a disappointment to those who had supported her deployment.

Although assurances of the continued support of the United States were extended to President Gemayel, the MNF and the mission to restore the sovereignty of the government had failed. The redeployment of the Marines to their amphibious ships was directed in February 1984. The other MNF units were also withdrawn, and the government of Lebanon was left to deal with their Syrian oppressors. The impact on the credibility of our assurances to others in the Middle East was clear. The emir of Bahrain put it simply to our ambassador in Manama, as reported in an embassy cable I drew from following our withdrawal: "Only the United States can solve the problems of Lebanon and the Middle East, and if the United States will not even stand up to Syria, there is not much hope for us in the future."

THE IRAN–IRAQ WAR AND THE SECURITY OF THE PERSIAN GULF

With the collapse of Rumsfeld's mission to Lebanon and the withdrawal of our Marines in 1984, the NSC staff responsible for Middle Eastern affairs became increasingly involved with issues arising from the Iran–Iraq War and the appearance that Iran was getting the upper hand. My focus as director of political affairs for the Middle East turned to prospects for containing Iran's ambitions in the Persian Gulf area. Lebanon had taught us that a significant dimension of the Iranian threat was its sponsorship of terrorism in the region. The case of Hezbollah in Lebanon, and the Iranian-Syrian complicity in attacks against our embassy in Lebanon following the redeployment of US forces, underscored our concern about dealing with Iranian ambitions and the reach of state-sponsored terrorism.

A significant interagency effort was launched in the spring of 1984 to examine our options and prepare a strategy to address US objectives in relation to the Iran–Iraq War. Ambassador Rumsfeld made another weeklong tour of the Middle East in late March 1984 that included stops in Kuwait, Saudi Arabia, Bahrain, and Iraq. I accompanied the ambassador on that tour and was present during meetings with ranking officials in the capitals of these countries. Among them was a meeting in Baghdad with Tariq Aziz, Iraqi minister of foreign affairs. I remember sitting in a large, beautifully appointed conference room with state-of-the-art, German-made audiovisual equipment. Aziz came into the meeting with ivory-handled revolvers on both hips. As we were seated, Rumsfeld quipped that he had come with peaceful intentions and was therefore unarmed.

The results of this trip were manifold. In the first place, our meetings in Egypt and Saudi Arabia with foreign and defense ministers confirmed that those countries were deeply concerned about the increasing prospect of an Iranian victory. Their requests for more dramatic demonstrations of US support led Ambassador Rumsfeld to ask whether they would accommodate more US forces in the region and especially land-based tactical air. Rumsfeld grew impatient with the reticence of the Saudis, who stressed the difficulty of hosting "foreign" military in Arab countries. Rumsfeld, tired of hearing repeated statements about the fragility and sensitivity of Arab public opinion, replied, "Excellency, we are a superpower, but we are not supermen!" He continued, asserting that we could not be expected to help in defending against sudden attacks from Iran if we were not allowed to base the required capability so that they could respond. It is important to note that at this time in history, the navy was adamantly opposed to operating aircraft carriers in the Persian Gulf for fear they might be trapped by mining of the Strait of Hormuz.

During our stop in Baghdad, we were unwitting witnesses to Iraq's apparent use of chemical weapons in their war with Iran. While watching the evening news from our hotel room, Howard Teicher and I saw footage of thousands of Iranian casualties near the port of Basra, stacked like cord wood. We had the distinct impression that the intact bodies had suffered death by chemical attack. Indeed, Tariq Aziz himself did not deny the use of chemical weapons to defeat human wave assaults by Iranian forces in southern Iraq.

Rumsfeld was quick to denounce the use of such weapons and to warn that their continued use would make it impossible for the United States to continue helping Iraq in their war with Iran. The "help," which Iraq needed desperately, was more and better intelligence on Iranian plans and activities. The establishment of a US interest section, or "mini-embassy" (my term) in Baghdad had always been intended to serve as a conduit for discreet intelligence support. (It was this office to which US ambassador April Glaspie was assigned at the time of her famous interview with Saddam Hussein, which preceded the August 1990 invasion of Kuwait.)

As we left central Baghdad for the military airport where Rumsfeld's aircraft had landed, our Iraqi escort pointed to the Euphrates River when we crossed one of the bridges. He remarked that the day before, an Iranian F-4 *Phantom* jet had made a low-level attack on that very bridge. It had obviously missed its mark. I also took note that almost every multistoried building that we passed had a manned anti-aircraft battery on its roof. The country was *very* clearly on a war footing.

Our next visit, to Bahrain, had two objectives. First, we were to discuss US operations in the Gulf proper with the Commander Middle East Force, Rear Admiral John Addams. Rumsfeld quizzed the admiral on his contingency plans and his readiness to respond to Iranian aggression against our ships or facilities in Bahrain.

As is so often the case, when senior civilians question military commanders about contingency plans or ROE, owing to the sensitivity of planned military operations the response is typically general and conditional. Addams's reply was no exception: "Although I can't share the details, the plans are well in hand." Rumsfeld reacted badly to what he considered an evasive response to his query. I was in a tough spot because I knew there was a more complete answer. Rumsfeld and Addams both looked at me with apparent annoyance, which made for an embarrassing moment. I had known Admiral Addams since the mid-'70s when he had served as our destroyer squadron commander (COMDESRON) and embarked in **Waddell**. Years after the meeting with Rumsfeld, Adm. Addams told me that he expected I would have explained the limits attending discussions of contingency plans with civilians outside the DOD. He did not appreciate that a former secretary of defense and the president's special envoy would not accept his reserve. The admiral would have understood Rumsfeld's expectations better had he read Rumsfeld's "rules"[56] before our meeting.

Our second objective was to explore Bahrain's ability and willingness to defend against Iranian incursions with the emir of Bahrain, Salman Al Khalif. In that meeting, the answers were more specific and forthcoming. For example, we learned about special systems in Manama Harbor to interdict hostile swimmers. The emir was especially thankful for the presence of the US Special Warfare personnel responsible for training Bahraini personnel and otherwise enhancing the security of the harbor and nearby facilities.

In the fall of 1984, just prior to my transfer back to the navy staff, I participated in yet another tour of Persian Gulf capitals as part of an interagency team led by Vice Admiral John Poindexter. Once again, we pressed regional leaders hard to permit more access for US forces and to concentrate their own efforts more directly on defending against Iranian- and Syrian-sponsored terrorism.

The Lebanon experience had seared our collective psyches. In a memorandum I prepared for Admiral Poindexter prior to taking my leave, I wrote that the cardinal lesson learned from the disaster that had befallen us in Lebanon was a realization that in a world populated by leaders bent on sponsoring terror to accomplish their goals, diplomacy without credible military means to undergird it is simply toothless.

* * *

56 Rumsfeld, *Known and Unknown*, 119. One "rule" that defined the role of the secretary of defense affirmed "his task is to exercise leadership and civilian control over the Department for the Commander-in-Chief and the country." As the president's special envoy, the rule was deemed applicable. Familiarity with the "rules" was a prerequisite to joining Rumsfeld's staff.

The Reagan administration had developed a huge rift. Secretary of State Shultz supported the president's recognition of the need for credible military means and the willingness to use these means to advance diplomatic objectives. Secretary Weinberger did not, and the six conditions that he insisted that must be met prior to the use of American military power made it virtually impossible to advance American interests in the Middle East.[57] Weinberger held the opposing view and made the case for noncoercive diplomacy.

It must be recognized that most, if not all, challenges to our national security interests—short of a direct assault on the United States or its allies—are unlikely to meet Weinberger's tests. The world we live in is simply more complicated than the setting implicit in Weinberger's "tests" and the challenges more nuanced.

I remain convinced that as was true of repeated bombings in Beirut and attacks on the Dhofar barracks in Saudi Arabia, Iraq's invasion of Kuwait and the violence wrought by al-Qaeda thereafter were predictable results of our inability to respond appropriately to repeated acts of terrorism against US interests in the Middle East. As Bruce Hoffman and Jacob Ware wrote in a recent commentary regarding the withdrawal of US forces from Afghanistan:

No one understood the significance of America's past retreats better than Osama bin Laden. In a 1997 interview, he recalled how the death of 241 [sic] US Marines in the

[57] 1. No commitment of forces to combat unless "vital" national interest are at stake.
2. Troops should only be committed with the clear intention of "winning."
3. Combat troops should be committed only with clearly defined political and military objectives and the requisite capacity to accomplish those objectives.
4. The relationship between objectives and the forces committed should be continually reassessed and adjusted as necessary.
5. US troops should not be committed to battle without "reasonable assurance" of congressional support and favorable public opinion.
6. The commitment of US forces should be considered only as a "last resort."

Beirut barracks bombing had compelled President Ronald Reagan to order a withdrawal from Lebanon...This led to the collapse of the multinational force in Lebanon... the main beneficiary was Hizballah.

I took my leave of the White House and the NSC staff proud of what we had endeavored to do. A few days prior to my detachment, I was invited with my family to meet with the president in the Oval Office after his daily national security briefing. We had photos taken with the president and he handed me a letter, which he signed in my presence, that I will long treasure. It recounted what we had attempted to do:

I am particularly grateful for the insights and perspectives you developed during your protracted trips to the region. I know that these ventures, particularly those to Lebanon, were not without personal risk. Despite the hardships and hazards of your mission, you were able to proffer skillful advice and sound judgments...This Republic has a long heritage of benefit from officers of the Naval service. You are among those in this gallant tradition.[58]

58 Letter from President Ronald Reagan to Captain Philip A. Dur, USN, October 31, 1984.

CHAPTER 9

AT THE RIGHT HAND OF A STRATEGIST AND MASTER OPERATOR

Executive Assistant to the Deputy Chief of Naval Operations (Plans, Policy and Operations)

Leaving the White House, I was transferred to the office of the Deputy Chief of Naval Operations (DCNO) for Plans, Policy and Operations (OP-06) as executive assistant (EA). The assignment was not a coincidence because I had been requested to serve in that position by none other than my former boss and great friend Vice Admiral James "Ace" Lyons. As described earlier, Lyons was famous in the navy both for his intellect and for his combative style. He was by any definition a master operator on land and at sea.

I had considered requesting an extension of my National Security Council (NSC) assignment, pending the results of a selection board that would meet in late 1984 to screen captains for major commands. Earlier that year, I had argued with

Lieutenant Colonel Ollie North, with whom I shared an office and a secretary (Fawn Hall), that a military officer could overstay an assignment to the president's executive office. My gut told me to get back to the navy. Coincidentally, Admiral Lyons asked me to serve as his EA, and that looked like a good place to await the results of the board. The White House years had been exhilarating and highly educational, but the navy is a jealous mistress, and I was after a big prize: I wanted another command at sea, and the special attraction was an Aegis guided missile cruiser of which there were only two in 1985.

Arriving back on the navy staff, I discovered anew the hidden influence of my position. The job of EA to the DCNO is tantamount to that of a chief of staff in an operational command. Arranging the admiral's calendar, attending many of his meetings, monitoring his phone calls, and relaying his instructions to his subordinates senior to me all made for an invaluable experience. After all, Admiral Lyons was the navy's operations deputy (OPDEP) and the Chief of Naval Operations' (CNO) surrogate in matters and issues before the Joints Chiefs of Staff (JCS). As such, I became very familiar with the briefing papers and the recommended navy positions on all the major issues before the JCS and the DOD.

The pace in OP-06 was frenetic! Admiral Lyons typically arrived in his office at about 6:30 a.m. and would remain at his desk until 5:00 or 6:00 p.m. each workday and on many Saturdays. Every day would feature meetings with staff and/or other divisions of the Office of the Chief of Naval Operations (OPNAV), briefings to the CNO in person and by phone, and countless other phone conversations. There were speeches to be prepared and letters to be written, edited, and cleared for the admiral's signature. All told, it provided me with yet another fascinating opportunity to serve the navy and my country.

One specific issue that I staffed still looms brightly despite the passing of many years. It had to do with Cuba's jamming of Radio Marti, a broadcast to the Cuban people transmitted from the Florida Keys that was intended to inform them of US policies that were often misrepresented in Cuban propaganda. Admiral Lyons advocated using drones carrying explosive charges to strike the offending jamming towers in Cuba. The idea had generated some interest in defense intelligence quarters, but it gained absolutely no traction in the JCS arena when it was tabled. Still, it struck me as an interesting response to an annoying and aggressive move by the Cuban government. Here again, though, the admiral emboldened his critics, in and out of the navy, who saw him as overly aggressive in his policy recommendations and too strident in the advocacy of his own ideas.

The admiral's special accomplishments while I served as his EA were the navy-to-navy discussions that he promoted with allies and in which he participated personally. Having reorganized planning and training while Commander of Second Fleet (COMSECONDFLT), he continued his efforts while DCNO to persuade the NATO navies in the Atlantic regarding the need to adjust their own planning, equipping, and the training of their forces for offensive operations against the Soviet Union. I accompanied him for talks with the Royal Navy (RN) in 1985, and there he tried mightily to continue advancing the case at Whitehall for an offensive maritime strategy. (His persuasive and logical arguments notwithstanding, I sensed in those meetings that our British counterparts, though generally accepting the logic, were not comfortable with his blunt arguments and brusque manner.)

Admiral Lyons was more successful in his meetings with the French and Norwegian Navy counterparts. The French, who at the time were undertaking to build their nuclear-powered aircraft carrier *De Gaulle,* were especially keen to upgrade their fleet's anti-air warfare (AAW) capabilities, especially the carrier-based fighters (at the time, ancient F-8 *Crusaders*) and their airborne early warning (AEW) system. French armed forces were not formally recommitted to NATO until 2009, but as demonstrated during exercise OCEAN VENTURE 81 in 1981, the Marine Nationale had always been prepared to operate and train with their US counterparts. In contrast with our British friends, French admirals did not seem at all concerned during bilateral meetings with Admiral Lyons who was leading the charge for offensive concepts of operations.

The Norwegians were arguably the most receptive to the veritable revolution in NATO's Atlantic strategy, especially the return of naval striking forces to the Norwegian Sea. They took great interest in Lyons's description of the AAW improvements afforded by the Aegis combat system. Notably, the Norwegian Navy eventually equipped several of their new frigates with the Aegis system.

Lyons also pioneered navy-to-navy talks with the Israelis. As is well known, for almost thirty years following the establishment of the State of Israel, the US military avoided, almost assiduously, any formal contacts with their Israeli counterparts. The latent and rather exaggerated fears within the military underlying this choice had to do with likely repercussions in the "moderate" Arab world.[59] The history of military relations between the two nations bears repeating. After the Six-Day War in June 1967 and despite lingering suspicions regarding Israel's "accidental" or mistaken attack on the USS *Liberty* during that conflict, the United States had replaced France as the principal provider of sophisticated weapons for the Israel Defense Forces (IDF).

59 In 1948, the JCS formally warned the Truman administration against the recognition of the State of Israel for that very reason.

During the Yom Kippur War in October 1973, the Israeli Air Force (IAF) suffered significant aircraft losses to the Soviet-equipped Egyptian Air Force. Israel had requested urgent replacements for losses during that short war, and the Nixon administration had ordered the DOD (specifically, the navy and Marine Corps) to draw from their inventories replacements for the more than one hundred fighter and attack aircraft that the IAF had lost. In addition to providing navigational guidance and air defense for the massive US emergency airlift of supplies and equipment to Israel, the Sixth Fleet was positioned to support Operation Nickel Grass, as the resupply effort was named. Owing to the sensitivities of all our European allies, save Portugal, regarding US wartime support to Israel and in the absence of land facilities, three Sixth Fleet aircraft carriers were positioned in the central and eastern Mediterranean. This was in part to provide contingency "lily pads" for replacement naval aircraft (A-4 *Skyhawks* and F-4 *Phantoms*) being ferried to Israel. Support for Israel was extended notwithstanding the competing presence of more than fifty Soviet ships in the Mediterranean, including twenty submarines.

In the years following 1973, direct relations between the US and Israeli militaries had remained very secretive and had centered primarily on the provision of significant weapons and assistance in their use and on the sharing of critical military intelligence. It was not until the Reagan administration in 1984 that the United States and Israel established a Joint Political Military Planning Group (JPMG) to develop closer cooperation between their respective armed forces and begin collaborative planning for well-defined contingencies involving the Soviet Union.

Working with then-Lieutenant General John T. (Jack) Chain, USAF, the director of the Bureau of Political-Military Affairs at the Department of State, I had participated in concluding the

JPMG agreement with Israel. We succeeded in overcoming the formidable reticence of the DOD. Admiral Lyons was a pioneer in this effort during his tenure as OP-06. The specific objectives he promoted were an increase in the frequency of US Navy port visits to Israel and the development of advanced training between the Sixth Fleet and the Israeli Navy and Air Force. Suffice to note that his support for improved military relations with the Israelis did not earn him any compliments from Secretary Weinberger, who had only grudgingly agreed to the creation of JPMG in the first place.[60]

Admiral Lyons was the force behind the establishment and employment of the Red Cell, led by then-Commander Richard "Dick" Marcinko,[61] who before this assignment had been the first commanding officer (CO) of the now-famous SEAL Team Six. The cell was created to prove and then correct the physical vulnerability of US naval installations to terrorist attacks, which was a great concern following the bombings in Lebanon.

Marcinko's team operated as commandos, and their penetrations of facilities were covert. Security forces protecting the installations were visited by Marcinko's team, every one of them a navy SEAL. The security forces were simply no match. The targets were notified in advance that they would receive a "visit" from the Red Cell, but except for base commanders and COs, they were not provided precise information on the exact timing or the method of penetration. The cell uncovered a woeful lack of readiness and porosity of perimeters at virtually every installation they visited. For example, waterborne access by swimmers to our main operating bases was shown to be a significant vulnerability.

60 Here again, Secretary Weinberger flashed his pro-Arab cards. He argued that any planning relationship with the Israelis would invariably leak and sound claxons of alarm throughout the moderate Arab world. I will note for the record that no such thing transpired, probably because most of the Arab world assumed we were already planning with the Israelis.

61 Richard Marcinko, *Rogue Warrior* (New York: Pocket Books, 1992), 281–307.

An incident involving the Red Cell in the spring of 1985 exposed the risks incident to this type of covert security test. The cell selected the headquarters of the Commander in Chief of the Atlantic Fleet (CINCLANTFLT) in Norfolk, Virginia, as a target installation. In mid-afternoon one day, I received an urgent alarm by buzzer at my desk in the office adjacent to that of Admiral Lyons. I hurriedly opened the door to his office and found one very excited and disturbed admiral. Before I could determine the source of his disquiet, he stammered several times before yelling, "Get Marcinko on the phone!"

Not knowing where Marcinko was exactly and not having any mobile phones available (cell phones were in their infancy), I repaired to my office and began dialing every number I had for the headquarters of CINCLANTFLT in hopes that I could locate Marcinko and his merry band. After what seemed an eternity, I finally got him on the phone and asked him to hold because the admiral wanted to speak with him. What transpired after that call was connected cannot be conveyed in polite language. Admiral Lyons was as emotional as I had ever seen him. His colorful instructions to Marcinko were to wrap up his exercise and return to the Pentagon at warp speed.

As I learned after the conversation, the deputy CINCLANTFLT, Vice Admiral Bernard Kauderer, had telephoned Lyons to inform him that Marcinko's team had captured and "imprisoned" several senior officers, including at least one flag officer. Kauderer described a weird scene that included the spectacle of these officers bound up and lying facedown on the floor of the fitness center. He also reported these details to his boss and thereafter to the CNO's office.

Although useful in pointing out the many weaknesses in our base security at home and abroad, the excesses that accompanied the Red Cell's efforts were criticized by many. The project was abandoned shortly after this incident. I am convinced that it took a move as bold as that organized by Admiral Lyons to convince the navy of the need to make huge strides in how we thought about and defended our critical installations against the growing threat of terrorism.

Another, more humorous, incident for which the admiral became famous had to do with a visit to the Washington Navy Yard by the naval attaché at the Soviet embassy in Washington. As one would expect, Admiral Lyons had a very high profile where the Soviet Navy was concerned. His efforts to train the fleet as it would fight in the event of war with the USSR were well publicized in many US journals, and they had even earned him some notoriety in the Soviet press. Just before Christmas in 1984, the Soviet attaché hand-delivered a box, wrapped in Christmas paper and containing a case of the finest liquors and wines from the Georgian Republic of the Soviet Union. The delivery was made to the main entrance to the Navy Yard, asking that they be delivered to Admiral Lyons's quarters. Before the gate sentries could inquire about the contents of the Christmas present, the Soviet vehicle left the entrance. The concerned Marine sentries called for an emergency ordinance disposal (EOD) team to inspect and remove the box, fearing it was some sort of explosive device. Taking no chances, the EOD personnel caged the case of liquor and destroyed its contents explosively. Hearing of the incident the next day, I received a call from the Soviet embassy explaining that it had been intended as a gift for Admiral Lyons.

During John Lehman's tenure as secretary of the navy (SECNAV), and while I was working for Admiral Lyons, the navy had undertaken the development of several weapons systems that fell into a category known as black programs. Those admitted into the details of these programs were exceptionally few in number. Admiral Lyons was among them; I was not.

Without disclosing anything about the programs to which he was privy, he would periodically leave the office for a few days for travel to unannounced locations. I was not informed about this type of travel, and only on leaving the Pentagon would he hand me a sealed envelope, admonishing that it was not to be opened except in case of an undefined "emergency."

During one of those trips, the EA to Vice Chief of Naval Operations (VCNO) Captain Bill Francis called me and said the VCNO was asking about the admiral's whereabouts. I was concerned that Admiral Lyons's nominal superior had not been informed about this trip, but I had my instructions. I replied to Francis that I did not know where he was. When would the admiral return, he asked? I told him that his calendar had been cleared through the following day, but that I could not be certain as to the exact time of his return. Francis was clearly annoyed by my response, and not long after, he stormed into my office to inform me, "The vice chief's hair is on fire!" He then suggested that I accompany him to the office of the VCNO, Admiral Ron Hays, and to explain Lyons's absence directly to Adm. Hays. I put the sealed envelope given to me by Adm. Lyons in the pocket of my uniform blouse and followed Captain Francis to the VCNO's office.

I explained to a calm but visibly disturbed VCNO that what I had recounted to Captain Francis was all that I knew. Admiral Hays then asked me who knew where Admiral Lyons was. I explained that I assumed that the office of the SECNAV was informed, but I did not disclose the contents of the sealed envelope in my pocket since no one had used the term "emergency." When Admiral Lyons returned to the office the next day, I told him what had transpired during his absence. He commended me for not sharing the "secret" contents of the envelope and for referring the VCNO to the secretary's office. I learned somewhat later that the relationship between Admiral Lyons and Admiral Hays had soured over this incident.

One relatively small event during the time I worked for Admiral Lyons illustrates the consequences that a military officer can face as the result of working for a superior who disagree with DOD principals. While on the NSC staff, I attempted to serve my superiors, the president, and successive national security advisors Clark and McFarlane. During that same time, General Colin Powell was serving as the senior military assistant to Secretary of Defense Caspar Weinberger. Admiral Lyons had already been a friend and mentor to me when I took the NSC position.

During the Lebanon crisis, Admiral Lyons and General Powell crossed paths and swords over policy on the US response to Syrian-led attacks on US and other multinational force (MNF) units. Lyons was an active proponent of the president's decision to take aggressive action against the Syrian and Syria-backed forces; Secretary Weinberger not only opposed any such actions but systematically ignored the president's directives.

When I was transferred to the navy staff in late 1984, as Lyons's EA, General Powell must have taken note because my sources at the White House later informed me that Deputy Assistant Secretary of Defense (ASD) for International Security Affairs (ISA) Richard Armitage, a very close friend of Powell's, and Powell himself had asked to be informed if I requested a White House clearance to return and meet with staff at the NSC.

In December 1984, however, I was unaware of these instructions when I was asked by Don Fortier, then a principal assistant to the president, to visit him in the West Wing. The meeting would serve to explore what options might be reasonable to counter Libyan dictator Gaddhafi's increasing use of terrorism against US interests. Fortier wanted to discuss "informally" what the navy's capabilities were and how one might begin developing plans for retaliatory strikes against Libyan facilities. With Admiral Lyons's approval, I went and met with Fortier, Admiral Poindexter, and others on the NSC staff.

Powell was apparently informed of my visit by one of his sources on the NSC staff. He then took the exceptional step of calling Admiral Lyons and warning him that "at the direction of the secretary of defense," I was not to make any more visits to the White House. Whether true or not, I was as surprised as I was disappointed. After all, I had gone to the White House for this meeting at the specific request of the president's assistant for National Security Affairs. I was obviously in an unofficial and informal capacity. It is a given in Washington policy circles that all sorts of meetings and off-the-record discussions take place among members of various agencies and even with members of Congress and the staff of congressional committees. My offering personal opinions and views to colleagues was neither treasonable nor disloyal.

Alas, this provided another lesson learned—namely, that by having carried out the instructions of my superiors at the White House, including those of the president himself, officials who had objected to the policies of the president held it against me personally after I had left the NSC staff. I also learned from informed sources that during the Tower Commission's review of the operations of the NSC staff in the wake of the Iran–Contra affair, General Powell had been critical of my role at the NSC during the Lebanon crisis.

Much later, after my selection to rear admiral in 1988 and under orders to my first assignment as a flag officer, I made a point to call on General Powell, who was by then commander of US Forces Command in Atlanta. The visit was primarily to discuss my forthcoming assignment as the US defense attaché in Paris, and in that capacity, I would be representing Gen. Powell once he assumed his future responsibilities as Chairman of the Joint Chiefs of Staff (CJCS).

We discussed his interests and the means for communicating with him while in Paris. But before leaving his office, I took the opportunity to discuss the above incident and, more generally, my tour of duty on the staff of the NSC. I explained to the general that notwithstanding the alleged criticism of my role in promoting the president's agenda for Lebanon, I had carried out my orders and executed my assignments exactly as directed by my superiors. I explained that I had a commendatory letter from the president that was signed in my presence as I left the White House in November 1984. I added that the president had been aware of the problems that the DOD had in executing his orders and instructions. I wanted the general to understand that I had never acted on my own or without the explicit approval of my superiors. General Powell acknowledged without further comment, and my working relationship with him while his representative in France was very good.

* * *

My relationship with Admiral Lyons was that of a loyal mentee. The admiral's style was abrupt and straightforward. He was a tough task master, and he insisted that his subordinates share his determination in the face of opposition from any quarter to advance navy positions and what he regarded as our service's interests. He once quipped only half-jokingly to me, "There is but one true god and that is Neptune; his chosen prophet was Mahan, and the navy is his holy church." As I described in earlier chapters, Admiral Lyons was most helpful to me at several critical points in my career, and I gratefully acknowledged as much following my retirement and in a conversation shortly before his passing.

One remarkable memory came as I neared the end of my tour as EA to Admiral Lyons: that of witnessing the process by which coveted four-star admiral assignments are made. (Subsequently, as EA and senior naval aide to the SECNAV, I saw more examples of the politics that attend three- and four-star assignments in the navy.) The case of Admiral Lyons's promotion is noteworthy because it was so controversial and even had an international dimension.

The logical progression to four-star rank in the case of Admiral Lyons would have been to command the US Atlantic Fleet (CINCLANTFLT). But until 1985, CINCLANTFLT was a "triple-hatted" assignment. The other two hats were command of the Unified Atlantic Command (USCINCLANT) and the exalted NATO Command, Supreme Allied Commander Atlantic (SACLANT). The triple hat was problematic in that assignment as CINCLANTFLT resulted in simultaneous appointments to the other two commands. Therein was the problem for advocates of the "reforms" eventually included in the Goldwater-Nichols Act.

As mentioned, Lyons had antagonized senior members in the RN by dismissing their advice and ignoring some of their sensitivities when planning for the Striking Fleet Atlantic (STRIKFLTLANT). At bottom, his straightforward and direct approach to allied command was apparently of concern to the RN. Given his well-known dislike for what he regarded as vestigial RN paternalism and the tutorials he had received from RN counterparts, the British were likely to object if Lyons were nominated for the job as SACLANT, and in this case, they clearly had a veto in NATO channels.

Nor were the CJCS, General Jack Vessey, and the secretary of defense, Casper Weinberger, likely to approve of Lyons as the unified commander, USCINCLANT. Vessey's opposition to Admiral Lyons had to do with his activism and strident manner while serving as the navy's OPDEP and working on joint matters. Admiral Lyons had earned the support of Admiral Watkins and his principal supporter for command of the Atlantic Fleet was the SECNAV, John Lehman. Weinberger's motivations for rejecting Lyons's appointment have already been described.

To circumvent the "triple hat" dilemma, the secretary of defense decided in early 1985 to separate command of the Atlantic Fleet, the navy component, from the other two commands. Under the revised arrangement, the unified command and the NATO command would remain a double-hatted position, and CINCLANTFLT would be the subordinate or component navy commander.

This change was consistent with the logic promoted in the Goldwater-Nichols Act, which elevated the authority and decision latitude given to the unified or "combatant commanders" and removed them from the service chain of command. Efforts both within the DOD and in Congress were already well underway to ensure that the unified or combatant commanders were responsible only to the president and the secretary of defense.

The stage was now set for the nominations, which I watched unfold. There were three navy vice admirals in line for promotion to four stars in the spring of 1985: Admiral Lyons, Admiral Carlisle Trost, and Admiral Arthur Moreau.

The decision makers responsible for selecting the candidates for nomination were (quite logically) CNO Admiral James Watkins, Navy Secretary John Lehman, and CJCS Gen. Vessey. The secretary of defense, and ultimately the president, would approve the nominations. Following that, the nominations would be sent to the Senate for confirmation. The "principals" sponsoring candidates for promotion were the CNO, the SECNAV, and the CJCS. It appeared to me that each had a candidate to advance.

After much maneuvering and many exchanges, the commander experienced in the Atlantic, Lyons, was nominated to command forces in the Pacific as Commander in Chief, Pacific Fleet (CINCPACFLT). The more experienced Pacific hand, Admiral Trost, was nominated to command the Atlantic Fleet as CINCLANTFLT. Admiral Moreau was nominated for the four-star command of naval forces in Europe and Allied Forces Southern Europe.

The details behind these nominations are indicative of the impact that personal loyalties and relationships play in the assignment of the most senior officers in our military. It is not widely understood outside the military establishment, but the last promotions of flag and general officers that are the result of legally constituted selection boards are those to rear admiral in the navy (and the Coast Guard) and to major general in the other services. Beyond that career point, nominations for promotion are made by the service chiefs and service secretaries and approved by the secretary of defense with input from a variety of other sources. In the post-Goldwater-Nichols era and the emphasis it has placed on "jointness" and the pivotal role of the combat commanders (COCOMs), service preferences may sometimes be overridden or overruled by the CJCS. Lyons, whose stellar record promoting sea power as a commander, strategist, and tactician, was almost a case in point.

In August 1985, I flew to Hawaii in the SECNAV's special mission aircraft to witness the CINCPACFLT change of command as Admiral Lyons took charge of the US Pacific Fleet. I was gratified to see the admiral rewarded for his many important contributions to our country and its security and grateful for the education and support he afforded me while I served at the right hand of one of the navy's most accomplished strategists.

On my return to Washington, I was detached from the navy staff and began a "pipeline" of training preparatory to assuming command of **Yorktown.**

CHAPTER 10

CLOSING THE LAST CHAPTER OF THE COLD WAR AT SEA

Commanding, USS *Yorktown* (CG-48)

The opportunity to command what was only the second ship in a new class of guided missile cruisers was exciting beyond description. After years of research and experimentation to improve anti-air and anti-missile defenses, navy-funded teams at RCA,[62] led by Admiral Wayne Meyer, had by 1984 fielded a transformational weapons system appropriately named Aegis. The system, comprising a solid-state phased-array radar driven by banks of computers that incorporated early forms of artificial intelligence and complex algorithms, could detect and track a large number of targets simultaneously. Missile launchers that could deliver precision ordnance against multiple targets were programmed to respond in seconds to the most challenging airborne threats. Owing to this development after more than forty years of effort, the fleet had finally solved one of its most vexing problems: that of defending against concentrated air and missile attacks by putative enemies, especially Soviet air and naval forces.

62 Later Lockheed Martin

In short, USS *Yorktown* (CG-48) was a state-of-the-art warship. The ship's engineering plant and much of her layout duplicated those of the *Spruance* class of destroyers. Because I had commanded the USS *Comte de Grasse* (DD-974), I was familiar with many of the systems and the compartmentation of the ship. The combat system, however, was entirely new to me and infinitely more capable and complex than those in earlier classes of cruisers and destroyers in which I served.

Prior to reporting for duty as a commanding officer (CO), I was required to complete a lengthy pre-command course syllabus, the longest component of which was a six-week engineering refresher at the Atomic Energy Commission site in Idaho Falls, Idaho. The Senior Officer Ship's Material Readiness Course (SOSMRC) was designed to upgrade and advance the engineering knowledge of non-nuclear-trained aviation and surface officers en route to command at sea. Glaring lapses in the matériel condition and readiness of several ships in the decades before had prompted the navy's leadership to require a SOSMRC certificate of every prospective CO of conventionally powered surface ships. (Nuclear-trained officers were rightly assumed to have had adequate engineering backgrounds.)

The course was taught by smart, nuclear-trained officers, and the instructional material centered on the proper operation and maintenance of ship propulsion plants and electrical systems. It was a tough course in a remote setting, but the instruction and the friendships forged across the aviation and surface warfare communities were invaluable.

Following our completion of SOSMRC, many of us were next assigned to a monthlong pre-command course at the Surface Warfare Officers School (SWOS) Command in Newport, Rhode Island. The emphasis there was to refresh prospective COs on fleet regulations and directives as well as personnel matters. The most valuable part of the curriculum was the "incident review" in which we were provided with details surrounding accidental groundings and collisions that befell our predecessors in command. These accounts afforded us an opportunity to reflect on, and prepare for, the challenges that lay ahead.

As the prospective CO of an Aegis ship, I was further ordered to attend a monthlong course of instruction at the Combat Systems Engineering Development Site (CSEDS) in Moorestown, New Jersey. Here, at a rural site near Philadelphia, the navy had built a functioning, prototypical combat system; because it had a superstructure that resembled a ship, it was known colloquially as the "cruiser in the cornfield." The installation was fitted with two installed AN/SPY-1A radar arrays staring out at the New Jersey Turnpike, positioned to track the hundreds of commercial aircraft in the busy air corridors around New York. We received a crash course on the Aegis combat system and the software doctrines that governed its performance. It was a valuable introduction that my experience aboard ship would refine.

The final pre-command course provided critical preparation for my forthcoming assignment. It was taught by knowledgeable and experienced officers at the Tactical Training Group Atlantic in Dam Neck, Virginia. Through this course, we became familiar with the latest intelligence on the capabilities and tactics of our putative enemies, the Soviet Navy and Soviet naval aviation. Experimental tactics and current fleet practice were reviewed in detail, and we were given practical exams to test our ability to deal with a variety of threats.

In June 1986, I took command of *Yorktown* in Norfolk, Virginia, in a ceremony presided over by Admiral David Jeremiah, then-commander, Cruiser-Destroyer Group 8 (COMCRUDESGRU 8).

I was relieving just in time to participate in a memorable Fourth of July visit to New York City. The occasion was a naval review by President Reagan to celebrate the centennial of the Statue of Liberty. My predecessor in command, Captain Carl Anderson, was a very senior captain, and owing to his seniority, the plan for the entry into New York Harbor had *Yorktown* in the lead as a formation guide.

Notwithstanding my lack of seniority, I was privileged to lead a column of twelve US and allied warships under the Verrazano Bridge into New York's Lower Bay. Following the same protocol, *Yorktown* was assigned one of the best anchorages in the harbor: we would be only a few hundred yards from the USS *Iowa* (BB-62) when, with President Reagan embarked, she would transit through the thirty or more anchored warships that comprised the naval review. Indeed, our assigned anchorage was as good as that of the largest ship present, the aircraft carrier USS *John F. Kennedy* (CV-67).

The evening of July 3 featured a spectacular show in the middle of the harbor on Governor's Island, which was managed by the Coast Guard. It included performances by several celebrities, including Frank Sinatra, Tony Bennett, and Liza Minelli. Presidents Ronald Reagan and François Mitterrand were in attendance, as were several thousand guests in the stadium. Although it was July, the temperature that night fell into the fifties, and with a strong northerly wind blowing, it was a chilling experience for sailors in our dress whites. From our seats in the stadium, we could see that both presidents and their wives had been provided with blankets to reduce their exposure.

Among my most humorous memories was our departure from Governor's Island following the concert, after both presidents had left by helicopter. Once we were cleared by the Secret Service to leave the stadium, we five COs of US ships in the harbor made our way to the boat dock to await our trip home in the captain's gig of *Kennedy*'s CO, Captain Jack Moriarty. As the boat approached the dock, we heard a loud complaint from none other than Frank Sinatra in the company of Liza Minelli. "Old Blue Eyes" was insisting that the Coast Guard team hail the boat that he had chartered and that it be brought alongside so that he and Minelli could leave, before our transportation could tie up. The Coast Guard chief in charge of the landing ignored Sinatra's pleas (now echoed by Minnelli), and we left the island with an unhappy Hollywood duo in our wake.

The naval review took place the next morning on the Fourth of July. As mentioned, all the ships, US and foreign, were anchored on either side of a channel through which the *Iowa* would pass with President Reagan embarked. I was up early that morning with my executive officer (XO), Commander John Kelly, to ensure that our ship was presentable and that our sailors were properly uniformed and ready to "man the rail." Just before the ceremonies were to begin, I received an urgent call from my quarterdeck watch, informing me that a small craft was alongside the brow, requesting to disembark two VIPs wanting to come aboard our ship. I was both surprised and somewhat annoyed and sent the XO to see who the VIPs were and why they wanted to come aboard at such an inopportune time.

Within minutes, the XO returned with none other than Senator John Warner (R-VA), then-chairman of the Armed Services Committee, and a charming British lady, whom he introduced as the granddaughter of Admiral Lord Jellicoe, the Royal Navy (RN) hero of World War I. Warner had been the guest speaker at the commissioning of *Yorktown* in Yorktown, Virginia, two years earlier, and as he explained to me, he wanted to show his guest around "his ship." I naturally agreed and left my perch on the signal bridge of *Yorktown* to give the senator and his date a proper tour of "our" ship. In any case, I made it back to the signal bridge just in time to render honors to our commander in chief as he passed close aboard in the magnificently laid-out *Iowa,* commanded by my good friend Captain Larry Seaquist.

After the two-hour naval review, *Iowa* reversed course, moving north in the harbor to anchor and embark several prominent guests of the secretary of the navy (SECNAV). At that point, I learned what it was like to be a junior captain in a privileged anchorage. We were hailed on the bridge-to-bridge radio with a message addressed to me from Secretary Lehman, who was still aboard *Iowa.* The message was short and simple: I was asked to clear my anchorage and informed that *Iowa* would take my spot. I informed my immediate superior and inquired where I was to go. He instructed me to proceed to a berth on the Brooklyn side of the East River.

The instruction was a difficult one to execute because after starting main engines and rousing my anchor, I had to work my way through literally hundreds of small pleasure craft that were anchored just off Battery Park, awaiting the firework spectacle planned for that evening. Contemplating how I could make this move safely, I contacted the Coast Guard, and they provided a small cutter to run interference as I approached the pier in Brooklyn. There were many inebriated small craft skippers who were very unhappy that they had to lift anchor to facilitate our passage through the East River. As it turned out, the berth in Brooklyn was a perfect place from which to watch what I re-member was the greatest fireworks display I had ever seen. The number of rockets, the duration of the presentation, and the noise echoing off the Twin Towers and other skyscrapers in the battery were simply spectacular.

On leaving New York City to return to Norfolk, we transited in company with *Iowa.* As we sailed together in a line abreast, with about thirty "tigers" (male guests of our crews) on the bridge, I took station about one hundred yards abeam of *Iowa*. We ran inert training missiles (Bluebirds) on the four rails of our missile launchers, and Seaquist responded by training all three of his massive sixteen-inch gun turrets pointing directly at our ship. My imaginative XO then ordered our bridge watch to play a popular song at the time on the top side speakers. The music, loud enough for those on *Iowa* to hear, was "Hit Me with Your Best Shot."

***

Following our return to Norfolk, we began an extended series of training exercise and inspections, including a September 1986 transit to the Puerto Rican Operating Area and the Atlantic Fleet Weapons Training Facility (AFWTF) for a battery of missile firings and anti-submarine warfare (ASW) training. In December 1986, we sailed south to conduct tests that would measure our acoustic signature and the effectiveness of systems designed to limit noise radiated through the hull—a critical factor in ASW.[63] After torpedo firing exercises in the Bahamas, in January 1987 we steamed south to the Caribbean in a battleship battle group comprising *Iowa, Yorktown*, and two destroyers. *Yorktown* was assigned duties as the anti-air warfare commander (AAWC) for the group.

***

63 Like the *Spruance*-class destroyers before them, *Ticonderoga*-class cruisers were fitted with noise-quieting features that complicated their detection by submarines.

While in this group, I came awfully close to what might be termed a career-limiting incident—one of my own making. In the decade before I took command of **Yorktown**, there had been considerable discussion in the navy regarding division of responsibilities in "composite warfare" (ASW, AAW, EW, and strike warfare, or STW) and the responsibilities of surface warfare officers in "major" combatant commands. Included in this category were commanders of destroyer squadrons (COMDESRON, honorific title "commodore") and COs of cruisers. The arrival of the Aegis cruisers, with their state-of-the art command-and-control suites, led some senior officers to consider sharing the cruisers' facilities with destroyer squadron commanders; the latter were routinely assigned duties as anti-surface warfare commanders or ASW commanders for battle groups. Cruiser COs were typically assigned duties as AAWCs.

The **Iowa** battle group was commanded by Rear Admiral Mike Kalleres, Commander, Carrier Strike Group 12 (COMCRUDESGRU 12), a colorful and rather outspoken flag officer famous for sending poignant critiques to his subordinates while commanding a destroyer squadron (DESRON).[64] When the admiral asked whether I could share my facilities with Captain Mike Loy, Commander, Destroyer Squadron 26 (COMDESRON 26), I recommended against it because one of Loy's destroyers in the group was designed specifically as a flagship for a commodore. I knew that Vice Admiral William "Scot" McCauley, his superior and in command of surface forces in the Atlantic Fleet, was solidly opposed to this practice, lest it confuse command responsibility and accountability in a combat situation. McCauley was famous for having argued strongly and successfully against embarking a destroyer squadron commander

---

64 Adm. Kalleres's messages were in the form of "Husky codes." To encourage excellence, for example, he would send a message to subordinates reminding that "only the lead Husky does not eat yellow snow." There were more than a dozen Husky codes to convey his assessment of performance.

in his cruiser, the USS *Halsey* (CG-23), during a deployment to the western Pacific in 1976. His argument had prevailed, and subsequently, there was a written policy in the Pacific Fleet that proscribed the embarkation of a destroyer squadron commander in a cruiser commanded by an officer serving in the rank of captain.

I knew of this policy and Adm. McCauley's views because at the time of that incident, I had been serving in the same Seventh Fleet task group as XO in *Waddell*. The story of McCauley's argument with Commodore Joe Nolan was well known. As he was now in charge of all surface combatants in the Atlantic Fleet, I felt comfortable resisting the embarkation of Commodore Loy in *Yorktown*.

Adm. Kalleres appeared somewhat startled by my response, and I could see that I had not changed his mind. My reasoning was precisely that of McCauley's ten years before; nevertheless, I lost the argument and was directed to embark the commodore for the six-week mini deployment. Inasmuch as I had not been formally subordinated to Loy's command even though he was senior to me, I decided that I would try to manage my relationship with the commodore as equals, which did not include breaking his burgee pennant on my mast (in lieu of my commissioning pennant), the practice when a ship's CO is subordinate to the embarked commander.

On leaving Norfolk and while still at sea detail, Loy went up to the signal bridge to ensure that his burgee pennant was flying from my mast. When he discovered it was not, he confronted me: "Where is my pennant?" I had done my research and replied, "Commodore, I am not under your command." Loy stormed off the bridge and went to his cabin to pen a message to Adm. Kalleres, recounting our conversation and my refusal to break his pennant.

The admiral radioed me and asked me to helicopter over to *Iowa* to discuss the matter as soon as we had cleared the sea buoy at the entrance to Chesapeake Bay. I could see that this was not going to be a friendly discussion. The admiral brusquely demanded an explanation for my refusal to break Commodore Loy's pennant. I explained that navy regulations supported my position in that I was not formally subordinate to Loy. He told me he would get back to me and I flew back to my ship. Kalleres sent a message to the assistant to the Chief of Naval Operations (CNO) for administration, detailing my argument and asking if it was consistent with regulations. The answer apparently came back in an operational immediate message from the office of the CNO, Admiral Carl Trost.

Although it reportedly recognized the correctness of my position, it advised Kalleres to assign **Yorktown** as a subordinate "task element" under Commodore Loy. (I was not copied on the message, but my immediate superior in command, Admiral Mike Boorda, recounted its contents to me somewhat later.) Kalleres took the CNO's advice, and so did I: I broke the commodore's pennant and calmed my wounded pride. I was chastened, and I worried that this event might not bode well for my future as I had come to Admiral Trost's attention again and not under the best circumstances. On balance, I had defended an important point in navy regulations. It would have been easy to abandon a seemingly quixotic position and acquiesce with direction that did not make sense, but that would have left the order unchallenged, enabling it to set a precedent regarding the relative responsibilities of commanders and COs. As we will see, this would not be the only occasion in which I contested attempts by my superiors to finesse what I considered a governing principle.

In conversation after I returned to Norfolk, Adm. Boorda assured me that I had been justified in taking a stand. Boorda, a close friend of Kalleres, supported my argument; he shared the concern that in a crisis or incident that might require action, the

CO of a cruiser should have the unchallenged latitude to defend his ship and crew. He agreed that with an embarked officer of the same rank but with little familiarity with the ship and its combat system and no formal responsibility, there was a clear risk of confusion and disagreement. His support was even more remarkable in that as a captain, he had opted to command a DESRON instead of a cruiser. Point made; I was never required to embark a commodore during the rest of my tour in command of *Yorktown*.

* * *

The cruise in the Caribbean as a battleship battle group was different from a carrier battle group in many respects. The training was minimal, inasmuch as there were no forces presented in opposition, other than the drug smugglers who plied their illicit trade through these waters. There were several ports of call in which *Yorktown* was to "show the flag": La Ceiba, Honduras; Cartagena, Colombia; and Colón, Panama.

In La Ceiba, I left the ship at anchor in the small harbor and, with the commodore, made protocol calls on the mayor and local military officials. While we were on land, a nasty storm hit the coast, bringing heavy winds and heavy surf. We were unable to get back to the ship, so we accepted an invitation from a United Fruit executive to spend the night in his hacienda. "Hacienda" is not hyperbole; the residence, with its magnificent mahogany paneling and floors, was a vestige of the quasi-colonial period in the early twentieth century when the interests of American companies, such as United Fruit and Dole, were ascendant in US foreign relations in Central America.

Our visit to Cartagena afforded a meeting with Colombian National Navy commanders. Our objective was to encourage more effort by the Colombians in stemming the outflow of narcotics from the Guajira Peninsula. Notwithstanding my best persuasive efforts in Spanish, the Colombian admiral made clear that the level of effort was limited by "political considerations."

As the spring of 1987 progressed, the exercises and the training increased in complexity and size. We worked to master and refine our shipboard doctrines for anti-aircraft and missile defense. At the same time, we were preparing for the rigorous battery of examinations and inspections scheduled before our deployment to the Mediterranean in the fall. It was in this time frame that we coined a nickname for our ship: "the Battlecruiser," a nickname that endured until *Yorktown* was decommissioned sixteen years later.

In the Atlantic Fleet of the 1980s, the carrier battle group preparing to deploy was to be challenged in the last major exercise to test the group's combat readiness. The opposing force, comprised of units drawn from other battle groups and designated "Orange," was configured to simulate a Soviet anti-carrier force. *Yorktown* was assigned to the Orange force, taking the role of a Soviet *Kynda*-class cruiser with a principal armament of SSN-3 anti-ship cruise missiles. Our tasking was to remain undetected until in position to launch a surprise attack against the USS *Saratoga* (CV-60) battle group, which now happened to be under the command of my administrative superior, friend, and reporting senior COMCRUDESGRU 8 Rear Admiral Jeremy M. "Mike" Boorda.

Adm. Boorda always prided himself as an expert ship handler, a surface warfare officer, a tactician, and most importantly, a forward-leaning and aggressive warrior. I regarded my tasking to simulate a *Kynda* with anticipation. I would be matching wits with Boorda.

A slight problem was that as COMCRUDESGRU 8 and the flag officer responsible for all the cruisers and destroyers in Norfolk, my homeport, Adm. Boorda could task his local staff to monitor my preparation for the exercise.

He did just that. He directed the CO of the USS *King* (DDG-41), Commander Steve Woodall, then operating independently and not under Boorda's operational command following an overhaul, to position himself at first light near the channel buoy at the entrance to the Chesapeake Bay. His orders were to "shadow" *Yorktown* and to report our position to *Saratoga* regularly. To be very clear, *King* was not part of the admiral's battle group, and thus the ship should have been a "neutral" in this FLEETEX.

But I had my own "intelligence" sources, who informed me unofficially of Boorda's plan, and I moved quickly to foil it.

Now my official schedule had me getting underway early one morning in early May. Departures were nominally scheduled after 0800 to coincide with the availability of harbor pilots and tugs. (The general practice for cruisers in Norfolk was to get underway with a pilot embarked and with the aid of at least one harbor tug.) I knew that if I left after midnight, I would, strictly speaking, be in conformance with the scheduled departure for sea. If I left just after midnight and in the dark without reliance of pilots or tugs, I might escape detection. And that is what I decided to do. I quietly recalled the entire crew to be back aboard ship by 2300. At 0001 hours, we took in our lines and backed out of our berth, independently proceeding in total electronic silence down the Thimble Shoals channel, past the sea buoy, and into the open Atlantic. The tattletale *King* was nowhere to be seen.

We steamed on an easterly heading, with lighting characteristic of a merchant ship, for about two hundred miles. We did not transmit on any of our normal communication circuits, although, as required, we transmitted on a high-frequency (HF) circuit every few hours to enable *Saratoga* to detect a bearing. To foil their listeners, we used Spanish on these transmissions. We also monitored their radio transmissions, and using our helicopter, the radars of the *Saratoga* battle group. After using passive targeting methods to compute a targeting solution, we had what we believed was the location of the *Saratoga*. After launching a simulated six-missile salvo, we broadcasted our aim point to the umpire, and then turned on all of our radar sensors in anticipation of a furious counterattack from *Saratoga*'s air wing.

The umpire's ruling came quickly. Our attack had been successful. As expected, we were subsequently attacked by more than twenty aircraft from the *Saratoga*. We engaged and simulated destroying ("splashed") all of them with our superb missile defense. Adm. Boorda was not happy with the results. In fact, he would not acknowledge our success in the exercise for many days thereafter.

Despite *Yorktown*'s success in this exercise, as we continued preparations for our fall deployment, I grew increasingly dissatisfied with one serious shortfall in our combat capability. The problem was that we could not effectively bring our 5"/54 gun batteries to bear against an air target because despite our state-of-the-art combat system, we did not have a gunfire control system capable of engaging a slow-moving air target above the horizon.

When the Aegis combat system aboard the *Ticonderoga* class was designed, the assumption had been that the gun armament was an anti-surface ship weapon or a naval gunfire support (NGFS) battery. Accordingly, the only radar installed to control fire from our five-inch guns was the AN/SPQ-9A fire control radar, which was in effect a two-dimensional system. The manager and founder of the Aegis program, the legendary Rear Admiral Wayne Meyer, had canceled the "guns in trail" software for the Aegis combat system's principal radar, the AN/ SPY-1A. Meyer's premise was that air targets would be assigned to the surface-to-air missile system and, in last-ditch situations to the Phalanx Close-In-Weapons System (CIWS), would destroy targets close aboard with rapid-fire twenty-millimeter gunnery.

The problem my combat systems officer, Lieutenant Commander (later Captain) Rick Easton,[65] and I recognized was those threats in the theater of operations to which we were about to deploy could very well include slow-moving aircraft. These targets would not be easily engaged with CIWS (target too slow and insufficient Doppler) and we might soon be forced to operate in an environment with rules that prohibited defensive action, unless and until we had a target that showed "hostile intent." Such a scenario had been typical in the early '80s off the coast of Lebanon, when our surface combatants were often confronted with slow-moving aircraft that approached close aboard or overflew our ships before we were able to establish "hostile intent." Without delving too far into detail, suffice to note that there was a minimum effective range for an engagement with SM-2 missiles, the primary Aegis weapons system. In short, a slow-moving aircraft in close proximity or diving on the ship might not be engaged with any effective system by the world's most sophisticated surface combatant.

In discussions with my combat systems team, it was clear that the missing link was the one between the SPY-1A radar and the MK-86 Gunfire Control System. Even though we had excellent tracking data from the SPY on all air targets, we could not get that targeting information to the system that controlled our guns.

---

65 Easton was the commissioning weapons officer in *Yorktown* and subsequently our combat systems officer. Later he went on to serve as the first executive officer of the first Aegis guided missile destroyer, USS *Arleigh Burke* (DDG-51), and later as CO of his own *Ticonderoga*-class cruiser, USS *Port Royal* (CG-73). Rick was an acknowledged expert on the Aegis combat system.

I sent Rear Admiral Tim Hood, who was the Aegis program manager at the time and my old friend from Destroyer School, a query regarding the possibility of providing us a software "patch" to move data from the SPY to the gun system. He told me there were other priorities for the software development teams, and the shortcoming that concerned me was not among them.

I then decided to challenge the technical community through my operational chain of command. It simply did not make sense to not provide our ship with targeting information for the gun system because the program office had deemed it "unnecessary."

We were the operators about to deploy and we needed the capability. I took the case up with my immediate superior, Adm. Boorda. Boorda considered himself an expert in gunfire control systems; he had taught fire control to destroyer department heads in the 1970s. He agreed completely. Taking up our cause, he brought the situation to the attention of COMNAVSURFLANT, now Vice Admiral Scot McCauley, and up the Atlantic Fleet chain of command. Our request received a new hearing in Washington.

Soon thereafter, the Aegis software experts in Dahlgren, Virginia, wrote a patch that enabled the instantaneous transmission of tracking information from the SPY radar to the MARK-86 system. We took the "fix" to sea in August 1987 and it proved incredibly effective in increasing the accuracy of the gun system. In our first test of SPY-directed gunfire, we were able to cut the wire behind the towed air target. This provided a good measure of the accuracy of our AAW gun capability.[66]

I abandoned another software "fix" that could have improved target discrimination by our SPY-1A radar system. While working up with the USS *Coral Sea* (CV-43) battle group, it

66 USS YORKTOWN MESSAGE DTG 261728Z JAN 88. This message, recounting our success with "Aegis AAW Gun Capability," was forwarded by COMSECONDFLT to all Aegis ships and to the entire chain of command.

occurred to me to ask the Aegis experts why this sophisticated combat system did not afford us means to distinguish air targets with large radar cross sections (RCS) from those with smaller returns. We were pushing our luck as operators by again questioning the technical community, but the tactical advantages seemed straightforward. For example, a capability to discriminate would help us to distinguish large air targets capable of launching anti-ship missiles (ASM) from the missiles themselves. We argued to the Aegis program managers that since the radar continuously measured the energy reflected from the targets it was tracking, it should be programmed to provide us at least a rough approximation of target RCS.

The response was discouraging. We were reminded that "many" variables affected the reflected energy returned from a target and were told that the data we sought would be made so unreliable by extraneous factors (e.g., target aspect and reflections from aircraft antennas) as to be useless. We further argued—in vain—that it seemed some of these variables (especially target dynamics) could be accounted for by the system and still provide useful information in prioritizing targets in the queue for engagement. Admonished to stick to our knitting as operators, we dropped the argument and moved on.

The most important milestone in our pre-deployment workup was our team's certification as the AAWC for the *Coral Sea* battle group. Throughout the summer months of 1987, we joined the *Coral Sea* in at-sea training with the carrier and her embarked air wing. As AAWC, it was important for us to familiarize the air wing fighter pilots with the Aegis combat system and the significant improvements, especially to air and missile defense, that it brought to the battle group. With each exercise, our air-intercept controllers (AIC) became personally acquainted with the fighter pilots and the airborne early warning (AEW)

air crews to understand their procedures and to refine our doctrines. I developed a close relationship with the battle group
commander, Rear Admiral Jack Ready, and his chief of staff,
Captain Will Story. The admiral accepted several invitations
to embark in *Yorktown* for air control exercises and missile
firings. He generally enjoyed his visits, and he reciprocated by
encouraging visits by *Yorktown*'s tactical action officers (TAOs)
to the *Coral Sea* and sending members of the carrier's fighter
squadrons and AEW personnel to get acquainted with our air
controllers. By the time we went to sea as a battle group for
our pre-deployment graduation exercise, FLEETEX 3-87, "the
Battlecruiser" was part of a well-honed team. We felt ready for
any eventuality that we might encounter on our deployment to
the Sixth Fleet.

In July 1987, we took a break from battle group exercises to
conduct ASW training in the Narragansett Bay Operating Area
with attack submarines based in New London, Connecticut.
After a series of one-on-one training with several submarines,
we put in to the old destroyer base in Newport, Rhode Island,
for a weekend visit. This was followed by another week of ASW.
Since we had earned a "special" port visit after a frantic schedule
of exercises at sea, I decided to volunteer us for a port visit to
Kennebunkport, Maine. That port is a charming spot on the
southern Maine coast that I had visited personally many times
in the '60s and '70s. As mentioned earlier, during a 1981 visit
by then-Vice President Bush aboard *Comte de Grasse* while I
was in command, the vice president had requested that the navy
consider sending a ship to Kennebunkport for a visit. He noted
at the time that it had been almost fifty years since a warship
had visited that town.

Although at the time the SECNAV and the assembled admirals had agreed that this should be arranged "soon enough," six

years later the visit had not yet been scheduled. I asked Adm. McCauley for permission (Adm. Boorda was deployed in the Mediterranean at this time) and he agreed to the visit, cautioning me to have my crew on their best behavior while in the vice president's "hometown." I then communicated directly with the vice president's naval aide to inform him that we would be coming for a weekend visit. To my surprise, a short while later, I received a personal letter from the vice president, welcoming me and my crew to Kennebunkport.

The vice president asked if I could embark his uncle George Walker for the at-sea voyage to Kennebunkport. He also asked me to arrange a visit for him to our ship during working hours the next day to meet some of our crew. He further suggested that it would be nice if I could host a reception on our flight deck for members of his family and some friends; my wife and I were invited to spend the night following the reception at Walker's Point. Last, he asked whether, prior to our departure on Sunday, a hundred and fifty of our crew could attend a "Texas-style" barbecue at Walker's Point.

As expected, my seniors allowed me to grant the vice president's request to embark the vice president's uncle for a few days for the voyage to Kennebunkport.

In Kennebunkport, Vice President Bush arrived in his cigarette boat, and the visit, in all its details, went off without a hitch. I have no doubt that every sailor, petty officer, chief petty officer, and officer in "the Battlecruiser" would attest that it was the most memorable port visit of our time together. Virtually every member of the crew received an autographed picture with the vice president in his working space in the ship. One of my officers, Lieutenant (now Rear Admiral) Mark "Buz" Buzby, was promoted to the rank of lieutenant commander by the vice president of the United States.

On completion of our visit, I submitted the obligatory after-action report to Adm. McCauley and others in my chain of command. McCauley informed me that because my visit had not been formally "approved" through channels in Washington, there was great interest in how this visit had been arranged. The situation was calmed by a congratulatory message from the vice president that had been transmitted to the SECNAV, the CNO, and the entire chain of command.[67]

In early August, we continued our preparations for deployment by conducting a variety of weapons exercises in the Virginia Capes Operating Area. The most difficult missile firings were during the VANDALEX events off Wallops Island, Virginia. These exercises featured firing a modified TALOS (VANDAL) missile with a maximum speed approaching Mach 3 from land to the vicinity of a defending ship. The target missile took a controlled, sea-skimming[68] flight profile, which was intended to simulate the latest variant of Soviet anti-ship cruise missiles. As defenders in the exercise, our challenge was to detect the VANDAL on the SPY radar quickly enough to develop a fire control solution and then intercept the missile before it arrived at its aim point (one nautical mile offset from the target ship). *Yorktown* conducted multiple VANDAL firings; our record against the target missiles was spotty because of repeated failures in the guidance systems of several of the target missiles, which put them well beyond our effective missile range.

One target presentation stands out. The low-flying VANDAL in question was detected just inside the radar horizon at about

---

67 I will note that "Washington" must have had advance notice inasmuch as Chase Untermeyer, the assistant secretary of the navy for Manpower and Reserve Affairs, a great Texas friend of the Bushes, also happened along in Kennebunkport as the "representative of the secretary of the navy." See Chase Untermeyer, *Inside Reagan's Navy* (College Station: Texas A&M University Press, 2015), 258–260.

68 A few feet above the ocean.

ten nautical miles. This caused our Aegis weapons doctrine to declare the target a "special" engagement, thereby focusing the radar and the entire combat system on intercepting a very urgent threat. The system responded beautifully; all four missile rails of the two MARK-26 launching systems were simultaneously loaded with SM-2 missiles. The forward launcher fired a two-missile salvo at the target and intercepted the VANDAL just as it arrived at the closest point of approach, a very small distance from our ship. I watched the engagement from the bridge and was truly impressed with the awesome response of our systems against this very realistic approximation of a late-generation threat.

The most significant conclusion I drew was that had we been equipped with a vertical launch system (VLS) and not our MARK-26 launchers, which could be depressed, we would not have been able to engage the target in time. The logic was straightforward. VLS-launched SM-2 missiles fly to a relatively high altitude before tipping down to intercept a sea-skimming threat. I reported by impressions to my superiors.[69]

* * *

Several months prior to our deployment, we had dodged Hurricane Charley. The circumstances were somewhat delicate. Homeported in Norfolk while in command, I was maintaining the family's residence in Springfield, Virginia, 150 miles away. I was home one weekend, attending mass, when my beeper went

69 In multi-ship formations, the deficiencies noted in the "detect to engage" challenge for VLS ships were corrected with the introduction of the Cooperative Engagement Capability (CEC) system. In single-ship engagements, the introduction of NATO Evolved Sea Sparrow missiles closed the gap in the effectiveness of VLS systems against supersonic sea skimming cruise missiles.

off (there were no cell phones in August 1987). I went to the pay phone in the back of the church and called my command duty officer (CDO), who informed me that an emergency sortie of ships in Norfolk was under consideration in view of the hurricane that was fast approaching the Virginia coast. There was no time for the three-hour drive to Norfolk, so I caught a commuter flight from Washington National Airport.

Because of the approaching storm, it was the last flight to Norfolk that day. While airborne, the captain announced that with winds increasing in Norfolk, it might be necessary for him to divert or return to DC. Worried, I hurriedly scratched a note to the captain on a cocktail napkin, explaining that I was a navy captain attempting to rejoin my ship, which was about to get underway for an emergency sortie. I waited anxiously for his reply until the flight attendant told me that the pilot (a former naval aviator) said he would make every effort to make Norfolk, safety permitting. We landed in a significant crosswind. To this day, I thank that pilot for the chance he took.

My driver met the flight and took me straight to the ship, where preparations by the watch team were already well underway. A recall of key personnel had been initiated and more than half the crew was already on board. In the end, the emergency sortie was not executed owing to the actual track of the hurricane, but warnings were issued to prepare for heavy winds. We were moored outboard of the USS *Mississippi* (CGN-40), and it in turn was moored outboard of the destroyer tender USS *Puget Sound* (AD-38), which was tied up on the southern side of a destroyer pier. I was very uncomfortable to be the third ship off the pier when the winds intensified as the outer bands of the hurricane approached Norfolk. The "whip" effect came to mind.

I requested the assistance of a tug to unmoor our ship and help move us to an open berth on the north side of the same pier.

We waited anxiously for the tug as the winds intensified. When the tug and pilot finally arrived, winds were already in excess of fifty knots. With the help of Lt. Cmdr. Buzby, who had returned to the ship and was the best ship handler in my wardroom, we broke our moor with *Mississippi*, and the winds from the east set us down quickly into the Elizabeth River. Using a standard bell, which results in fifteen knots under normal circumstances, we inched our way to the open berth on the opposite side of the pier and moored safely, with the tug holding us on to the pier as we made up our lines. It was a harrowing experience to say the least and one that *Yorktown* veterans still discuss.

At the end of August, we completed the last in the long series of pre-deployment milestones, a Defense Nuclear Surety Inspection (DNSI), which is highly exacting: a failure results in the loss of certification. It should be noted that the only nuclear capability in the Baseline 1 Aegis cruiser was the rocket thrown depth charge (RTDC). With the Cold War at its peak, we maintained that capability, even as we doubted its real tactical value—we took great care maintaining our readiness and demonstrating the ability to handle and protect these weapons as directed. Our combat system organization prepared thoroughly, training in the handling and securing of mock missiles at every opportunity. We received a satisfactory score with no major discrepancies and many compliments from the inspecting party. Our performance made me immensely proud of the entire crew inasmuch as every department had contributed to this milestone accomplishment.

* * *

After an uneventful crossing of the Atlantic, the *Coral Sea* battle group comprised of seven ships arrived at the Strait of Gibraltar and were immediately forced to defend against a surprise "attack" from the air wing embarked in the carrier we were relieving, the *Saratoga*, under Adm. Boorda's command. Knowing Adm. Boorda as I did, I had anticipated the high likelihood that an "attack" would be launched against us. Owing to the congestion in the strait, the *Coral Sea*'s fighter aircraft could not be launched, so *Yorktown* had to single-handedly simulate "intercepting" all sixteen attacking aircraft with our Aegis system. Mission accomplished!

* * *

Before detailing more experiences during this eventful deployment to the Mediterranean, I cannot fail to discuss some of the ports of call that we made. As the essential air defense platform for the *Coral Sea* battle group, *Yorktown* was required to visit the same ports as the carrier, or at least ports that were in a short steaming distance from *Coral Sea*. This was done in recognition that we needed to be close should we be required to be underway in the event of an emergency. Accordingly, we joined *Coral Sea* in visits to Palma de Mallorca, Naples, Athens, Alexandria, Toulon, and Barcelona.

An element of our unexpected good fortune was the number of visits we made to French ports. As mentioned earlier, the French consider the battles of Yorktown and the naval battle at the Virginia Capes featuring the Comte de Grasse as signal events in their own military history and highwater marks in their competition with the English. Visits to France by *Yorktown* were especially welcomed by the citizens of the ports we visited. In fact, *Yorktown* was "adopted" by the city of Le Cannet in December and every member of the crew received a gift from the mayor of the city.

Nowhere, however, was the welcome more genuine than during our calls in Villefranche-sur-Mer. When the carrier was scheduled to visit Cannes or Marseille, I was granted permission for *Yorktown* to visit "Ville," where I became reacquainted with my old friend from *Comte de Grasse* days, Mayor Joseph Calderoni. I think we set a record for Sixth Fleet ships by making four visits to that beautiful port in the course of one sixth-month deployment. Our crew received a very warm welcome on each return, and the bars and restaurants even extended *les prix spéciaux* to *Yorktown* sailors.

One tradition we maintained during all our visits to Villefranche is remembered fondly by older residents to this day. At 0800, as we executed morning colors, we played the "Star-Spangled Banner," followed by the French national anthem, "La Marseillaise," on our topside speakers. The music could be heard throughout the town as it echoed against the homes and hotels on the hillside above the harbor. No one complained about the music, even at such an early hour on weekends. Villefranche became the home away from home for the crew of "the Battlecruiser."

* * *

Our close relationship with the French was not limited to social or protocol visits. In January, we were given an opportunity to test our electronic support measures against EXOCET cruise missiles, which had figured prominently in Argentine attacks on

RN destroyers and frigates during the Falklands War. In view of the tragedy that befell the USS *Stark* (FFG-31), attacked by an Iraqi EXOCET in May 1987, developing effective counter-measures against that missile had become a high priority for the navy. Precisely because the Marine Nationale's cruise missile simulator, the ARPEGE, used against us was able to gauge and assess the effectiveness of our defensive systems, we were able to develop tactics to confuse and divert several variants of the EXOCET missile. Thanks to the cooperation of the Marine Nationale and the French government, we took giant strides toward that end.

Importantly, we broke new ground in the development of tactics to prove the effectiveness of the Aegis combat system in support of strike operations by carrier aircraft. The exercise that afforded us this opportunity was nicknamed African Eagle, and it featured low-level airstrikes against Moroccan targets well inland. During an intensive three-day exercise and in the coordination with the battle group commander's staff, we positioned *Yorktown* close to the Moroccan shore and proved that the SPY-1 radar was very effective in maintaining solid tracks on friendly aircraft well into their routes toward targets inland.

The carrier aircraft's sorties also provided the Moroccan Air Force an opportunity to train in defending their airspace against air attacks. As a result, we were also able to gain early detections on the "bogeys," Moroccan aircraft attempting to intercept our strikes. Finally, we proved that the system was invaluable in "delousing" the returning aircraft by calling out "bogey" aircraft attempting to mix with *Coral Sea* aircraft to simulate attacks on the carrier. Our tactics were detailed in a tactical note to the Commander of US Sixth Fleet (COMSIXTHFLT), which resulted in doctrine governing the stationing of Aegis cruisers in overland AAW and in support of power projection.

The highlight of the Mediterranean deployment in this intensive period of the Cold War was a voyage through the Turkish Straits into the Black Sea to conduct a freedom of navigation (FON) operation through closed Soviet territorial waters. Under international law, warships are entitled to transit through claimed territorial waters of another nation while exercising the right of innocent passage.[70] The issue that prompted our tasking to transit Soviet territorial waters was a regime, established in 1983, restricting the right of warships to conduct innocent passage transits through well-defined narrow sea lanes. This effectively closed a large portion of the northern Black Sea south of the Crimean Peninsula to all foreign warships. International law provides that unless declared navigational restrictions are challenged, the simple passage of time confirms legitimacy to the closures that may be declared by riparian powers. The United States therefore traditionally challenges what are deemed illegal regimes.

Unbeknownst to us, the Soviet Foreign Ministry had delivered a *note verbale* to our State Department following an earlier challenge by the USS **Caron** (DD-970) and **Yorktown** during their previous deployment in 1986. The note had apparently warned that any future transits of the closed area would be challenged, forcibly if necessary.

On our way into the Black Sea, we passed by the beaches of the Gallipoli Peninsula and the hills above, where so many British, Australian, and New Zealand soldiers who met their untimely ends there in 1916 are interred. After passing through the Dardanelles, a narrow passage ringed by mountains on the north side, we transited the Bosphorus strait on February 10,

---

70 Coincidentally and ironically, while serving on the NSC staff as one of two naval officers, I was given responsibility for the FON program. To be assigned a critical FON mission while in command of **Yorktown** was remarkable but coincidental.

1988. We were met by the Soviet Navy destroyer *Bezzavetny* at the entrance to the Black Sea. A ship of the *Krivak* class, she displaced about 4,800 tons and was armed principally for ASW. As he took station on our port beam, an English-speaking voice came up on the bridge-to-bridge very-high-frequency (VHF) radio, welcoming *Yorktown* to the Black Sea and informing us that the destroyer would be our "escort" while in the Black Sea. I acknowledged the transmission with a "Roger, out."

Two days later, a cold and blustery morning, *Yorktown* and *Caron* were prepared to begin the FON challenge as directed. We reviewed our rules of engagement (ROE) carefully and the guidance we had from the chain of command. Nowhere in that guidance was there a reference to the warning that had been issued by the Soviets the year before.

We began our innocent passage transit at approximately 0900 in a position in the Black Sea outside of territorial boundaries, about three miles south of *Caron*. It was a cold and clear morning in very calm seas. On signal, both ships came to an ordered course of 090 (due east) at a steady speed of advance of seventeen knots. As we commenced our transit, we were tracking fourteen Soviet aircraft, including several TU-16 *Badgers*, at least one MI-24 helicopter gunship, and several SU-35 *Fitters* and MIG-29 *Floggers*. The marvel of the SPY radar was that we could track these aircrafts with fire-control precision without changing the discernible mode of the radar. (Use of a fire-control radar with "lock-on" features would have been a violation of conditions allowed during innocent passage.)

Over the course of the next hour, *Bezzavetny*, which had taken a station approximately five nautical miles north of *Yorktown*, began issuing a series of warnings as we approached the twelve-mile territorial sea limit. The warning on channel sixteen began with direction to move south immediately as we were entering a submarine exercise area. Subsequent warnings were issued regarding impending gunnery exercises. I personally responded to each warning with the following statement: "I am a United States warship engaged in the right of innocent passage." That said, I was committed to maintaining my course and speed.

As we entered Soviet territorial waters, *Bezzavetny* began closing our position, and a warning came over the radio that if we did not come south immediately, "our ship is going to strike yours." Now, the Russian verb "to strike" (ударят, or *udaryat*) can be translated as "hit," "punch," or "attack." Knowing Russian but not knowing exactly what kind of "strike" the Soviet commander had in mind, I alerted my Combat Information Center (CIC) to the possibility of an actual firing incident. I admonished our Condition Three watch teams that all our weapons, while ready, would remain "tight" unless I personally ordered a response to an actual attack on our ship.

It is difficult to exaggerate the tension we felt, knowing that with the sky full of Soviet combat aircraft and our proximity to the main base of the Soviet Black Sea fleet at Sevastopol, any live firing accident would require us to act quickly to deal with multiple threats while transiting at best speed to clear the area. My nerves were especially rattled when the cryptologic intelligence officer came to me in CIC to explain that we had intercepted an order from one of the aircraft to the MI-24 helicopter gunship aircrew to maintain visual surveillance and to take our helicopter "under fire immediately" if it was rolled out of the hangar. Knowing the ROE as they applied to innocent passage transits, I had no intention of moving my SH-2D *Sea Sprite* helicopter, but the warnings in Russian on their radio circuits were indeed ominous and indicative of the danger we confronted.

When *Bezzavetny* closed to within two hundred feet, it was clear that the threat "to strike" us meant that he would try to ram or shoulder us out of Soviet waters. I assumed the conn, knowing that if there was to be a collision with the Soviet ship, it would be prudent for me to be in control of our maneuvers. After all, any collision at sea would be grounds for a formal investigation, and I was responsible; I didn't see the need to have one of my junior officers sharing in the responsibility. Holding the conn while simultaneously answering questions from COMSIXTHFLT, Vice Admiral Ken Moranville, on a secure radio circuit as I controlled the ship made the situation even more complicated.

At one point, with our ships about twenty feet apart, a dozen uniformed KGB border guard personnel under the command of a colonel took station on *Bezzavetny*'s starboard bridge wing. At the same time, the Soviet skipper, Captain Vladimir Bogdashin, stepped out of his pilot house and took a position on his starboard wing. He pointed to me (because I was the only one on our bridge with "scrambled eggs" on my ball cap) and raising his hand to heaven, he gestured for me to move out, pushing both hands in my direction. I looked back at him and shook my head no while saying "*nyet,*" whereupon he again lifted his hands to heaven to signal his exasperation. He closed the distance between our ships and made contact on *Yorktown*'s hull at 1003. As we were doing seventeen knots when we touched, he drifted aft and the bullnose of his bow began taking down the lifelines on my port quarter. It also knocked the exhaust funnel for number three gas turbine generator off the deck.

Finding myself "in extremis" and no longer bound to maintain the ordered speed, I called for "Flank Three" and immediately began accelerating away from *Bezzavetny*. Reacting to my maneuver, Bogdashin started another gas turbine engine (evidenced by a lot of white smoke) and turned his bow into my port quarter (left rear section of the hull). The unhoused anchor, dangling on a very short scope of chain (which I assumed was intended to put a hole in our ship), became entrapped on the frame of our Harpoon missile launcher. The chain tightened and then snapped, leaving the anchor teetering on our deck. At the same time, the bow of *Bezzavetny* surged upward and impacted two Harpoon missile cannisters on the gun deck at the stern. The top third of the two missiles fell on the deck, spilling guidance-and-control electronics over the fantail. In addition, although I did not learn of it until months after I had left *Yorktown*, the bulbous bow of *Bezzavetny* contacted the port screw, tearing away the "masker air" channel on the five blades. I maneuvered *Yorktown* away from *Bezzavetny* and secured the aft array of the SPY radar to minimize the risk of an explosive or "hero" incident leading to radar energy which could detonate elements of the broken Harpoon missiles, whose high-explosive warheads and electronics were now exposed.

The track for our passage completed by 1100, we took a southerly heading and completed our mission in the Black Sea. I was very proud of the crew as we began our exit through the Bosphorus. We had come close to an actual shooting incident in the "bear's lair" and we had kept our wits about us under extreme circumstances. We received supportive messages from my CRUDESGRU commander in Norfolk, Adm. Boorda, and another from my immediate operational superior, Adm. Ready. As we passed through the strait approaching the Fatim Sultan Mehmet Bridge across the Bosphorus, we looked up to read a banner in English congratulating us for having challenged the Soviets in the Black Sea. The Turks were clearly impressed with our defiance of Soviet attempts to limit freedom of navigation in the Black Sea. The incident, however, was far from closed.

Then, as if we had not had enough excitement, as we transited the Dardanelles back into the Aegean Sea, we detected several Soviet TU-22 *Backfire* bombers conducting simulated strikes against **Yorktown** and **Caron.** This was not an ordinary occurrence, but with the marvels of our radar systems, we were able to observe this activity from afar. Among the other marvels of the SPY radar is the ability to reconstruct the tracks of aircrafts encountered, including three-dimensional flight profiles. While those *Backfires* were simulating attacks on us, we could record their speed, altitude, and the simulated weapon release points. We printed the data and forwarded it to responsible and interested commands.

The Black Sea incident resulted in an unscheduled port visit to Haifa, Israel, to repair the damage to the ship and to offload the broken Harpoon missiles. Somewhat ironically, the Haifa shipyard repairing the damage was manned largely by Russian-speaking immigrants from the Soviet Union. While escorting the party who had come to investigate the incident, I overheard two shipyard workers wondering (in Russian) "who" had caused the damage they were repairing. When I explained in Russian that it was the Soviet Navy, they seemed astounded that they had been tasked to repair the damage.

After completing repairs, rendering safe the broken Harpoon missiles, and installing two replacement missiles, we began a transit back to the western Mediterranean in company with **Coral Sea.** The transit was uneventful with one exception, the offload of what remained of the broken Harpoon missiles in the containers that had brought us the two replacement missiles. Because of the exposed high-explosive warheads, the transfer was deemed too dangerous to be done while in port. Instead, the offload of the damaged missiles was performed at sea by our SH-2D LAMPS helicopter. The load slung under the aircraft approached the absolute maximum the helicopter was certified to lift. I watched the entire evolution from the flight deck and remember vividly how the entire rotor plane flexed as the helicopter began lifting the canister off the deck. The shape of the rotor plane resembled that of an open umbrella, and I could only gasp as our intrepid aviators slowly lifted the load and "slid" to the port side, headed for *Coral Sea*, where a huge CH-53D *Sea Stallion* helicopter awaited their arrival before transferring the containers to facilities ashore. The *Sea Stallion* helicopter was deemed too large to hover over our flight deck while lifting the missile containers.

While in transit, I received a message from Adm. Boorda, who was back in his headquarters in Norfolk, informing me that the newly nominated SECNAV had asked that I come to Washington to be interviewed for an assignment as his senior naval aide and executive assistant (EA). I was flattered to have been nominated by my community (surface warfare) and to be among the candidates the secretary wanted to interview.

The situation was complicated. First, I was deployed in command of a cruiser scheduled for at-sea exercises in the same time frame that I was now required in Washington. My operational commander, Adm. Ready, who was informed of the secretary's request, agreed that I should go to Washington and leave my executive officer (XO) in command of *Yorktown* while I was away. This suggestion meant to be helpful to me, seemed fine to him as a naval aviator because in that community the XO of a squadron has been preselected to command the squadron and relieve the incumbent. In the surface navy, however, the captain is aboard if the ship is at sea.

Although I tactfully replied to the admiral that I could not leave my ship while she was underway, Adm. Boorda quickly agreed and requested that I be scheduled for a port visit in the western Mediterranean so that I could fly to Washington for the interview with Secretary Ball. Arrangements were made and we put in to the French naval base in Toulon. I flew to Washington from Nice and returned two days later.

The second complication was that we had long been scheduled for the first operational propulsion plant examination (OPPE) to be conducted during the return transit to Norfolk. That inspection was scheduled to begin a few weeks later. The secretary had indicated to the Bureau of Naval Personnel (BuPers) that he would make his choice within thirty days and that he expected his EA to be aboard immediately thereafter.

When I returned to Toulon and to my ship, I had mixed feelings about the interview that I had with Secretary Ball. On the one hand, I had been candid and sincere about the honor to have been considered for this assignment, which was among the most coveted for a line captain. Admirals Boorda and Ready both had made clear what I already knew: If the probability of selection to flag was about 10 percent for a successful cruiser CO, history showed that it was better than 70 percent for the EA to the SECNAV. I had spent almost seven years of my career in Washington assignments, and I was not overly enthused by the prospect of another grueling assignment in the Pentagon as a captain. After all, I had successively served in the navy staff (twice), the Office of the Secretary of Defense, and the Executive Office of the President. My sense was that from a career standpoint, my operational record at sea and previous assignments in the capital had qualified me for selection to flag rank—that is, if I were ever to be admitted to that senior fraternity.

Indeed, as mentioned, when the 1987 flag board selections were announced in January 1988, revealing that I had not been selected as a "below the zone" candidate, I placed a telephone call from Naples to Admiral Hunt Hardisty, the president of the 1987 selection board. He was on old friend, and I felt it appropriate to inquire of him why I had failed selection. He explained that I had been "in the mix" until the very end of the board's deliberations but that my community had deferred in my case owing to the fact that I was "below the zone." Admiral Hardisty's acceptance of my call and his candid appraisal were very much appreciated. I was disappointed in part because I could not imagine what job I could ask for after command of **Yorktown** that would enhance my prospects for selection to flag rank. Admiral Hardisty agreed that it would be difficult to enhance my career profile at sea and ashore, although he mentioned specifically that a senior EA position in Washington or assignment as chief of staff to a numbered fleet commander should be my goals.

During my interview with Secretary Ball, we covered several subjects, most of them having to do with issues facing the navy and the options before the new secretary. He also asked me specifically why I wanted the job as his EA. I replied that every line captain in the navy, regardless of his community, would be delighted with the role. I told him that I thought the range of my assignments in Washington and my current operational experience might qualify me, although I knew that many others had comparable "tickets."

His next questions raised uncertainty in my mind as to how the interview was going. He asked that if someone else were chosen for the job as his EA, what assignments I would list in priority on my preference card. I responded without hesitation that I would ask for consideration for an assignment as chief of staff to the Sixth or Seventh Fleet commander. Failing that, I would request an assignment as the naval attaché to France. The latter preference surprised the secretary because like most people familiar with the importance the navy ascribed to attaché duty, he understood that attachés were rarely selected for flag rank. Sensing his surprise, I gingerly explained that my command of the French language and my earlier dealings with senior French military officers led me to believe that I could be of value in such an assignment. Secretary Ball smiled and took note of what I had said. Much later, he would play back what I had said to him during that interview.

In sum, I was not overly optimistic when I left the secretary's office. Admiral Boorda had asked me to call before I boarded the plane back to France and I told him I thought the interview had gone well, but I didn't think the secretary had decided one way or another. Boorda explained that I was the "last surface captain" in the hunt, but the secretary still had an aviator and a submariner to interview. He explained that were I chosen, he would personally intercede to see that I could bring *Yorktown* "home" to Norfolk and preside over the critical OPPE to be administered while in transit. I was grateful and relieved because in my mind, we had completed a very successful deployment and I wanted "the team" to stay together until we got home. As things turned out, we completed the propulsion exam with flying colors and the record will show that we were the first surface combatant to have taken and passed this critical engineering milestone at the end of a six-month deployment. COMNAVSURFLANT, Adm. McCauley, had wanted to prove that this could be done, and we had met the challenge.

The new SECNAV flew out to *Coral Sea* as our battle group arrived in Hampton Roads. He met with Adm. Ready and addressed the crew of the carrier. He did not visit *Yorktown* or the other ships in the battle group, and I took this to mean since I had not received any indication from the secretary or his staff, I would not win assignment as his EA. About a week after our return to homeport and a few days of leave, I was meeting with my XO and department heads when a call came in. The caller was the Marine aide to the secretary, Colonel Pierpan, informing me that the secretary was sending his plane to Norfolk the following day to bring me to Washington for another interview.

That interview was to inform me that the secretary had chosen me to serve as his EA and senior naval aide. I was as gratified as I was surprised. As mentioned, the position had a marvelous track record for promotion to flag rank. In a phone call following this meeting, Adm. Boorda, now chief of naval personnel, had championed my candidacy and seemed as happy as I was. He remarked that my path to flag rank had become much easier but stressed it was by no means a done deal. (Actually, the record the crew amassed in *Yorktown* was likely the key to both my nomination to serve as EA to the secretary and to my subsequent promotion.) Ending the call, the admiral told me he was working on finding me a relief on *Yorktown* within two weeks!

I returned to Norfolk the same day and informed my wardroom of the impending change of command. The initial indications from Adm. Boorda had been that Captain Fred Moosally was expected to be my relief. (Instead, Moosally relieved Captain Larry Seaquist in command of the battleship *Iowa*.)

The subsequent, and successful, candidate to relieve me was Captain Peter O'Connor, a seasoned and well-respected surface warfare officer whom I considered a great choice. The change-of-command ceremony was organized on very short notice without much of the usual fanfare. Adm. Boorda agreed to speak at the ceremony, which took place in the hangar of the ship. In his remarks, the admiral could not have been more generous and complimentary to me, my wardroom, and the crew. To my pleasure, after Adm. Boorda presented me with the Legion of Merit, he recognized the entire team that had brought us so much success.

I still consider that command of *Yorktown* was the best assignment I had in the navy.

* * *

As an epilogue to my account of the incident with *Bezzavetny*, after returning to Washington, I attended a garden party in the home of Admiral Bob Hilton, one of my former bosses, in April 1988. Secretary of Defense Frank Carlucci was a neighbor of the Hiltons. During the party, Admiral Hilton brought me to the secretary and introduced me as the former captain of *Yorktown* who had been in command during the FON operation in the Black Sea. The secretary asked me what I thought about the program and whether the benefits were worth the risk, especially where Soviet territorial waters were involved. I answered strongly in the affirmative. Then he asked me whether we should modify or change the way we conducted these challenges. I thought for a minute and replied, "Absolutely." I told him that we should conduct challenges in the future at thirty knots. He looked surprised, and I explained that I did not think any ship could lay alongside of me if I were making thirty knots. Secretary Carlucci nodded in agreement. Interestingly, ships of the Sixth Fleet have now resumed challenges to Russian attempts to close the same territorial waters south of the Crimea. The most recent accounts of Russian attempts in June 2021 to deny passage to transiting US destroyers indicate that they were carbon copies of what I encountered some twenty-five years ago. This time, Russian sensitivity is that we profess to be transiting "friendly" (e.g., Ukrainian), not Russian, waters.

CHAPTER 11

POLITICS AND LEADERSHIP AT THE NAVY'S SUMMIT

Executive Assistant and Senior Naval Aide to the Secretary of the Navy

Leaving *Yorktown* in mid-April 1988, I reported to the office of the secretary of the navy (SECNAV) and assumed duties as executive assistant (EA) and senior naval aide. As mentioned earlier, the secretary, William L. (Will) Ball III, had only recently assumed his duties, following the "resignation" of his predecessor, James L. Webb.[71]

The Chief of Naval Operations (CNO), who occupied the adjacent suite of offices in the Pentagon's "E" ring, was none other than Admiral Carl Trost, whom I had come to know and not under the happiest of circumstances. As I previously recounted, I had been assigned at Admiral William Crowe's request as the action officer with the charge to keep OP-06 (the

---

71 Webb resigned in March 1988 following a very public disagreement with Weinberger over the decommissioning of the *Garcia*-class frigates. President Reagan appointed Will Ball, who was serving as the president's assistant for legislative affairs, immediately thereafter.

Plans, Policy and Operations Directorate) in the lead as the responsible staff element for long-range planning at a time when then-Rear Admiral Trost, who was the director of the Systems Analysis Branch (OP-96), seemed equally determined to assume the mantle as the navy's long-range planner. The competition had been intense and often charged. I had later come to Adm. Trost's attention again when, while I was in command of *Yorktown*, I challenged breaking the pennant of Captain Mike Loy during our Latin American cruise. In short, Adm. Trost knew who I was, and as his EA, Rear Admiral Tom Paulsen, informed me, he was none too happy to learn of my assignment.

Others on the immediate staff included the undersecretary, Henry L. "Larry" Garrett, and the assistant secretary for Manpower and Reserve Affairs, Chase Untermeyer, who had been a guest in the home of the vice president when *Yorktown* visited Kennebunkport in July 1987. The 29th Commandant of the Marine Corps was the famously gruff and hard-nosed General Alfred (Al) Gray; his EA at the time was Colonel (later General) James (Jim) Jones, the future 32nd Commandant of the Marine Corps and the former SACEUR and first National Security Council (NSC) advisor to President Obama. The administrative assistant to Secretary Ball was then-Lieutenant Commander (later Admiral) Gary Roughead, who would eventually become CNO.

Working for Will Ball was as much a pleasure as it was an honor. In the first place, the secretary was a former naval officer and a destroyerman to boot. He understood the challenges of life at sea and the pressures on sailors and their families while on distant deployment. His own tour of duty in the navy as a surface warfare officer in USS *Sellers* (DDG-11) and in the navy's Office of Legislative Affairs had also prepared him for the responsibilities of his position.

The secretary was clearly an expert in congressional relations, so vital for the support of our ships, aviation squadrons, and most importantly, our people. His service on the Hill, which had culminated in the position of chief of staff of the Senate Armed Services Committee (SASC), had made him an expert in the ways of Congress. That service as congressional staff was then followed by successive appointments as assistant secretary of state for Legislative Affairs during George Shultz's tenure as secretary and as assistant to the president (Reagan) for legislative affairs. Secretary Ball's contacts on Capitol Hill, and more generally in Washington, were to be of great value during his tenure as SECNAV.

On several occasions, I was invited to tag along when he met with Senator John Warner, then-chairman of the SASC, and with Senator Ted Stevens, chairman of the Senate Appropriations Committee, as well as other committees. I was continually fascinated by Ball's knowledge of the issues before committees and the special interests of key legislators. I observed that he had specific objectives for each meeting on the Hill, and he generally obtained the outcomes he sought; the navy profited as a result. My education in legislative affairs while working for the secretary stood me in good stead in later years as a flag officer and as a corporate executive.

While I was serving as EA, several events occurred that required the careful attention of and deliberate decisions by the secretary. I will review several of the most important as I remember them.

The first of these arose from the secretary's responsibility in the assignment and promotion of vice admirals and admirals to forward nominees to the secretary of defense. Among the first senior flag officer assignments the secretary faced was that to Vice Chief of Naval Operations (VCNO). In this instance, the incumbent VCNO in the summer of 1988 was Admiral Hunt Hardisty, who had been confirmed as commander in chief of the Pacific Command (CINCPAC). He was expected to assume his command in September 1988, so the selection of a relief was a priority. However, because the CNO, Admiral Trost, was a submariner, the VCNO nominee was likely to be an aviation admiral, if the usual protocols were followed—especially given the number of issues then confronting naval aviation, not the least of which was the selection of the next generations of fighter and attack aircraft. Several names were thus in play for the position, including Chief of Naval Personnel Vice Admiral Leon Edney, and Sixth Fleet commander Vice Admiral Kendall (Ken) Moranville, both naval aviators.

I had become acquainted with Admiral Moranville while commanding *Yorktown*. After I had taken up my duties as the EA, he called me on the phone to encourage my support for him in the VCNO position. Although I recognized that my input in this matter would not weigh heavily, if at all, in the final decision, I nonetheless mentioned to the secretary that I knew Moranville, that he was a respected tactician, and that if the past was prologue, he certainly had the requisite experience having commanded both the Third Fleet in the Pacific and the Sixth Fleet in the Mediterranean. Unfortunately, my input to the secretary came to the attention of Vice Admiral Edney, who was ultimately chosen for the VCNO slot. I learned about this later by way of some friendly advice from Admiral Mike Boorda, who succeeded Edney as the chief of naval personnel: to remain "invisible" in the future regarding senior flag officer nominations.

A second event, another example of the secretary's role in such matters, arose with the vacancy in the position of commander in chief, US Central Command (CINCCENT) that resulted from the retirement of General George Crist. Because Crist was a

Marine, the informal protocols of the "joint" process called for his successor as CINCCENT to be an army general. The army's nominee was none other than General Norman Schwarzkopf.

With Adm. Crowe serving as Chairman of the Joint Chiefs of Staff (CJCS) and given his preference for a navy candidate, the CNO and the SECNAV undertook a challenge to the informal protocol. They advanced the name of Vice Admiral Henry (Hank) Mustin as a candidate for the command. That nomination elicited a sharp reaction from the army chief of staff, General Carl Vuono, and Secretary of the Army John Marsh. I watched with interest as Secretary Ball discussed with Adm. Crowe the nomination of Admiral Mustin. (By coincidence, a high school classmate of mine, Colonel [later Lieutenant General] Rich Timmons, was holding the same job I held with the secretary of the army. I had a clear view of how the army was reacting to the navy's attempt to "usurp" what the army regarded as their position.) In the end, the Joint Chiefs of Staff (JCS) as a body and Secretary of Defense Frank Carlucci together decided that a ground combat expert was a better choice for the vacancy than a sailor. It is interesting nonetheless to speculate about how Desert Storm might have been fought had "Hammering Hank" Mustin been the head of the Central Command.

A third important event, associated with the secretary's relationship with Admiral Crowe, which demonstrated Ball's deference to officials responsible for units engaged in combat operations, occurred in the aftermath of the destruction of Iran Air Airbus Flight 655 by the USS *Vincennes* (CG-49) in the Persian Gulf on July 3, 1988. The tragic loss of the 290 passengers and crew of the Airbus resulted in a major international crisis.

As Adm. Crowe explained to the secretary immediately following the incident, the circumstances that led Captain Will Rodgers III to order an engagement of the airliner were complicated by the fact that the ship had entered Iranian territorial waters to engage several Iranian gunboats. The gunboats had reportedly taken the *Vincennes*'s embarked helicopter under fire, which then led the ship and an accompanying frigate, USS *Elmer Montgomery* (FF-1082), to respond. While the *Vincennes* was returning fire on the Iranian gunboats, an air target was detected, originating from the coastal town of Bandar Abbas—and at almost the same time that the *Vincennes* electronic warfare (EW) team reported detecting a radar signal, peculiar to an Iranian F-14, that was coming from the same bearing as the radar target. The coincidence of an air target and the electronic signature of an Iranian fighter led Captain Rodgers and his team to engage the commercial airliner with SM-2 missiles. Later, it was reported that the officer manning the anti-air warfare (AAW) console on the cruiser had erroneously reported that an ascending air target was descending as if to attack the ship.

The Navy Department was in a difficult position, inasmuch as the navy's Aegis experts doubted the explanation that the ship's combat system would have misrepresented the flight profile leading system operators to conclude the aircraft had presented a threat while descending on a profile to attack the *Vincennes*. Secretary Ball rightly deferred to Crowe, the JCS chairman, in issuing the initial public statement on the event. Adm. Crowe then personally held a press conference to explain the tragedy and the circumstances that led to it.

Later, I traveled with the secretary to the Aegis facility at Wallops Island, Virginia, where we witnessed a reconstruction of the situation as described by *Vincennes*.

Adm. Crowe subsequently provided a lengthy account of the incident and the basis for his decision not to hold the commanding officer (CO) responsible.[72] He said that when all the analyses and post-mortems had been completed, the technical and behavioral experts had concluded that the stress confronting the combat team in *Vincennes* had weighed heavily on their ability to interpret the radar data and their ultimate decision to engage the Airbus.

The reconstructed sequence of events that contributed to this conclusion was as follows. The Iranians had initiated the hostilities by firing at the LAMPS helicopter, which had then led to the surface gunfire engagement which occupied the CO even as the operators in the Combat Information Center (CIC) had begun tracking the Iranian Airbus. The engagement of the Iranian gunboats had brought the entire crew to general quarters and a combat footing. The resulting tension and confusion had caused the cruiser's radar operators to mistakenly associate the Airbus with the radar signature on the same bearing that belonged to an Iranian fighter. That faulty association had led to the declaration of the Airbus as "assumed hostile." An erroneous series of reports from several console operators had then led to a mistaken conclusion that the target (the Airbus) was descending and tracking toward *Vincennes*, when it was in fact ascending. Thus, human error—and not systems error—had delivered faulty information, and given the gun engagements in progress, the captain, who had been able to focus on the air picture for only less than two minutes, approved the missile engagement.

My own knowledge of the Aegis combat system gave me some insight into this tragedy. Before assuming command of *Yorktown*, I had traveled to San Diego and embarked in *Vincennes* to observe a live-fire missile exercise in the Southern California Operating Areas. I noted at the time that the weapons

72 Admiral William J. Crowe Jr., *The Line of Fire: From Washington to the Gulf, the Politics and Battles of the New Military* (New York: Simon & Schuster, 1993), 206–209.

doctrine in *Vincennes* (developed following the commissioning of *Ticonderoga*, the first Aegis cruiser) allowed console operators who were at separate consoles and beyond observation by the CO and the tactical action officer (TAO) to designate a target as "assumed hostile." As it was explained to me, preparing for action in the presence of aircraft designated "assumed hostile," the CO or the TAO would enable the firing circuit with a key at their common console. Thus, in a combat setting, a critical factor in any engagement sequence was the designation of targets as "unknown" or "assumed hostile." In the case of targets designated "hostile," the firing circuit was enabled. Confronted with multiple "assumed hostile" contacts, target prioritization and the selection of firing doctrine was delegated to the combat systems coordinator and the ship's anti-air warfare commander (AAWC), who were seated at separate consoles.

* * *

Among the most interesting aspects of my job was the opportunity to sit in on many of the secretary's meetings. One topic that was frequently discussed was the status of the A-12 (McDonnell Douglas A-12 *Avenger II*) program under development.

Before getting to the specific issues, I need to give my perception of the organizational and bureaucratic contexts for those discussions.

The A-12 program had its roots in the administration of John Lehman. As is well known, Lehman was a strong supporter of dedicated long-range "attack" aircraft, and he was himself a Reserve A-6 *Intruder* bombardier/navigator. His preference for dedicated long-range attack aircraft in the navy's air wings was shared by a segment of senior naval aviation, especially both active and retired members of the "medium attack," or A-6 (Grumman A-6 *Intruder*), community.

Coincidently, the retirement of "light" attack aircraft (the A-7E *Corsair II* and A-4D *Skyhawk*) and the arrival of the dual-role F/A-18A/C single-seat *Hornet* had given rise to another school of thought in naval aviation, which held that the investment priority for new aircraft should be dual-role aircraft. Prior to the introduction of the F/A-18 series, the postwar navy—unlike the air force—had maintained a division between types specialized for air combat, fighters, and those built for attacking ships and targets ashore. Although earlier generations of fighters such as the F-4J *Phantom II* had limited ground attack capability, the fighter community generally preferred to keep the missions distinct. Advocates of dual role pressed the case for "fighter and attack" represented by the F/A-18, which had entered the navy's aviation inventories in the early 1980s. The F/A-18 was billed as the successor to the A-7E and the A-4D "light" attack aircraft.

It was also argued that the *Hornets* would serve a dual role as a "low-cost fighter" to supplement the comparatively expensive F-14 *Tomcat*. An important supporting argument was the economic benefit that should accrue if the number of different aircraft types comprising a carrier air wing were reduced. This school of thought was championed by Vice Admiral Kent Lee, commander of the Naval Air Systems Command.

The result of these developments in naval aviation was strong support for the F/A-18 from the "light attack" community of active-duty airmen and retired veterans.

Vocal opposition to exclusive reliance on dual-role aircraft came from the two-seat, mission-specialized F14 and A-6 communities. Inasmuch as the F/A-18 was championed by veterans of three single-seat aircraft, the senior aviation community included many more veterans and retired proponents of the single-seat fighter/attack aircraft. The dominance of that community became even more obvious later, during discussions of the replacement for the F-14D *Tomcat*. Later, a scandal surrounding leadership at Grumman Aircraft Corporation, which had developed plans for a modernized and improved long-range fighter (the *Super Tomcat* 21) to replace the F-14D, helped settle matters in favor of the navy's future reliance entirely on a shorter-range fighter attack aircraft, the F/A-18 E/F *Super Hornet*.

Just as the F/A-18 A/C began entering the fleet in increased numbers, the progress toward a successor to the A-6, a stealthy long-range attack aircraft designated the A-12 *Avenger*, began in earnest. McDonnell Douglas won a lengthy competition in 1988, several months before Secretary Ball took office. Throughout 1988 and well into 1989, there were frequent A-12 meetings in the secretary's office with senior aviators, including the VCNO, Admiral Edney, who was a light attack pilot in his own right; Vice Admiral Richard (Dick) Dunleavy, a medium attack veteran and the deputy CNO for air warfare. Representing the acquisition community, the meetings were also attended by the commander of the Naval Air Systems Command. (Interestingly, the CNO was only an infrequent participant at these meetings, having apparently delegated the uniformed navy's role in overseeing the A-12 program to the VCNO.)

The senior civilian member after Secretary Ball in these intra-navy meetings was the undersecretary of the navy, Larry Garrett. Garrett had also served as the "under" to the previous secretary, Jim Webb; as a result, he was quite familiar with the genesis of the A-12 program and the heated controversies among aviators that had accompanied it. Indeed, Secretary Garrett had a close relationship with Adm. Edney, who had been director of the Office of Program Appraisal in Webb's secretariat. He had been a participant in the A-12 discussions while in that position. Although it was early in the A-12 program's troubled history, much of the agenda that Secretary Ball dealt with already had to do with pressured budgets and missed program milestones.

At one of the meetings that I attended, the secretary was informed by those managing the program of the possibility that a major issue with the design was on its way to resolution. When I heard the optimistic forecast, I was surprised. In advance of the meeting I had provided the secretary with a document from the Naval Air Systems Command Program Office that had seemed much less optimistic regarding a resolution to the problem. I had included a note from the program office that had been attached to the document. Following the optimistic forecast, I pointed to the note on the memorandum and quietly called the secretary's attention to it to ensure that the secretary was properly informed should he now be asked to approve the recommended course of action. My gesture was noticed by the undersecretary, and his reaction after the meeting was pointed. Passing through my office, he admonished me to "never again undermine his role in advising the secretary." I replied respectfully that I had sought merely to remind the secretary that there was a pertinent document in his staffing that addressed the issue under consideration.

The undersecretary then invited me to follow him to his adjacent office suite. There, he made clear to me that I was "jeopardizing" my future by my action. At that point, I am afraid that I did let my pride get the best of me. By way of reply, I explained that I saw my role as EA rather differently than did the undersecretary: I had been hired by the secretary to assist him, and I was doing just that. Moreover, I told him that I was not intimidated by his threat to my career.

Having provoked a frosty glare, I took my leave and returned to my office, questioning whether I should report the encounter to Secretary Ball. I found out later that the undersecretary had made his disappointment with me clear to the secretary and that he had also conveyed it to the VCNO. It was not long before Adm. Edney called me into his office and admonished me to keep my advice and comments to the SECNAV "private."

This disagreement with a senior only served to remind me that the controversial issues that required the secretary's attention were serious bureaucratic contests, with hard-nosed protagonists on each side of the issues. I had studied the behavior of bureaucracies at Harvard as one of my PhD fields under the acclaimed authority, James Q. Wilson, so I was not surprised by what I discovered in the Pentagon setting. The most troubling aspect was the extent to which personalities and the threats of retribution figured in the resolution of serious issues.

* * *

One further area of intense activity and focus for the secretary was the preparation of the annual Program Objective Memorandum (POM) and the budget process itself. By law, the SECNAV presided over the formal preparation of the Department of the Navy budget and its presentation to the Office of the Secretary of Defense. The Navy Department is unique in that the budget submission comprises the accounts for two services, navy and Marine Corps. The budget includes "blue" dollars for the navy, "green" dollars for the Marine Corps, and "blue in support of green" dollars for navy programs that support the Marine Corps, all consolidated in one budget submission.

Naturally, the secretary's support for Marine programs is a subject of great interest to the leadership of both services. There are often controversies regarding program priorities. During my stint as EA, the senior Marine Corps aide to the secretary was Colonel (later Major General) David Richwine. Dave was a friend and a colleague; he was always in close touch with headquarters to ensure that the secretary was informed of Marine Corps priorities and kept sensitive to issues deemed critical to the corps. Issues of greatest concern to the Marines were "blue in support of green" dollars for such joint items as shared aviation programs and amphibious assault shipping. The allocation of dollars between the two services was the most contentious issue between the uniformed leaderships of the navy and Marine Corps.

With General Al Gray serving as commandant, the secretary himself was of necessity in frequent touch with Headquarters Marine Corps (HQMC). In several meetings while finalizing the FY89 budget request, Gen. Gray, suspicious of the Office of the Chief of Naval Operations (OPNAV) staff's efforts to husband "blue" dollars at the expense of programs critical to the USMC, called on the secretary in person to underscore his concern. In a testament to his diplomatic skills, the secretary was able to strike a fair balance in the budget while retaining the confidence and respect of both service chiefs.

As with most bureaucratic undertakings, the process by which the Navy Department budget was staffed and finalized for the secretary's approval was indeed complicated. The document prepared for submission to the Office of the Secretary of Defense (OSD) is frequently delivered as late as the deadline allows. Just as frequently, it is returned thereafter to the navy for rework if it is deemed to be not compliant with OSD direction. All of this makes the annual process a case study in crisis management.

As the June 1 deadline for submission of the FY89 budget approached, Secretary Ball was in England, visiting the headquarters of the deputy Commander in Chief US Naval Forces Europe

(CINCUSNAVEUR), Vice Admiral Ed Martin. At Martin's residence outside London, the secretary received a visit from a delegation led by the navy's civilian associate budget director, Charles Nemfakos, that included the Marine Corps budget director and other senior financial managers. The purpose of their hurried transatlantic visit was to obtain Secretary Ball's last-minute signature on the budget, which was a compromise hammered out in protracted, down-to-the-wire negotiations given the extraordinary lengths necessary to force agreements among the claimants.

***

In the summer of 1989, I received word of my selection to the grade of rear admiral, lower half. The secretary conveyed this wonderful news to me himself after he had formally approved the recommendations of the selection board. I was then very surprised to receive literally a hundred or more congratulatory letters from navy and Marine flag officers; I put these into a three-ring binder to remind myself of the responsibilities that would follow.

Having been selected for flag rank, my days as the EA to the secretary were now numbered; the new rank meant a new assignment. I would be required to attend the required CAPSTONE General and Flag Officer Course with all the other flag selectees from the four services and the Coast Guard. This I would do in the late summer of 1989.

As for my next assignment, I was hoping I could follow the well-beaten path of other EAs who had preceded me and obtain orders to command a cruiser destroyer group and a carrier battle group as my first flag assignment. I relayed my preference to

Secretary Ball and Vice Admiral Boorda, the chief of naval personnel, but circumstances intervened and my preference was not to be.

When I had first interviewed for the job with the secretary the year before, he had asked what assignment I would request if not selected as his EA. I remembered I had mentioned the position as naval attaché to France as my second choice. The secretary had not forgotten.

Shortly after my selection to rear admiral, the secretary received a phone call from General Colin Powell, now the CJCS. He recounted a conversation he recently had with General Maurice Schmitt, the chief of the French General Staff and thus his French counterpart. Gen. Schmitt had conveyed his unhappiness with the fact that Gen. Powell's representative in Paris, a navy rear admiral and the US defense attaché, could not communicate with him in the French language. Powell explained to the secretary that Schmitt, who spoke excellent English, resented the fact that he had to speak English with an attaché accredited to France. Because the navy had pressed hard to have one of its flag officers assigned to the defense attaché post (historically, it had always gone to an army officer), Powell was giving the secretary the opportunity to find a navy replacement who spoke French.

After the conversation with Powell, the secretary called me into his office and told me of the call. He then asked how my French was. It was rusty I said, but I could manage. The result of the secretary's conversation with General Powell was his advising me that my preference to command a carrier battle group would have to wait. As chief of naval personnel, Adm. Boorda concurred that I would be nominated for assignment as the US defense attaché in Paris.

This turn of fate was significant in retrospect. It kept me from being in command of a carrier battle group during the first war with Iraq, Desert Storm. As the next chapter will recount, I generally enjoyed my assignment in Paris, but I also came to regret, near the end of my naval career, that I had not been in command while engaged in combat operations.

* * *

Just before I took my leave of the secretary's office, I was privy to a sad spectacle—one that ultimately led to a change in the civilian leadership of the navy Department. That spectacle was the nomination and failed confirmation of Senator John Tower as secretary of defense. Secretary Ball was a close friend and a longtime assistant to the senator who chaired the SASC. Tower was a navy veteran of World War II and a strong proponent of sea power. The navy was overjoyed that the former boatswain mate first class, short in stature but a giant of the Senate, had been nominated to lead the Defense Department.

Secretary Ball worked closely with several other experienced Hill staffers who were close to the senator to prepare him for his confirmation hearings. Included in the group who gathered frequently in Secretary Ball's office to work on the Tower confirmation were Jim McGovern, the secretary of the air force; Paul Wolfowitz, the undersecretary of defense for policy; and Senator John McCain. Senators Ted Kennedy, Sam Nunn, and several other Democrats declined to vote in favor of confirmation, paving the way for the accession of Dick Cheney to the secretary of defense position. At that point, it became clear that Will Ball would leave the department. He had fought too hard for Senator Tower.

* * *

Before moving to Paris, I was fortunate to participate in the CAPSTONE course. CAPSTONE was intended to introduce newly selected flag and general officers to the responsibilities that accompany selection to senior ranks in the armed services. Each class is taught by retired four-star generals and admirals representing all the uniformed branches of the DOD and Coast Guard. Among the most valuable seminars were those dealing with public relations and the press. Congressional relations and the expectations of members of Congress were discussed in detail. At the end of the course of instruction, we were all feted in the Indian Treaty Room of the Old Executive Office Building and introduced to the president and Mrs. Bush.

Because I was ordered as the defense attaché to France, I requested to join the European Command group for travel to one of the DOD areas of responsibilities (AOR). The timing was fortuitous because the Cold War was ending; the tectonic plates underlying European security were already moving. Our traveling group included several army and air force colleagues who were also destined for tours in Europe, including the future CJCS, General John Ralston, USAF. The briefings that we received at the army headquarters in Heidelberg, the air force headquarters in Ramstein, and the navy headquarters in Naples all centered on the portentous developments underway on the continent following the apparent collapse of the Warsaw Pact. We listened carefully to the implications of these changes for the respective commanders, and the NATO alliance in general.

Our eyes were opened wide in Stuttgart at the US Commander in Chief Europe (USCINCEUR) headquarters, where, in a classified briefing, we learned of the obvious decline in the readiness and posture of Eastern European armies and air forces. Although Soviet forces based in Poland and Germany seemed intact for the moment, public attitudes and the reliability of the host governments were clearly in doubt. All of this was welcome news to veterans of decades of Cold War, including the calamity that befell us in Vietnam.

Our last stop on the CAPSTONE tour was Berlin. We crossed Checkpoint Charlie, which was soon to disappear, into East Berlin. A striking moment came while we were having lunch in an East German restaurant in the inadvertent company of a loud and discourteous group of Soviet Army officers, who made clear their resentment of uniformed Americans in their sector. We were given tours of museums in the Soviet-occupied sector of the city, where we were allowed to witness and record the heroic victory of the Red Army in World War II, including film and still-photo documentaries of the brutal "liberation" of Berlin. On the western side of Checkpoint Charlie, the museums featured images of the hundreds of escapes across the border both before and after the erection of the famous Berlin Wall; sadly, there seemed to be more instances of failure than there were of successes in escaping through the Iron Curtain. On a brighter note, signs were already in evidence of the liberating effects of *perestroika*. It would be less than six months before thousands of East Germans began escaping through Hungary and Austria and before the wall came tumbling down. I obtained a piece of the Berlin Wall a year later that still adorns my desk.

To Capt. Phil Dur – With appreciation, Every good wish & Very Best Regards. Ronald Reagan

Farewell call on President Reagan in the Oval Office, December 1989

To Phil Dur – with high esteem Geo. Bush

Briefing the National Command Authority, January 1984. From left to right: Mike Deaver, Judge William Clark, President Reagan, Vice President Bush, Ambassador Richard Fairbanks, Howard Teicher, and me

For Phil Dur
With best wishes,   *Ronald Reagan*

Briefing the president. From left to right: Ed Meese, President Reagan, Judge Clark, Howard Teicher, and me

Luncheon in honor of President Amin Gemayel of Lebanon, 1983

Greeting President of Lebanon, Amin Gemayel. From left to right: President Gemayel, Howard Teicher, Ambassador Reginald Bartholomew, me, and President Reagan

Promotion to captain, National Security Advisor Bud McFarlane presiding, September 1984

Admiral James
Aloysius (Ace)
Lyons

Yorktown ("the Battlecruiser"),
1986

Yorktown and her Battle Efficiency Awards, 1987

Vice President George H. W. Bush aboard *Yorktown* in Kennebunkport, Maine,
July 1987

Vice President and Mrs. Bush cutting a cake baked in his honor by our galley chiefs, July 1987

My wardroom in "the Battlecruiser"

Soviet *Krivak* destroyer *Bezzavetny* preparing for collision (notice the anchors are out of their hawses), February 1988

Yorktown firing a low-elevation SM-2 missile from the after MK26 launcher

CHAPTER 12

A SAILOR AMONG DIPLOMATS

United States Defense Attaché, Paris

In preparing for my new assignment in Paris, I studied the regulations and directives that defined my duties as defense attaché. My representational duties were to represent the secretary of defense and the Chairman of the Joint Chiefs of Staff (CJCS) to the French Ministry of Defense (MOD) and to the French General Staff. Operationally, I reported on intelligence matters to the Defense Intelligence Agency's (DIA) Attaché Directorate. In addition, I was the reporting senior for the three service attachés from the army, navy (inclusive of the Marines), and the air force. These officers were responsible for promoting relationships with counterpart services in the MOD and for reporting on developments within the French military branch of interest to both their respective services and the DIA.

Arriving at the American embassy in August 1989, I began my assignment by making a series of calls. At the embassy proper, there was a call on the ambassador, Walter J. P. Curley, preceded by a call on the deputy chief of mission (DCM), Mark Lissfelt. The call on Lissfelt was instructive. This senior Foreign Service officer was well known and respected for his diplomatic skills and expertise in NATO affairs. He made clear that the reputation

I had made dealing with State Department and Foreign Service officials while on the National Security Council (NSC) staff was well known to him. He stressed in that first encounter that I was subordinate to the ambassador (which I clearly understood) and to him as the DCM. He went so far as to imply that in the embassy protocols, I was subordinate to the political officer, Kim Pendleton.

My call on Ambassador Curley went a little more smoothly and was indeed a warm welcome. The ambassador had served as an officer in the Marine Corps during World War II, including service as a platoon commander during the Iwo Jima campaign. Among the assignments he was most proud of was a stint as aide-de-camp to Generalissimo Chiang Kai-shek of the Republic of China. In my first conversation with him, the ambassador reaffirmed that my reporting relationship in the embassy was to him.

I mentioned the complexities of my representational duties because there was a curious anomaly at the American embassy in Paris, as well as at our embassies in London and Bonn. The tenure of Assistant Secretary of Defense for International Security Policy (ISP) Richard Perle featured intense negotiations in NATO and with the Soviet Union regarding the intermediate nuclear forces (INF) in Europe. Perle had insisted on the assignment of a trusted "political-military attaché" from the civilian side of the Office of the Secretary of Defense (OSD) to each of the three European embassies cited in order to protect DOD equities in the negotiation process. The Department of State, which had led the negotiations with the Soviets and for coordinating US positions with the principal NATO allies, insisted that the political-military liaison officer (or attaché as he was mistakenly called) at each embassy was to be subordinate not to the defense attaché but to the political officer.

This complicated situation had come about precisely because the office of the assistant secretary of defense (ASD) for international security affairs (ISA) did not trust the defense attaché system to adequately represent the department in the complicated arena of arms control. The logic, as it was explained to me by the DCM, was that the attaché system operated under the direction of the DIA and that the attaché's connection to that agency would therefore make the addition of an arms-controlled portfolio unworkable.

The problem that I confronted was that no one had bothered to modify the defense attaché's role as the accredited representative of the secretary of defense or to clarify how the defense attaché related to the "political-military attaché." Nor had it been explained why, since the INF negotiations had been successfully concluded four years before, there was an enduring need for a separate representative of the DOD who was without formal accreditation to the French MOD.

The rubber met the road on my watch during official visits to Paris by senior DOD officials and during the intensive preparations preceding their visits.

Following my arrival, my able and experienced executive assistant (EA), Gail Pugh,[73] arranged calls for meeting with the chief of the French General Staff, General Maurice Schmitt, and with senior civilian and military officials in the French MOD. These calls tested my rusty French, but my visit with Gen. Schmitt, which was especially important given his complaint about my predecessor, went very well, and he remarked that he was pleased to work with an officer of the US Navy who could communicate in the French language. In addition to my call on Gen. Schmitt, I

---

73 Gail, an alumna of the University of Minnesota, had served in the defense attaché system for more than twenty years when I arrived. Her French was impeccable and her knowledge of embassy politics and the centers of gravity in the French government was encyclopedic. She was of inestimable help to me from the beginning of my assignment.

met with the senior military officer in the prime minister's office, Vice Admiral Ghislain de Langre. I also called on Marc Perrin de Brichambaut, an expert on US policy and defense politics, who was the Ministry of Foreign Affairs' representative in the MOD. In that call, de Brichambaut hinted that his preferred point of contact at the embassy was the Defense Department civilian, the "political-military attaché."

The most eventful acquaintance early in my tenure came about at the request of the *chef du cabinet particulier*, the national security assistant in the immediate office of the president of the French Republic. Admiral Jacques Lanxade, the incumbent, called my office and invited me to the Élysée Palace to make his acquaintance. I was delighted to oblige, and I informed the ambassador of this unusual and unexpected opportunity. Ambassador Curley was as intrigued as I was by Lanxade's request, and he asked me to come by and debrief him following my call.

I soon discovered why Lanxade had asked me to come by. In the first place, he explained that he, as a sailor who had worked frequently and closely with the US Navy,[74] trusted me as sailor to respect his confidences and to assist him in relationships with certain US officials: General Brent Scowcroft, the national security advisor to President George H. W. Bush; Secretary Cheney and other senior DOD officials; and Gen. Powell, the CJCS. I was surprised when he explained that he did not "trust" the civilian side of the American embassy because they were not "reliable correspondents"—they were "too close" to their counterparts at the Quai d'Orsay. Lanxade was convinced that US Foreign Service officers were predisposed to inform the Quai of any discussions he had with them. He stressed that some of his

---

74 Lanxade had served tours as the operations director at CECMED, the French Mediterranean command, and as the flag officer in command of French naval forces in the Indian Ocean (ALINDIEN). In both assignments, he had worked closely with and befriended his US counterparts.

discussions with US officials had turned up in State Department cables and were subsequently discussed in the "corridors" of the Quai d'Orsay.

The admiral took the time to explain that his brief was to serve the president of the republic. The constitution of the Fifth Republic had conferred responsibility for national security to the president, but "bureaucrats" in the Ministries of Foreign Affairs (the Quai d'Orsay) and Defense (la Rue Saint Dominique) made it difficult to advance the president's policies. He explained further, "Some do not understand, and others are determined to obstruct the president's directions." He wanted to ensure that correspondence from the Élysée remained "outside" normal diplomatic channels. Lanxade allowed that I might keep the ambassador informed of his views, if I felt that it was necessary, and I explained that I would have to do that. He asked me to inform the ambassador when he described the information given to me as "privileged." This was especially pertinent regarding messages that he might send through me to his counterpart, General Brent Scowcroft.

Lanxade could speak modest English, and he much preferred to work with me in French; he felt that my ability to translate his French into English would make for more precise communication. I will mention now, with details to follow, that my relationship with Adm. Lanxade was the highlight of my tour in Paris. I do not believe it an exaggeration to say that I gained unique insights through my frequent collaboration with Lanxade, one of President François Mitterrand's closest advisors and a future chief of the French General Staff. My understanding of critical aspects of European security and how France's leaders regarded their role in the post-Cold War era was passed through reporting channels.

My role and my responsibilities were tested early in my tour during a visit to Paris by Secretary of Defense Cheney in the fall of 1989. At the ambassador's direction, I participated in several planning meetings, during which it became clear that Lissfelt, the DCM, wanted the political section of the embassy to arrange the itinerary, the agenda, and virtually all the staffing for the secretary's visit. True to my charter and as I understood my role, I took exception. Lissfelt insisted that precedents had been established during earlier visits to France by senior civilian leaders of the DOD. I asked for a meeting with the ambassador regarding the matter to explain my concerns.

The visit by Cheney at this juncture was indeed very important. On the one hand, the end of the Cold War was in sight, following the massive defections of East Germans through Hungary and Austria during the preceding summer and fall. Those developments were having a convulsive effect on European politics, and the implications for the NATO alliance and our defense relationship with the French were already apparent. Each evening, the French television channels featured stark images of thousands of East Germans rushing the Austrian border. The headline was that a transformation of postwar Europe was in the offing.

Of lesser consequence, the French government at the time was in the throes of a decision to replace the heart of their naval aviation, their fleet of aged F-8 *Crusader* aircraft. Many senior officers in the Marine Nationale favored the purchase of the US-built F/A-18 *Hornets*, but the ministry, with the active support of the French Air Force, insisted on replacing the F-8 with the French-built *Rafale*, which had already been chosen as the next-generation fighter for the French Air Force. As Cheney's visit approached, it was clear that the MOD and the prime minister's office would soon decide the matter. In my dealings with Marine Nationale leaders, some held hope that the secretary's visit might help the case for an early replacement of the F-8 fleet with F/A-18s. The alternative would be waiting a decade or longer for a "navalized" *Rafale*. I was asked to intercede and to encourage a timely alternative.

I was granted an audience by the ambassador, but it was in the company of the DCM and the political officer. We discussed the matter at length, and the ambassador's decision was to split responsibility for planning the secretary's visit between the Defense Attaché Office (DAO) and the political section. I would attend all the preparatory discussions and help prepare Cheney for his meetings with the French minister of defense and the prime minister. The political section would have the leading role in preparing staffing and for recording the results of the meetings.

Subsequently, I met privately with the ambassador, who explained to me that senior Foreign Service officers simply did not trust the uniformed military to prepare this visit. I told the ambassador that I found the argument insulting in both a personal and professional sense. My job description included representing the secretary to his counterpart in the French government. There was no such accreditation for anyone in the political section of the embassy. As the son of a career Foreign Service officer, my position regarding this matter was not meant to question either the competence or the motivation of other embassy officers. I felt that my background as a director of political-military affairs on the staff of the NSC, however, had provided me the expertise to meet the terms of my appointment as the US defense attaché.

During a subsequent visit to Washington for meetings at the Pentagon and at the DIA, I met with ASD (ISA) Stephen (Steve) Hadley (subsequently national security advisor in the George W. Bush presidency). He was clearly uncomfortable with my principled position on this subject, and he cautioned me not to "rock the boat." Hadley did acknowledge that the arrangements made by Richard Perle had created ambiguity at best and a very awkward situation for me at worst. All of that said, the State Department was happy with the arrangement, and undoing it was now in the "too hard" box.

Following several later encounters with Lissfelt and at the suggestion of Gail Pugh, I reached out to one of my most illustrious predecessors, General Vernon Walters. Walters had grown up in France and had served as the deputy director of the CIA and later as UN ambassador. He was now the US ambassador to Germany. He was a frequent visitor to the French capital, where he owned an apartment on the Champs-Élysées and where he had many French friends.

I meet with Ambassador Walters for lunch at a hotel on the Rue de Rivoli and explained my predicament regarding the "other" DOD representative attached to the political section of the embassy. He allowed that he had found that the same curious arrangement existed in his embassy when he assumed duties as the US ambassador in Bonn. He informed me that he had instructed the "political-military attaché" at his embassy to keep the defense attaché apprised of his activities and that he had directed that the defense attaché would be the responsible official for all visits to Bonn by Washington-based DOD personnel. He encouraged me to stand my ground and to make clear to Lissfelt and the ambassador that the fact that I served as a uniformed member did not in the least disqualify me from representing and supporting the civilian leadership of the DOD. He promised to convey his solution to the problem to Ambassador Curley, and I suspect he did.

Secretary Cheney's visit went off without complications. His meetings with French minister of defense Jean-Pierre Chevènement and with Prime Minister Michel Rocard were for the most part rather cordial with two exceptions. In his meeting with

Chevènement, Cheney noted the ready availability and reasonable cost of the F/A-18 as a replacement for the Marine Nationale's fighter. Protecting Dassault, the French aerospace company, seemed to be of overriding importance to the defense minister; the Marine Nationale would simply have to wait. Cheney replied that this "industrial policy" would come at a high cost. Chevènement replied, *tempi*, or so be it. Then, in Cheney's meeting with Rocard, the prime minister also reacted testily to Cheney's argument that French government subsidies to the Airbus consortium were having a detrimental impact on the competition for commercial aircraft sales with Boeing. The prime minister noted that because Boeing was a major supplier of military aircraft, it enjoyed only thinly veiled subsidies bearing on its own commercial contracts. Airbus, he explained pointedly, had no defense work.

I took advantage of Cheney's visit to organize a Franco-American celebration of the anniversary of our victory over the British at Yorktown during our War of Independence. Having joined the prestigious *Cercle de l'Union Interalliée* club in Paris, I had access to a special venue to host a celebratory dinner for the French military leadership. To this end, I requested uniformed representation from the US Army, Navy, and Air Force in Europe who were joined by a cadre of Marines from the embassy's Marine detachment. Forty servicemen, outfitted in their best service dress uniforms, lined the *escalier d'honneur* at the *Cercle* as our French guests came up the stairs and into the ornate banquet room. I had invited more than fifty French general officers and admirals plus a dozen US flag and general officers from commands in Europe. The dinner was a hit with the French, who I knew would enjoy joining Americans in acknowledging their contribution during our Revolutionary War. It was not such a great hit with my British counterpart in Paris, who complained that he had somehow missed my invitation to dinner.

Following Cheney's visit, there were many others in the months that followed by ranking civilian officials of the DOD—especially Paul Wolfowitz, the undersecretary (policy); Steve Hadley, ASD (ISA); and Andy Marshall, director of net assessment. Military visitors included General Colin Powell, DIA Director General Harry Soyster, USA, and the J5 on the Joints Chiefs of Staff (JCS), Lieutenant General Lee Butler, USAF. By the time of those visits in the late winter of 1989 and early 1990, I had solidified my position on the embassy team and my relationships with Adm. Lanxade, Gen. Schmitt, and Adm. De Langre. Meetings that I arranged for visitors with these leaders were instrumental in promoting a broader and deeper dialogue between them and their American counterparts. As the integrity of the alliance, and the future of European security more generally, grew in importance, the bureaucratic hijinks in the embassy subsided and we got on with the business at hand.

The first six months of 1990 were rather frantic because our discussions with French counterparts centered on the "German question" (i.e., prospects for the reunification of Germany), the future of NATO, and France's role in a post-Cold War Europe. Now, thirty years later, it is easy to discount the anxieties that accompanied the tumultuous changes in Germany and Eastern Europe in January 1990. The French began by attempting to slow down (*freiner*) the drive to unification being championed by Chancellor Kohl of Germany.

At the same time, there was considerable discussion in the French press and in French political circles of prospects for the dissolution or the disintegration of NATO. This issue was fueled in part by Soviet insistence on the "neutrality" of a reunified Germany. Privately, certain French officials made a point of describing how "other" Europeans found the "unbridled military potential" of a reunified Germany "indigestible." During my discussions with Admiral Lanxade and other senior French military, they were none too subtle in pressing the point that the United States should be careful to join in slowing the drive to reunification and join in deliberate preparations for the impending withdrawal of Soviet forces from Eastern Europe. It was abundantly clear that the withdrawal would prove faster than had been envisaged in the agreement signed in November 1990, titled Conventional Armed Forces in Europe (CFE).

As mentioned, in the wake of Secretary Cheney's meetings with Defense Minister Chevènement and Prime Minister Rocard, there were successive visits to Paris by the undersecretary of defense (policy), Paul Wolfowitz, and the assistant secretary (ISA), Steve Hadley. These visits were clearly prompted by mounting concern in Washington on the future of European security and related measures. Both officials met with French counterparts in the MOD and at the Quai d'Orsay. One issue of critical importance in discussions with Admiral Lanxade was the future following reunification of the French Army division based in Germany. Lanxade made clear that the French were adamant that unless a multinational (Franco-German) corps were to be created under the auspices of the West European Union (WEU), French forces in Germany would be repatriated. Owing to the long-standing exclusion of France from the NATO military structure and the impending collapse of the Warsaw Pact, Lanxade said that continuing their deployment in Germany was no longer "rational"; the basis for the presence of French forces in Germany had been to "deter or to slow" a Warsaw Pact drive toward France.

A related topic for discussions with ranking US visitors was the role of French tactical nuclear weapons in eastern France. The French had never accepted the NATO strategy of flexible response, insisting instead that the success of a purely conventional defense of NATO Europe was problematic. In the event of conflict, the intended use for their tactical nuclear weapons had been as a "last resort" (*l'ultime avertissement nucléaire*) before launching a riposte from strategic forces, in their own version of the TRIAD. Given the demise of the Warsaw Pact, the basis of French strategy was bound to change in a fundamental way. In short, with the pact in disarray, the future strategic logic for NATO and France's relationship to NATO were very hot topics for discussion during the first half of 1990.

A side note: With the collapse of the German Democratic Republic (GDR) and with reunification increasingly likely, the Soviets undertook to enlist the support of France and French critics of NATO. In March 1990, Soviet defense minister Dmitry Yazov visited Paris, and Admiral Lanxade, who had been present in the meetings with Yazov, reported that the Soviet minister was seeking the "imposition of guarantees" by the Four Powers on a reunified Germany. Included among these were a formal renunciation by Germany to accessing nuclear weapons, and clear limits on the future size and configuration of German armed forces. Yazov delivered a speech to French military officers attending the *École de Guerre*, during which he reiterated a condition demanded by President Gorbachev and Foreign Minister Shevardnadze that a unified Germany not remain in NATO. Yazov's party also included several Soviet generals and admirals who in turn had extensive meetings with their counterparts in the French General Staff. A full court press was on![75]

The Soviets were hosted aboard the French aircraft carrier **Clemenceau** and at the French Air Force base at Saumur, near Reims. Our sources on Gen. Schmitt's staff kept us abreast of the meetings and their content, and I reported them in detail to the DIA and other interested commands. Just after the Yazov

---

75 Maurice Schmitt, *De Dien Bien Phu a Koweit City* (Paris: Bernard Grasset, 1992), 159–161.

delegation left Paris, I received an unusual invitation from my Soviet counterpart in Paris, a Soviet general (a GRU officer, I am sure). Over a classic Russian lunch of borscht, caviar, blinis, stuffed cabbage, and plenty of vodka, the general was at pains to inform me of the Soviet tour de force in Paris. His intent remains a mystery, but he must have hoped that if the French warmed to supporting the dissolution of the NATO military structure, it would throw a wrench into US plans for the future of the alliance. I took the opportunity to remind the general that differences in US and French views regarding NATO and its structure were long standing. I also stressed that we believed the future of NATO was inextricably bound to the reunification of Germany and to the changes sweeping the former protectorates of the Soviet Union in Eastern Europe.

The Soviet visit to France was followed by reciprocal visits to the Soviet capital by Gen. Schmitt and Adm. Lanxade. For their part, and as later explained to me by Gen. Schmitt and his staff, the French visitors wanted to appear supportive of the CFE while in Moscow. During a speech to Soviet officers at the Voroshilov Academy, Schmitt supported the objectives of the CFE and stressed the importance of measures to reduce the "risk of surprise attack" and of others to establish a "degree of parity" in conventional forces, based in a zone described as "from the Atlantic to the Ural Mountains."

By May 1990, with preparations well underway for the NATO summit convened to deal with the German question and the future of the alliance, US visitors listened to views of what the French sought in the forthcoming summit. Among the most important were future NATO policies and strategies regarding the role of conventional forces, the role of nuclear forces in Europe, and the role of the Commission on Security and Cooperation in Europe (CSCE). It became abundantly clear that there was considerable divergence in the views and objectives of the US and French counterparts.[76] Admiral Lanxade and the French General Staff provided insight into the objectives of the French. Preparing for visits for Hadley and Wolfowitz scheduled for February 1991, one could see that there was considerable daylight in the objectives of the two sides. There were also significant differences between the views of the Quai d'Orsay—aligned with those of Minister Chevènement and the MOD—and the uniformed military leadership.

As conveyed by Lanxade, the most important differences were those that divided the Élysée and the Quai. The Élysée, determined to participate in the evolution of the alliance while sensitive to France's status outside the integrated military structure, proposed that work in the areas of interest be done by the North Atlantic Council. The Quai and the MOD, on the other hand, wanted discussion of these matters to take place in an ad hoc organization created specifically for this purpose. The logic was that matters discussed in the North Atlantic Council—namely, reviews of conventional forces and nuclear force posture—would inevitably draw France more closely into discussions of NATO's military organization. Lanxade described the concerns of "bureaucrats" in the French ministries as "archaic and dysfunctional."

Putting aside questions of the proper venue for these deliberations, the imperative for President Mitterrand, as Lanxade explained it, was the creation of a "strong" Western European union to "anchor" a unified Germany solidly in a European security framework. The German attaché in Paris, my counterpart attaché, advised me that this was also the position of Chancellor Kohl and the chief of the German General Staff, General Klaus Naumann. Privately, Lanxade shared with me that

76 Jacques Lanxade, *Quand le monde a basculé* (Paris: Nil Editions, 2001), 244–250.

he and Naumann were close collaborators and aligned during these critical discussions of post-Cold War Europe.[77]

One of the French trump cards during these discussions was the future of the French Army division garrisoned in West Germany. The Germans were anxious to keep French forces in their garrison. Quite apart from discussions of future NATO force structure, the German side felt that the establishment of a purely European security framework that included France would reinforce the premise that a reunited Germany's future was in a European union.

One other related incident of note occurred in the early summer of 1990. While sensitive negotiations were underway within the French General Staff regarding the future of NATO and the WEU, the Supreme Allied Commander Europe (SACEUR), General John Galvin, made one of his occasional and discreet visits to Paris. The agenda for Galvin's meetings with the French (the future of French forces in Germany) was not disclosed to the ambassador or to anyone at the embassy. The Department of State was very sensitive and insistent that US policy objectives in meetings with the French be synchronized and coordinated with the "country team" in Paris. Having gotten wind of Galvin's impending visit from sources in the French military, I had communicated the ambassador's sensitivities to Galvin's EA before the general arrived in Paris.

This was a long-standing issue with the embassy in Paris, inasmuch as this SACEUR, like several of his predecessors, was following a practice that had annoyed past US ambassadors to France. The embassy's view was that any senior US official undertaking negotiations with the French should coordinate with the ambassador, the leader of the country team. During the tenure of one previous ambassador, the issue had arisen while General

77 Lanxade, *Quand le monde a basculé*, 255–256.

Alexander Haig held the vaunted SACEUR post. Hearing of an impending visit by Haig to Paris, President Carter provided a letter to the ambassador, instructing him to report back to the White House directly if any serving US military commander came to France without the ambassador's approval. Succeeding presidents had apparently followed suit.

Learning of Galvin's visit after the fact, Ambassador Curley called me into his office and held up the sitting president's letter, which he kept in the top drawer of his desk. He instructed me to inform General Galvin that were he to visit Paris again without first notifying and obtaining the ambassador's approval of the visit, Curley would report the breach of protocol immediately to the president himself. I listened carefully and thought hard about how to convey the ambassador's message.

I waited a few days before calling the general's EA again and passing on an abbreviated version of Curley's warning. The colonel and I both understood that the issue was far from resolution. From the standpoint of SACEUR, the contention was—and probably still is—that he came to France not as a senior US military commander but rather as a major NATO commander representing the alliance. It may well be that this issue remains unresolved to this day, although with the French now reintegrated into the NATO command structure, separate meetings between SACEUR and the French military may not be as sensitive a matter to the State Department.

French concerns about military relationships, and European security more generally, figured prominently during a visit to France by CJCS Gen. Powell in September 1990. This visit was clearly the defense attaché's office to manage, and our entire team worked hard to prepare the chairman for his meetings with the ambassador and the top leadership of the French military. I concentrated on preparing Powell for his meetings with Lanxade and Schmitt.

As expected, these meetings featured wide-ranging discussions on the future of NATO and the impact of the end of the Cold War on US force structure and our presence in Europe. From the beginning, the meetings confirmed that there remained considerable differences in US and French views that would not be easily resolved.

We did make solid progress on other topics, including expanding military-to-military cooperation. For example, we were granted provisional use of French live-fire training facilities at Canjuers in the South of France and Marine Nationale facilities near Toulon. The latter served to facilitate exchanges between US Navy SEALS and their French counterparts. For their part, the French were most appreciative of our decision to share information on Soviet submarine activities and to allow French participation in tracking Soviet submarines when discovered in maritime areas important to France. The French were also grateful that we arranged for several services and exercises with the French carrier *Foch* and her escorts while they were deployed in the western Atlantic. Although recognizing that agreement with the French on future courses of action would not be easy, Gen. Powell seemed pleased with his visit and the relationship he had advanced with Gen. Schmitt.

As the summer of 1990 progressed, the emphasis in our political-military dialogue with the French shifted from the future of Europe to our reaction to increasingly bellicose moves by the Iraqi government. Our response included regular offensive strikes by allied aircraft against Iraqi air and air defense sites that were tracking our flights patrolling the so-called no-fly zone established in reaction to Iraq's chemical attacks on its own population. In addition, Iraqi maneuvers along the frontier with Kuwait made an attack against that country increasingly probable. As the criticism of Iraq and its maneuvers intensified in our press and official statements, the French government seemed at pains to restrain their own criticism. This was the result of long-standing sensitivities in a country hosting a large Arabic-speaking minority and of the privileged relationship that France enjoyed as Iraq's second most important arms supplier. Ironically, Minister of Defense Chevènement, who was also the serving mayor of Belfort, a city in eastern France with a large Muslim minority, was the president of a Franco-Iraqi friendship society.

Events reached a climax in August, when Iraqi armored columns invaded Kuwait. Immediately following the invasion, the focus of our entire embassy shifted to working with French counterparts to coordinate our response to this Iraqi aggression at the diplomatic level. My own focus turned to planning the combined military action that would soon follow. President Mitterrand was determined that France join in pressuring Iraq to withdraw, but he preferred diplomatic efforts under the auspices of the UN Security Council. He was also inclined to argue that should diplomacy fail, France would participate in "an international military response." The condition Mitterrand stressed was that any military action against Iraq would be taken under UNSC Resolution 698, then under consideration by the Security Council. Fortunately, the resolution was passed with only Cuba and Yemen dissenting. Lanxade explained to me that he had informed Gen. Scowcroft on behalf of his president that France's participation in operations to liberate Kuwait was conditional: "French blood" would not be shed in order to restore the absolute monarchy, Al-Sabah, in a liberated Kuwait. I asked Lanxade how Scowcroft had replied; Scowcroft, in a terse message, had acknowledged the point without comment.

During the anxious days before Desert Storm was launched, in a period our military labeled Desert Shield, the United

States undertook the massive movement of forces from Europe and the United States to Saudi Arabia. At their request, I spent many hours at French military headquarters, keeping them informed of movements and basing arrangements in the Kingdom of Saudi Arabia. For their part, the French sought to demonstrate their intentions by sailing the carrier *Clemenceau*, with a large contingent of French Army helicopters and a battalion of infantry, to the Persian Gulf, while at the same time negotiating beddown arrangements for French forces in Qatar and the United Arab Emirates. Later, as plans progressed, and as the number of US and UK forces in the theater grew apace, the French marked the beginning of a serious commitment to confront Iraq with the deployment of an armored division (Operation Daguet) to the western reaches of Saudi Arabia.

The significance of this deployment cannot be understated. Although there was never a question that the large British corps deployed to Saudi Arabia would operate under US command, the status of French forces, and their relationship to the combined US-UK force, was a difficult and delicate matter. A long-standing Gaullist aversion to the subordination of French military units to foreign command was alive and well in Mitterrand's Socialist government. It was especially apparent in the meetings that the political section of the embassy had with the Quai d'Orsay and the civilian leadership of the MOD.

Gen. Schmitt, Adm. Lanxade, and virtually all the military leaders with whom I dealt (the sole exception being Defense Minister Chevènement) understood that when offensive operations against Iraq began, French forces would perforce operate under the control of Commander in Chief Central Command (CINCCENT) General Norman Schwarzkopf and his Saudi deputy. There was simply no way to finesse or mask this requirement.[78] I attended several meetings with Gen. Schmitt and his operations staff to undertake detailed planning for the eventual change of operational control to USCINCENT.

An additional wrinkle in US-French planning appeared after President Mitterrand had given his approval to the subordination of French ground and air forces to the coalition commander as preparation for the ground offensive was intensifying. At meetings in Saudi Arabia, Schwarzkopf offered Chevènement two options regarding the employment of the Daguet Division. One was to be incorporated into the major US-UK thrust into Kuwait ("the left hook"); the other was to operate to the west of the major thrust as a "covering force." These options were forwarded through the chain of command to President Mitterrand and his war cabinet in Paris. The General Staff, supported by Lanxade, was clearly inclined to have Daguet included in the major axis of advance.

Foreign Minister Roland Dumas and Chevènement held a clear preference for Daguet operating independently as a detached "covering force." They argued that it would be easier for French authorities to retain "command" of their forces and, by implication, geographically limit French military operations to Kuwait. Under this scheme, "operational control" of French forces would pass to the coalition commander, but "command" in the strictest sense would remain with the French authorities. Lanxade explained to me that after a tense meeting, the reluctant ministers prevailed and persuaded the president to overrule his military advisors. As is well known, the result was that the French operated separately and met with little opposition in their march north from their garrison in Saudi Arabia into northern Kuwait.

78 Lanxade, *Quand le monde a basculé*, 70–71; Schmitt, *De Dien Bien Phu a Koweit City*, 190–191.

Even as preparations went forward and with extensive discussions underway between US and French military at the headquarters level and in the theater proper, the defense minister was hedging his bets. In several public venues, Chevènement took pains to emphasize that whereas the invasion of Kuwait had been a violation of international law, France would not be party to any "offensive" operations against Iraq proper. His public statements to that effect were a constant irritant to the Élysée, with the president and his cabinet attempting to maintain a cooperative posture within the coalition. The president himself was not hedging on his commitment to join in the liberation of Kuwait by whatever military action made sense.

Matters came to a head on January 16, 1991 as air strikes began, the first objective being the neutralization of the Iraqi air defense system and the destruction of the Iraqi Air Force.

Chevènement's concerns were widely supported by the leftist French press, which had predicted significant collateral damage in the event of an air offensive against Iraqi targets. In a round of calls Admiral Lanxade made in a visit to Washington, during which I accompanied him, we were provided a briefing by Admiral McConnell, the responsible intelligence director on the Joint Staff. The briefing included detailed satellite imagery of potential targets in Iraq. Lanxade was duly impressed with the quality and fidelity of the imagery that had been annotated to highlight items of interest.

Following our return to Paris and after the air campaign was underway, Lanxade revisited the issue of the imagery. There were several instances of adverse press coverage of strikes in Baghdad and several ministers, including Defense Minister Chevènement, claimed significant collateral damage and civilian casualties had resulted. Another claim was that the United States was concealing intelligence regarding the accuracy and efficacy of our air strikes.

Lanxade explained the president's concern about these charges, and he asked whether imagery of the quality he had seen at the Pentagon could be shared. I passed the request along to DIA director Lt. Gen. Soyster and to Gen. Powell's EA. Gen. Soyster responded very quickly that he would be sending me annotated bomb damage assessment (BDA) imagery to share with President Mitterrand and a select few. The courier arrived on February 4 with fifteen large (36" x 36") images of targets in and around Baghdad that had been struck by Tomahawk missiles and precision guided munitions delivered by US aircraft. I showed the images to the ambassador before proceeding directly to the Élysée Palace, where Adm. Lanxade met me. We proceeded to a waiting area outside the enormous and ornate office of the president.

Entering the office with Lanxade, I had sensed that we had a very interested audience, one limited to President Mitterrand and Jean-Louis Bianco, his chief of staff. Their reaction was one of astonishment at the quality of the imagery, the accuracy of the strikes, and the fact that there was no obvious evidence of extensive collateral damage.[79] To my surprise, following a review and discussion of the imagery, the president invited me to sit down on the couch in his office to discuss the progress of the air offensive. He began by saying that he was most impressed by our weapons and our intelligence. Our reliance on unmanned Tomahawk missiles, with their range and accuracy, seemed astounding (étonnant). I summarized some of the most recent intelligence and operations reports of developments and described the performance of the sea-launched Tomahawk missile in understandable terms.

This request to provide a half-hour briefing to the president of the country to which I was accredited was an enormous

79 Lanxade, *Quand le monde a basculé*, 86.

privilege and an honor. I was especially proud, as the grandson of a French immigrant, that my presentation and conversation, both entirely in French, had not required the presence of an interpreter!

In the weeks preceding the air offensive, I had assisted in preparing a visit to France by the director of the National Security Agency, Admiral William (Bill) Studeman. I had known the admiral for many years as he had been the director of naval intelligence in 1985 while I was serving as the EA to Adm. Lyons. Adm. Studeman's objective in going to France was to encourage the French to cooperate in the planning of our forthcoming air offensive against Iraq. The Iraqi air system, named KARI,[80] was a network of radars, communication facilities, missile sites, and air defense aircraft. Engineers and technicians from the French defense industry had designed and built KARI and thus had detailed knowledge of the system. I arranged and attended some of the meetings that Adm. Studeman had with counterparts, including a critical meeting he had with Adm. Lanxade over dinner at the *Cercle de l'Union Interalliée*.

Studeman's visit was a resounding success as measured in part by the successful air campaign that preceded the ground offensive.

* * *

I digress to record a fascinating moment in my tenure during those historic times. I have referred to Minister Chevènement's reluctance to associate France with attacks on Iraq proper. Indeed, it was at Chevènement's insistence that the French air forces in

80 KARI was the reverse spelling of IRAK, the French spelling of IRAQ.

Saudi Arabia were based at some distance from other coalition
air forces so as to avoid any guilt by association were the latter
to be employed in attacks against targets in Iraq proper. After
strikes in Iraq had commenced, the minister was still insisting
publicly that France was not a party to operations against Iraqi
forces beyond Kuwait. A few days later—on January 21, to
be precise—I was summoned to the Élysée for a meeting with
Admiral Lanxade.

The conversation that ensued involved a most unusual request. He reminded me of the *petit problème* that the Élysée
was having with the minister and his posture regarding strikes
in Iraq. I acknowledged that it had been noted by our side and
that it seemed an awkward stance by the minister of defense.
Here came the surprise.[81]

Lanxade implied that what he was about to ask would likely
result in a political crisis. He nonetheless wanted me to convey
to Gen. Powell the following request: France would appreciate
it if the commander of French air forces in Saudi Arabia could
be "assigned" targets to strike in Iraq at the earliest opportunity.
Lanxade explained that Gen. Roquejeoffre (the Commander
of Opération Daguet) was not a "commander in chief" by any
definition. He could not make that recommendation nor, under
French regulations, could Gen. Schmitt order such an action. A
request for approval of an offensive action had to be tendered
to the Office of the President for approval.

I immediately returned to my office and placed a call to
Gen. Powell, relaying Lanxade's message. The chairman was
puzzled and asked me why the request wasn't made "in theater"

---

81 Lanxade, *Quand le monde a basculé*, 82–83; Schmitt, *De Dien Bien Phu a Koweit City*,
228. Curiously, Gen. Schmitt in his memoirs failed to mention Chevènement's refusal to
approve French strikes against targets in Iraq. Instead, he cited the supposed vulnerability
of French *Jaguar* aircraft to Iraqi air defenses as the reason for keeping French aircraft
out of Iraqi air space.

by the French commander. I explained that I had anticipated the question in my call on Lanxade, and I gave Gen. Powell the explanation I had received regarding how decisions were made in the French chain of command.

On January 24, a formation of French *Jaguar* aircraft struck Iraqi Revolutionary Guard targets in Basra.

What had transpired illustrates the complexity built into command and control under the constitution of the Fifth Republic. In practice, only the president of the republic can approve *planned or preemptive* military action against an opponent. In this case, in order to obtain that approval, the message chain went from Powell to Schwarzkopf; from Schwarzkopf to USAF Lt. Gen. Chuck Horner, the coalition air commander; and then from Horner to Gen. Roquejeoffre. As explained, Gen. Roquejeoffre had no authority to comply, so he passed the request he had received to Gen. Schmitt, who in turn forwarded it for decision to the minister of defense (Chevènement), the prime minister, and the president.

Knowing that he could not disapprove the request, Chevènement deferred to the Élysée, clearly hoping that Mitterrand would support his public statements and deny the request. In Lanxade's memoirs, he writes that he outlined the position of the defense minister to President Mitterrand and asked for his decision. Mitterrand's reply, with a "knowing smile," was "affirmative."[82] The rest is history, and shortly thereafter, on January 29, Chevènement resigned. Pierre Joxe, formerly the minister of the interior, was named as his replacement.

* * *

82 Lanxade, *Quand le monde a basculé*, 83.

The other event of major significance that occurred during Desert Storm was almost as remarkable. France had withdrawn from the NATO military organization in 1968, and with that, NATO had abandoned several large air force bases in France. No US aircraft had operated from bases on French soil since then, and the overflight of French territory by US military aircraft carrying weapons payloads had been "by request only."

In late January 1991, with air operations against Iraq well underway, I passed a request from the Joint Staff to the French General Staff (and separately to Adm. Lanxade) to allow the overflight of French territory by B-52 bombers operating from bases in the United Kingdom and en route to strike targets in Iraq.

At the same time, although recognizing it was a long shot, the United States asked for permission to base KC-10 aerial refueling tankers at a base in the South of France. The mission was to launch out of France, rendezvous over the eastern Mediterranean with the B-52s en route to Iraq, refuel them, and return to base in France.

On February 1, we received the answer we were looking for. The ambassador was summoned to the Quai d'Orsay to meet with Foreign Minister Dumas. Simultaneously, I was summoned to the office of the new minister of defense, Pierre Joxe. The only conditions to the approval that each of us received were that there would be no nuclear weapons in the B-52s and (this was for French public consumption) that the base would be an isolated facility at Montmarson, "distant from the large Arab population centers" in the southwest of France. Lanxade called me subsequently to gauge our reaction. I allowed that "euphoric" was not too strong a word.

By the end of February 1991, with the coalition victorious in Kuwait, the discussion of the postwar posture toward Iraq and the security of the Gulf seemed of minor interest to the French.

This may have been a reaction to the restoration of the monarchy in Kuwait as they repatriated their forces. Our French counterparts conceded that the *après-guerre* regional order was seen as the responsibility of the United States and the United Kingdom, both of which had "historical interests" in and ties to the area.

***

During the delicate period following the collapse of the Berlin Wall and while discussions regarding the terms of German reunification were in train, there were two instances that captured French views regarding their recent history and future role in European security arrangements.

The first was a remark attributed to President Mitterrand, possibly apocryphally, when he was queried by a reporter to explain how he viewed the prospect of a reunited Germany. Mitterrand was reported to have responded, "*Moi, j'aime les Allemands tellement que j'espère q'uil, y aura toujours deux Allemagnes!*" ("Personally, I love the Germans so much that I hope there will always be two Germanies!").

The pain of German occupation from 1940 to 1945 was still evident during my tour in Paris; even today, many Frenchmen struggle with the reality of a strong Germany aspiring to European leadership. One incident demonstrated to me the memories and residual antipathies and memories that remained, forty-five years after the end of the war. In the middle of my Paris assignment, my assistant received a request from a military museum in Nantua, a small town in eastern France, which was dedicated to preserving the history of the wartime exploits of the Resistance. The museum wanted to display a bazooka that had been air-dropped by the United States to the French Resistance fighting in that area; it had been used very effectively to destroy German trains and truck convoys that were moving supplies across France to bolster German defenses in Normandy. With the help of the Department of the Army, we obtained the bazooka, which was on display in a small museum in Kansas. I traveled to Nantua to deliver it in person to an elderly colonel who had commanded the Resistance in eastern France.

Following the ceremony, I was invited to a luncheon in a local restaurant that the colonel was hosting on behalf of a veterans organization. During the meal, which was being served by several elderly women, the colonel suddenly stood up at the table and yelled in a grave voice, "*Salope!*" ("Slut!") while pointing at one of the servers. The server glanced at the colonel, burst into tears, and quickly hurried back into the kitchen. Once calm had been restored and the meal service had resumed, the colonel turned to me and explained that the woman had been a collaborator who had befriended and "serviced the *Boches*." After the liberation, he had personally shaved her head in view of other residents of Nantua to shame her. Not all the scores and the trials of the war with Germany had subsided entirely.

A second event that demonstrated residual tensions among Frenchmen and Frenchwomen in relation to the historic past occurred during an Independence Day commemoration at the tomb of the Marquis de Lafayette in the Picpus Cemetery, located in a northern district of Paris. This cemetery, on the grounds of a Catholic hospital, is also the burial ground of more than thirteen hundred nobles and clergy who were guillotined in the Place du Trône in 1793. The ceremony on July 4, 1991 that I attended included the participation of Admiral Jonathan Howe, then the Commander in Chief US Naval Forces Europe

(CINCUSNAVEUR), representing the United States, and Adm. Lanxade, representing France.

As we stood for the national anthems of both countries, I observed a dozen or more nuns watching the opening ceremonies from the second floor of the hospital. When the French military band finished playing the "Star-Spangled Banner," the nuns were smiling and clapped their approval. But as the band played the French anthem, the "Marseillaise," which celebrates the Revolution, I noticed that the same group of nuns turned their backs on the proceedings. I learned later that nuns and priests in the hospital during the Revolution had hidden many nobles there; when this was discovered, the clergy had been executed, along with the aristocrats they had hidden, and all were buried in a common grave. Clearly, their successors two centuries later were not fans of Republicans—the political heirs to those in charge during what is still remembered as the Terror.

* * *

An observation on the state of Franco-German relations illustrates the close cooperation between France led by Mitterrand and Germany under Chancellor Kohl. As mentioned previously, it appeared in the early spring of 1990 that the conditions attending the pending reunification of Germany would include the dissolution of the Warsaw Pact and the reciprocal withdrawal of US and Soviet forces. The French assumed that a fundamental restructuring, if not a parallel dissolution, of the integrated NATO military structure in Europe was imminent as well. With respect to that restructuring, I obtained an interesting revelation.

As was my custom, I had a friendly relationship and occasional meetings over breakfast at the embassy restaurant with my German counterpart in Paris, General Freidel. (Interestingly, Freidel spoke English poorly and preferred to converse with me in French.)

At one of these breakfast meetings, he told me of an exchange he had recently had with Adm. Lanxade. The admiral, he said, had asked him to communicate with the German Inspector General, General Klaus Naumann, to inquire "informally" how the Federal Republic of Germany would regard a French SACEUR. The question evoked great surprise from the German attaché, but he nevertheless communicated it to his superiors in Bonn.

Several months later during another breakfast meeting, I asked Freidel what Naumann's reply had been. He looked at me with a sheepish grin and said that Naumann had replied, "*Oui, pourquoi pas, mais pas pour toujours*" ("Sure, why not, but not forever"). Naumann was hinting that such an arrangement would entail reciprocity that would allow for a future German SACEUR. I communicated our exchange to the Pentagon. In a subsequent meeting with Gen. Powell in his office, he instructed me to tell Lanxade to "stop messing with my SACEUR," indicative of how the chairman saw his relationship to the American commander in that post.

* * *

Our work at the embassy shifted anew to the future of Europe, inasmuch as German reunification was by that time a foregone conclusion.

The French position on the future of European security was, in summary, premised on several principles:

1. NATO would be reorganized in light of a greatly diminished threat to Western Europe and the anticipated withdrawal of many, if not all, US forces from Germany, which they expected might be considered as a condition for the withdrawal of Soviet forces from Eastern Europe.
2. The CSCE would become the appropriate forum to safeguard peace in post-Cold War Europe.
3. The WEU could establish a formal command structure and designate multinational European forces, to be called the Eurocorps, to operate outside Allied territory covered under Article V of the NATO Charter·

The burning issues for France were the future of NATO and, by extension, the role of France and that of French forces stationed in Germany. As noted earlier, the French pressed hard for the establishment of a multinational force under the auspices of the WEU and not subordinate to NATO command. Pressure on these points was mounting, but at the London NATO Summit in 1990, the United States and United Kingdom succeeded in shutting down any serious consideration of a Eurocorps under an expanded WEU.

Immediately following that summit, President Mitterrand announced the withdrawal of French forces from Germany. The likelihood of such a decision had become clear even before the cooperative interlude of the Gulf War. France was facing considerable pressure on multiple fronts. The Soviets, though now posing a much-reduced threat to France, maintained their determination to force the withdrawal of all NATO forces from a reunited Germany. In light of a significant redeployment of US forces in Germany and continuing public reluctance to rejoin the integrated NATO military structure, Mitterrand could see no logic to justify French forces remaining in Germany proper.

As I prepared to leave Paris near the end of April 1991, the discussions between the embassy's political section and their contacts at the Quai d'Orsay on the future of NATO, the WEU, and France's role continued. Competing factions in the French government were apparent. Lanxade led the charge for a separate WEU defense corps (Eurocorps) that would relate to but not be subordinate to NATO; he hinted that in return, France would return to the military organization of NATO. The Quai, on the other hand, rejected any possibility of *any* formal association with NATO.

Lanxade continued his correspondence with Gen. Scowcroft and Gen. Powell, but the differences in the positions of the two governments (the United States opposed the WEU/Eurocorps proposal) were not changed. At my farewell cocktail party, which was hosted by Gen. Schmitt, Lanxade explained publicly that I had contributed to taking postwar US-French relations to a high-water mark. However, he continued sadly, "the ebb tide had set in," just as I was taking my leave of Paris. He knew I had orders to command a battle group; he wished me fair winds and asked that I not forget what I had learned during this remarkable tour of duty.[83] As of this writing, I have neither forgotten nor discounted the important events to which I was a witness and a contributor. My induction into the Defense Attaché Hall of Fame in Washington is testament to the contributions of our entire team at a critical juncture in US-French relations.

83 Inside the cover of his book, *Quand le monde a basculé,* Lanxade wrote the following inscription to me: "To Philip Dur, a great friend of France who has contributed in an exceptional manner to relations between the Élysée and Washington during the Gulf War. He has witnessed events that he knows well. In recognition of his help and friendship. Very Cordially, Jacques Lanxade."

CHAPTER 13

CRUISERS, DESTROYERS, TAILHOOKS, CATAPULTS, AND TRAGEDY AT SEA

Commanding, Cruiser-Destroyer Group Eight and *Saratoga* Battle Group

In April 1991, I left Paris bound for the command I had sought two years earlier: administrative command of a cruiser-destroyer group and operational command of a carrier battle group.

I recognized that I had reached this goal with the support of the chief of naval personnel, Vice Admiral Mike Boorda. His support had been critical, and he had kept me abreast of his intercessions with Secretary of the Navy (SECNAV) Larry Garrett, who had admonished me a few years before while he was the undersecretary of the navy. By the time I received my orders, I felt I had mended my fences with Garrett after he came to Paris on an official visit near the end of my Paris tour. I had done whatever I could to host him appropriately, including arranging meetings with the French chief of the navy staff, Admiral Coatena, as well as with Admiral Lanxade. The French government does not provide an exact counterpart for our service secretaries, so the protocol for calls during visits by a SECNAV to France is a little complicated. I had managed a visit to France for Secretary Ball in 1988, and I replicated the itinerary for this visit by Garrett.

I thought I had also cleared up any earlier misunderstandings with Admiral Bud Edney, who by now was wearing the CINCLANT/SACLANT hat in Norfolk. He, too, had come to Paris to meet with Marine Nationale leadership, and he had left confident that we had improved US and NATO relationships during his visit to France. The Marine Nationale's relationship to NATO's Atlantic commander has always been very important, and during the unsettled period in alliance politics described earlier, Adm. Edney's visit was helpful in reassuring that its long-standing arrangement of closer cooperation with NATO would endure, despite the uncertainties in European security.

I relieved Rear Admiral Nick Gee as COMCRUDESGRU 8 in August 1991 at sea and while embarked in the USS *Josephus Daniels* (CG-26), which was conducting counternarcotics operations in the Caribbean Sea and the eastern Pacific. My responsibility was command of the naval forces in Joint Task Force Four, engaged in drug interdiction operations. Command of the navy element (Task Group 4.1) was assigned to CRUDESGRU commanders in the Atlantic Fleet, who rotated in that assignment.

Our quarry was seaborne traffickers (for the most part Colombian) who were smuggling cocaine and marijuana in boats, aircraft, and even crude submarine vessels from South America to Puerto Rico and Florida, and through Mexico to California. I was familiar with the genesis and the details of these operations because I had helped to initiate them when I was working on the South Florida Task Force while assigned to the National Security Council (NSC) in 1982!

My goals as I took command were straightforward and based on my rather intimate feel for the challenges I would face while assigned to the largest of the six such cruiser-destroyer groups in the navy. There were three groups in the Atlantic Fleet and three in the Pacific Fleet, but CRUDESGRU 8 was by far the largest. Adm. Boorda, one of my predecessors, liked to brag that while he commanded the group in 1988–1989, it was "the fifth largest navy in the world" since he was responsible for fifty ships. By the time I arrived, there were only thirty-three cruisers, destroyers, frigates, and one battleship, all homeported in Norfolk, Virginia. I mention my predecessor because one aspect that made command of CRUDESGRU 8 most appealing was the record of successes earned by former commanders, including Admirals Metcalf, McCauley, Jeremiah, and Boorda. I knew all these gentlemen well because the two ships I had commanded in the previous decade, *Comte de Grasse* and *Yorktown*, had both been assigned to this group.

I was mindful that all these predecessors had attained higher rank and great responsibilities. I also knew the ship maintenance and repair business in the Tidewater area well, and I was very familiar with the fleet training and support establishment that serviced our ships. At bottom, the duty of the administrative commander in the fleet homeports was to see to the combat readiness and certification of the surface combatants assigned. I felt that I was well prepared for the task ahead.

My own experience in commanding two surface combatants had taught me that gauging the readiness of any single ship for combat at sea is a challenging task. The navy has always maintained an extensive array of inspections and certifications to ensure readiness, and moreover, there was a series of independent ship exercises meant to measure combat readiness in the primary mission areas of anti-submarine warfare (ASW), anti-air warfare (AAW), and surface warfare (SUW). Growing up professionally in this environment, I had come to appreciate that measuring readiness in these mission areas was indeed critical because they form the very basis of our profession and our raison d'être as cruiser-destroyermen. That said, as I took command, I felt that the individual ship exercises as they were administered in 1991 did not provide an adequate measure of the actual combat readiness of the surface combatants for which I was responsible.

The exercises meant to demonstrate proficiency always seemed to be canned and overly structured. Combat at sea is anything but. Moreover, because the exercise syllabus was scheduled well in advance, there was virtually no element of surprise. Knowing what was in the offing, ship commanding officers (COs) could arrange things so as to put their best foot forward at the time the exercises were observed by their superiors. It was, simply put, easy to game the system. Finally, given that each mission area was addressed separately, there was little by way of metrics to accurately gauge readiness across warfare areas. For example, could a ship conduct ASW while under air or missile attack? How ready was a single warship to conduct multi-ship operations in various multi-threat combat scenarios? These questions were a concern.

Upon our return from the Caribbean deployment, I decided to design a set of exercises to better assess combat readiness. I asked my staff to build scenarios and plans for short-notice, multi-ship exercises in the Virginia Capes Operating Areas that would provide advanced training in the three most important mission areas. And because multi-ship formations would require an officer in tactical command (OTC), I decided to use "major commanders," both destroyer squadron commanders and the

COs of the twelve cruisers assigned to the group, to serve as OTCs for the exercises we planned. The name chosen for the exercises we proposed was Fast Break. As we designed it, each exercise would feature four ships that were in port and in a matériel condition that mandated a four-hour readiness to be underway. This condition was the prescribed norm for all ships not in a repair or maintenance availability or other status that extended their readiness condition beyond four hours.

My staff would arrange for a submarine target to be available in one of the operating areas; a fast surface gunnery target would be available in another. We would then arrange for fighter aircraft from nearby Oceana Naval Air Station to provide both friendly fighters for ships to control and opposing (bogey) aircraft for air intercept training and for tracking and fire control simulation by our guided missile destroyers (DDGs) and cruisers. Where possible, we would arrange for the exercise units to be cleared for actual gunfire in an operating area, where they could conduct surface gunnery and anti-air gunnery against towed air targets or drones. When all the exercise services, area clearances, and target presentations had been scheduled and arranged, we would send a message to the designated OTC. To provide a margin of comfort, the participating ships were directed to be underway in eight hours (not four) after receiving warning of a Fast Break exercise. We also provided a task organization and a movement order for the participating units. The exact sequence of operations and the targets to be presented were provided only to the designated OTC.

The first Fast Break exercise was not a resounding success, inasmuch as two of the four ships tasked were not able to get underway because their engineering plants could not meet the eight-hour readiness for sea notice, never mind the four-hour notice that was actually prescribed. One of the ships that could not get underway (a nuclear-powered cruiser [CGN]) was commanded by a captain who had been designated as the OTC. I substituted a destroyer squadron commander to take charge of the exercise. The two ships that did get underway for the exercise profited from the experience, as did the commodore assigned as the OTC. The exercise and the services provided were enthusiastically acclaimed by the two COs, and both stated that they had found a better measure of their readiness in the primary mission areas.

One problem the exercise uncovered was that the four CGNs assigned to CRUSDESGRU 8 had been given dispensations from the usual readiness for sea requirements owing to the "special demands" imposed by their nuclear power plants. My superior at the time, Commander, Naval Surface Forces Atlantic (COMNAVSURFLANT), Vice Admiral Paul Reason, himself a nuclear-trained surface officer (a "surface nuke"), retained personal responsibility for the engineering readiness of the CGNs nominally assigned to my command. Adm. Reason was especially solicitous of his "nukes," and after the experience with this first exercise, he directed me not to include the CGNs in Fast Break exercises without his clearance. I assume he felt that I could not be appreciative of the challenges faced by the COs of CGNs or of the reasons for exceptions made in their case. If that was the logic, he was correct.

We did conduct several more of these exercises in the fall of 1991, but I concluded that the assumptions I had used in developing the exercises were somewhat ambitious. Before sending ships into unscheduled exercises, we needed to dig more deeply into each ship's actual readiness condition before sailing her, instead of assuming that readiness for sea and readiness in general were as reported. It seemed that while Fast Break may have been a good idea, its time had not come.

The bulk of my tenure as a group commander was taken up with ensuring that the twelve cruisers for whom I was the reporting senior were ready to deploy in every sense. This entailed careful monitoring of the inspections, shore training, and underway exercises by me and my very capable staff. It also required that my staff and I become familiar with the abilities and the needs of the COs, executive officers (XOs), and even the department heads of these cruisers. As to the frigates and destroyers, I was fortunate to have two superb readiness destroyer squadron commanders who reported to me and were responsible for overseeing the readiness of their assigned ships.[84]

In 1992, the navy's practice was to assign CRUDESGRU commanders and carrier group (CARGRU) commanders to operational command of the six battle groups in the Atlantic Fleet when deployed. The term "CARGRU commander" begs explanation because there were only six carriers in the Atlantic Fleet and there were four CARGRU commanders. The number of commands had something to do, I assume, with the aviation community's historical allotment of flag officers. In any case, three of the four CARGRUs and all three CRUDESGRUs served as battle group commanders during my tenure as Commander, Cruiser-Destroyer Group 8 (COMCRUDESGRU 8).[85]

A carrier battle group generally comprised the carrier, two to three cruisers, two to four destroyers and/or frigates, and two attack submarines. Each group also included a tactical destroyer squadron commander. In practice at the time, the CO of the carrier and the carrier air wing commander (CAG) reported to the battle group commander, regardless of whether the latter was

---

84 Readiness squadron commanders, DESRON TWO (steam-powered ships) and DESRON TEN (gas turbine-powered ships) did not deploy. Instead, they looked after the matériel readiness of their assigned ships.

85 The fourth CARGRU commander was designated the training coordinator for deploying carriers. That commander did not deploy.

a surface officer ("black shoe") or an aviator ("brown shoe"). In my case, the carrier assigned to COMCRUDESGRU 8 was the USS *Saratoga* (CV-60). The air wing embarked was CVW-17, which comprised nine squadrons: two F/A-18C *Hornets*, two F-14B *Tomcats*, one S-3B *Viking*, one A6-E *Intruder*, one EA-6B *Prowler*, one E2-C *Hawkeye*, and one SH-3G *Sea King*.

Now, the *Saratoga*, the oldest CV in service at the time, was a ship with a very checkered past. I had personally experienced several near collisions involving the *Saratoga* in my career. The first was in **Little Rock** in 1967, when a faulty communication and a mistake by the captain in command of our cruiser almost resulted in the **Little Rock** being cut in half while the carrier was conducting flight operations at thirty knots. The second near-miss occurred in November 1969, when I had the conn in the destroyer **C. H. Roan** while deployed to the Mediterranean. In that instance, after sunset and recovering the last aircraft for the day, the carrier attempted to rejoin a large formation including six destroyers by passing between the two lead destroyers in a circular "screen" on a reciprocal course and at high speed. After realizing the mistake in this approach, the *Saratoga* made a hard turn to port, immediately in front on our destroyer. We missed her by thirty yards while backing "emergency full!" Both incidents resulted in the relief of the captains of the cruiser and carrier, who had committed serious maneuvering errors. *Saratoga* had also collided with the USS **Waccamaw** (AO-109) in 1978 and had suffered a disastrous fire and later flooding in one of the engine rooms a few years before that. During the deployment preceding ours, twentyone *Saratoga* sailors had drowned when a rented liberty launch sank while the carrier was anchored off Haifa, Israel. The reader will appreciate that I felt somewhat star-crossed embarking in *Saratoga* as my flagship.

Of great concern to me as we began a series of pre-deployment inspections of the carrier was the poor condition of the engineering plant. *Saratoga*, or *Sara*, as she was affectionately known in the fleet, was powered by one of the first 1,200 PSI steam plants in the navy. In the thirty years since she had been placed in service, time had taken a huge toll. There were steam leaks and water leaks throughout the engineering plant, and there were serious fuel oil leaks that became painfully apparent during our deployment. As the date of our departure approached, I became increasingly concerned about engineering readiness. Then, almost miraculously, *Sara* passed her operational propulsion plant examination (OPPE), notwithstanding several uncorrected deficiencies that would have kept surface combatants with the same engineering problems alongside the pier.

The inspectors' reasoning was straightforward. Carrier deployments were (and remain) a critical concern because the navy makes force "commitments" to the unified commanders pursuant to decisions by the unified chain of command. There were no replacements for *Sara* in the master CV schedule, and so she was declared ready to deploy. I had taken a tough stand on the ship's engineering readiness and had stressed the need for command attention to the deficiencies noted. The CO, who by law was an aviator with limited ship engineering experience, felt that the attention that I was paying to "his" engineering department amounted to "micromanagement." He complained to his administrative commander, Commander Naval Air Force, Atlantic Fleet (COMNAVAIRLANT), to that effect. In addition, the messages I sent to that commander outlining my concerns were described to me as "unhelpful" and appeared to have been filed without comment. Conventionally powered carriers were held to very different engineering standards than cruisers and destroyers and certainly not to the standards of their nuclear-powered counterparts. But in the end, I had to accept that a marginally ready *Saratoga* would be the carrier and that the battle group would press ahead with preparations for deployment.

One of the pre-deployment milestones that I found particularly enjoyable and most educational for a "black shoe" was the movement of the entire carrier air wing to what was called "Strike University" at the Naval Air Station, Fallon, Nevada. The Strike Warfare Center at Fallon had been designed as a center of excellence for training an air wing in the rigors of planning and successfully executing bombing and missile attacks against targets ashore. It was established in 1985 at the insistence of Secretary John Lehman following the disastrous strike against Syrian forces during the Lebanon crisis in 1983.[86] The dedicated center was modeled after the "Top Gun" model at Miramar Naval Air Station where fighters and airborne early warning (AEW) aircraft trained for aerial combat.

I accompanied the air wing and members of my staff to Fallon, flying cross-country from Oceana Naval Air Station in the right seat of an A-6E *Intruder*. My intent was to better understand the principles, tactics, and other operational considerations that determined the success of air strikes. I took the opportunity to fly in every type of aircraft in CVW-17 while at Fallon. The F-14B, A-6E, EA-6B, and E-2C aircraft were configured for two or more crew, so finding a seat in these aircraft while training was easy. Both of our F/A-18C *Hornet* squadrons, however, were single-seat airplanes. To ensure that I witnessed the strike and tactical profiles optimized for the *Hornets*, I asked the commander of the light-attack community, my good friend Rear Admiral Jack Moriarty, to "loan" us a two-seat variant, the F/A-18D. He obliged, and I flew several strikes in the back

86 Lehman, *Winning the Cold War at Sea*, 328–332.

seat of an airplane flown by an instructor pilot who happened to be a Marine first lieutenant.

The week we spent at Fallon was exhilarating. Days were filled with strike planning sessions, live weapons deliveries, opposition by "hostile" fighters, and post-strike debriefs and critiques. The pace was brisk, and the days simulating combat operations ran from dawn to dusk. This may have been the most valuable piece of training for a battle group commander. Sadly, owing to a tragic mishap that befell another CRUDESGRU commander, Rear Admiral Jay Prout, some three years after I flew with the air wing, "black shoes" are no longer encouraged to fly in tactical aircraft while training.

The entire group did well in our final pre-deployment evaluation, the FLEETEX. The three cruisers assigned, USS *Thomas S. Gates* (CG-51), USS *Philippine Seas* (CG-58), and USS *Biddle* (CG-26) were commanded by accomplished captains who were proficient sailors and tacticians. Similarly, the destroyer squadron commander (COMDESRON 24) was a professional; the destroyers and frigates assigned to him were not lacking in readiness, and their performance at sea was solid and professional.

The two submarines assigned, USS *City of Corpus Christi* (SSN-705) and USS *Billfish* (SSN-676), were never really integrated into the group. As things stood in 1992, the submarine element remained under the operational control of the submarine operating authority. Although generally responsive to our tasking during training and while en route to the Mediterranean, once there, they often operated independently. To be frank, I was never exactly sure where they were after we joined the Sixth Fleet.

The carrier air wing was the heart of the battle group because it provided most of the offensive potential, and it was far and away the most visible element. I was fortunate to have CVW-17 embarked. It was a superbly well-balanced air wing. All nine squadrons were frontline assets. The F-14B aircraft of VF-74 and VF-103 were the latest variant of *Tomcat* in the Atlantic Fleet, and our A6-E squadron, VA-35, comprised nine brand-new *Intruders* and four vintage KA-6D tankers. Commanded by an experienced and exacting captain, the wing performed flawlessly during our deployment. In addition to the ships and aircraft assigned, we were also the first carrier battle group to embark a SEAL platoon from SEAL Team Eight.

Early in May 1992, we passed through the Strait of Gibraltar as scheduled, and I reported for duty to the then-Commander of US Sixth Fleet (COMSIXTHFLT), Vice Admiral Bill Owens. I had met Adm. Owens in Washington while he served on Admiral Trost's staff, and while I was with Secretary Ball, Adm. Owens had interviewed to head up the Department of the Navy's Office of Program Appraisal. A submariner by trade, Adm. Owens was highly regarded in the navy for his intelligence and outstanding performance, which ultimately led to four-star rank and as-signment as vice chairman of the JCS. It was not long, however, before I had a difficult encounter with him.

Shortly after arriving in the Mediterranean, Adm. Owens instructed me in a message to form a maritime action group (MAG), as he styled it,[87] and directed that I be prepared to detach a destroyer and submarine from our group to proceed on duties that he and his staff would assign. Furthermore, he directed me to assign Captain William "Woody" Sutton, the COMDESRON, to command the MAG. The logic for creating this separate and detached organization was to conduct a series of minor exercises with some of the smaller navies in the Mediterranean. Pursuant to his orders, I detached my former command, *Comte de Grasse*,

87 In NATO doctrine, there are provisions for a "surface action group" (SAG). The creation of a MAG, which included maritime air patrol and a submarine, however, was not a recognized tactical formation at the time.

the *Billfish*, and COMDESRON 24. The rump battle group remaining would be *Sara*, the cruisers, and one FFG, USS *Jack Williams* (FFG-24).

My problem with the MAG construct had to do with issues of command and control. Admiral Owens was instructing me to detach a group that would be tasked by him, while keeping me responsible for their operations and safety. I struggled with this construct and informed him by message of my concern. I explained that I did not feel that I could be responsible for ships under his operational control. Rules of engagement (ROE) and the direction of the group in the event of hostile action while in the vicinity of not-so-friendly littorals such as Algeria, the former Yugoslavia, and Libya came to mind. Admiral Owens was quick to respond to my message.

He sent his personal C-12 aircraft to Palma where *Saratoga* was conducting a port visit to fetch me. I flew to Naples, and to my surprise, as I descended from the airplane, he was on the tarmac to greet me and showed me onto his personal helicopter, where the rotors were already turning. Thirty minutes later, we were aboard his flagship, USS *Belknap* (CG-26), in Gaeta, Italy. After attending the admiral's morning brief, we repaired to his office with the chief of staff. The admiral was gracious in probing the basis for my concerns with his MAG concept. After listening carefully, he made it clear that the MAG would be formed and detached as he had directed. The only concession he made to address my concern about responsibility for operations in a crisis setting was that in the unlikely event of danger, he would immediately shift operational control of the MAG back to me. I took a deep breath while mulling over how I could help the MAG commander if he were distant from the carrier and already in harm's way with inadequate defenses.

I mention this experience to illustrate yet another instance in which senior naval officers had become accustomed to finessing what I felt were hard points in navy regulations and were indeed inconsistent with the principle of accountability while in command.

In the end, however, the MAG was short lived. Although Admiral Owens was COMSIXTHFLT, his superior was Adm. Boorda, a surface warfare officer, headquartered in Naples. Boorda told me of his discomfort with the construct, and he saw to it that the MAG as a separate task group in the Sixth Fleet was a short-lived experiment.

The first several months of our deployment featured rather routine operations and exercises with allied forces. One memorable set of exercises, named DASIX, pitted our F-14B fighters against French air forces in the Gulf of Lyon. This training was valuable for our fighter pilots because the Mirage 2000 fighter, then the mainstay of the French Air Force, was a formidable challenge in air-to-air combat. I took the opportunity to take the back seat of a *Tomcat* during one exercise. I had been in the second seat of the F-14B many times before, and I had learned the basics of operating the controls for the AWG-9 air intercept radar in earlier flights. As we hooked up to the catapult, I looked forward to testing my mettle as a radar intercept officer (RIO).

We were catapulted off the angle on a clear, sunlit afternoon and quickly climbed to about twenty thousand feet, assuming an orbit at our assigned Combat Air Patrol (CAP) station. After only a few minutes, a call came over the air control frequency from the E-2C, vectoring us to intercept a "bogey" inbound at high speed to the battle group. We made a hard turn and lit the after burners, pulling a lot of Gs in the process. The controller called the bogey as being on our "nose" at five nautical miles. I searched frantically with my head in the radar boot for the contact but could not see anything in the forward hemisphere. The pilot kept encouraging me, and growing more anxious by the minute, I looked up from the scope to see the Delta wing fighter in a sharp turn to starboard, less than a mile from us. The radar immediately locked on and we simulated firing a heat-seeking Sidewinder missile into his after burner. The Mirage was so stealthy that a head-on profile had not shown up on our radar, and the pilot explained that he had not gotten a "visual" until the aircraft had closed in to within a couple of thousand yards.

During the same exercise series, I accepted an invitation from the Marine Nationale to exercise our SEAL platoon in a combat search-and-rescue (SAR) exercise. The plan was to gauge the readiness of our battle group to extract a downed aircrew from enemy territory while engaged in offensive strike operations. Since air strikes on several inimical countries were in our contingency plans, we constructed a scenario that featured an Aegis cruiser and a submarine positioned twenty-five miles off the coast of southern France, holding the carrier fifty miles off the coast, with two cruisers and two destroyers providing local air defense and ASW support for the carrier. Before the *Philippine Sea* began moving to its station near the coast, the SEAL platoon embarked in the cruiser with their equipment.

While conducting simulated strikes against targets inland after sunset, we stationed two F-14B fighters in a CAP station under control of the *Philippine Sea* between the cruiser and the coast of France. Upon receipt of a simulated "aircrew down" in enemy territory, we flew one specially configured SH-3G from *Sara* to the *Philippine Sea*. Elements of the SEAL platoon embarked in the helicopter, and under fighter cover, the SEALs flew inland some thirty miles to "rescue" two pilots that we had prepositioned in a very rural setting north of Toulon. Using GPS and emergency beacons from the "downed" pilots, the SEALs established a security perimeter and extricated the pilots within minutes, returning them directly to the carrier via the SH-3. Because our strikes were "opposed" by French aircraft, the scenario took on an air of realism when a formation of French *Jaguars* attempted an airstrike against the carrier, and the intruding aircraft tried to mix with some of our strike aircraft that were returning to the carrier. They were successfully identified as intruders, "deloused," and designated "hostile" by the *Philippine Sea*. Accordingly, the aircraft were engaged and were simulation-"splashed" by missiles from the *Thomas Gates* before they could attack the carrier.

I felt the exercise had illustrated the real value of embarking special warfare experts to conduct combat SAR in the event of hostilities. Before this, there had not been any organic combat SAR capability in deployed carrier battle groups. The fate of our downed aircrew in Syria back in 1983 might have been different had we had such a capability in the *John F. Kennedy*. Reviewing a file drawer full of contingency plans that might have been executed during our deployment, I felt much better about our readiness in the event we were ordered to execute one of those plans.

Before I leave mention of the SEAL platoon, I would like to stress that the challenge was to provide frequent and realistic training for this very energetic group. We did succeed in providing imaginative tasking for them, including rappelling covertly onto our assigned replenishment tanker, parachuting with their rafts out of the C-2A *Greyhound* carrier-onboard-delivery (COD) aircraft, and conducting a variety of small boat insertion exercises while the carrier conducted port visits. At the deployment's end, the CO of SEAL Team 8 congratulated us for setting a precedent for future battle group-embarking SEAL platoons. I have an honorific SEAL paddle in my den that reads, *"Lead Scout for*

Naval Special Warfare and Carrier Battle Group Integration. Future Battle Groups now need only to follow the trail we've blazed. Much thanks for your support!"

* * *

Following exercises with the French, we enjoyed a favorite pastime of ships deployed to the Mediterranean: the group conducted a series of port visits in the South of France during the month of July. I took the opportunity to schedule a port visit to Villefranche for the **Thomas Gates**, commanded by Captain Chip Boyd, and I broke my flag in his ship so that I could participate in this visit. As mentioned earlier, I was very familiar with Villefranche, having visited many times while in command of my own ships. The mayor in 1992 was still Joseph Calderoni, my great friend of ten years standing and a much-decorated hero of the French Resistance in World War II. Because we were in port for our Independence Day celebration, **Thomas Gates** hosted a magnificent champagne reception on the flight deck for the mayor and more than one hundred citizens of "Ville." Our guests were most appreciative, expressing their fondness and admiration for our country and our navy.

Meanwhile, *Saratoga*, anchored off Sete, was awaiting clearance to begin a weeklong visit to Cannes. This port visit was special because we would be in Cannes during the July 14 Bastille Day celebration. We were even asked to provide marching units of sailors and Marines for the municipal parade through the city. At the "sunset parade" hosted in *Saratoga* the day prior, I had taken the opportunity to invite General Maurice Schmitt, the former chief of the General Staff, whom I had befriended in Paris and who was now retired in the South of France. We also hosted many senior French military personnel, including the commander of the Mediterranean Fleet and the commander of French air forces in Provence.

The next phase of our deployment brought us into the Adriatic Sea, where we would spend the better part of August and September conducting flight operations off the coasts of Italy and the former Yugoslavia. Hostilities were already underway between the Croats and the Serbs, and the extension of the conflict to Bosnia-Herzegovina had just begun.

The stated logic for this movement into troubled waters was "to underline our concern" over the situation in the former Yugoslavia. Our passage through the Strait of Otranto marked the first for a US aircraft carrier since June 1951, when the *Coral Sea* had ventured into the Adriatic to embark the Yugoslav leader Marshall Tito for a demonstration of carrier airpower.[88] Our tasking was to conduct "routine" operations, including airborne surveillance of the eastern littoral by our camera-equipped F-14Bs. When night fell and we were able to observe from our ships the coastline between Montenegro in the south to Croatia in the north, we could see fires and explosions. It was a tragic testament of the disintegration of the former Yugoslavia. On one occasion, flying parallel to the coast of Croatia in an F14B aircraft from VF-104, I observed what looked like a river of fire running down the side of a small mountain in Croatia. It was clear that a flammable liquid load was being poured onto a village on the coast from the hill above. The incident provided graphic evidence of the horrors visited on civilians during this civil war.

After we had been in the Adriatic a few weeks, Serbian Air Force fighters began reacting to our surveillance flights. We took great care to remain twelve nautical miles or more from the coast,

88 Dur, *The Sixth Fleet: A Case Study*, 31.

but at one point our embassy in Belgrade forwarded complaints to the State Department and US Commander in Chief Europe (USCINCEUR) alleging that *Saratoga*'s aircraft had violated Serbian airspace. Fortunately, we had Aegis-generated tracks of all our flight activity and could prove convincingly that no flight had violated Serbian airspace. In addition, we maintained a watchful eye and a vigilant watch for Serbian submarines and coastal patrol vessels. The combat systems in our surface combatants, submarines, and on *Saratoga* were manned and ready for action at Condition THREE. (This readiness condition, which I directed on all ships while operating in the Adriatic, figured prominently in a tragic incident in the Aegean somewhat later.) On several occasions, we encountered Serbian and Croatian patrol vessels, although there were no resulting incidents.

While in the Adriatic, we received a special assignment that proved to be a bonus for both of our F-14B squadrons. Our intelligence community was interested in gauging the altitudes at which our fighters could be detected by space-based infrared sensors when operating in after burner. To that end, we received a generous increase in the fuel allotted to our fighter squadrons to cover the significantly higher expenditures that were required due to extraordinarily long periods of flying with after burners lighted. On the final night of a three-day exercise, I decided to ride in the back seat of an F-14B piloted by one of the more senior officers in VF-74. We were catapulted off *Saratoga*, proceeded to a designated point a few miles from the carrier, and began a nose up climb to about forty thousand feet with the burners powering our vertically ascending aircraft. We attained a speed considerably greater than Mach 1. On reaching the designated altitude, the pilot leveled the airplane and began a slow roll. As we alternated between horizontal flight and inverted horizontal flight, the bright lights of the Italian coast and the comparatively dim lights of the Croatian coast contrasted with the starlit canopy of the Adriatic sky. Witnessing this exhilarating spectacle, I could only exclaim, "WOW!" The pilot then called out to me on the intercom: "Hey, Admiral, what do you think your 'black shoe' buddies are doing tonight?" Whatever "they" were doing could not match what this "black shoe" was experiencing.

During our time in the Adriatic, we frequently replenished fuel and consumables from our assigned logistic support ship, the USS *Detroit* (AOE-4). *Saratoga* also conducted port visits to Trieste in the northernmost reaches of the Adriatic Sea. The surface combatants were scheduled for port visits to Venice. These interludes provided us a wonderful opportunity to rest and maintain our ships in ports rarely visited by US warships deployed to the Mediterranean. Trieste, which had been a flashpoint between Italy and Yugoslavia in the early days of the Cold War, is a beautiful city. Although not well known to Americans, the city had been the most important naval base for the Austro-Hungarian Navy before World War I. Personally, I spent some quality time ashore visiting castles, museums, and monuments dating back to the Austro-Hungarian period. I also rented a car and took a quick day trip to Slovenia to have a look at the breeding farm in Lipica that is home to the famous Lipizzaner horses of the Vienna Riding School. Slovenia seemed quite a contrast to the rest of the former Yugoslavia: peaceful, serene, and almost bucolic.

We left the Adriatic in late September 1992 and transited east into the Aegean Sea, where the battle group conducted port visits to several Greek islands. *Saratoga* spent five days in Rhodes, the historic Greco-Turkish island. The visits were preparatory to the battle group's participation as an element in the defending "Brown" force in exercise Display Determination. The exercise scenario had my task force (TF-60) operating as a covering force for the amphibious landing force (TF-61) that would conduct a landing exercise to put US Marines ashore in Saros Bay in northern Turkey. The "Brown" force would be opposed by "Green" forces, including Greek air forces and a collection of NATO surface combatants, including Spanish, Turkish, and Italian ships. During the exercise, Commander in Chief, Allied Forces Southern Europe (CINCSOUTH), Adm. Boorda, in his NATO hat as the officer conducting the exercise (OCE), sent a message to all the players just before the beginning of Phase Two, the opposed transit to the Amphibious Objective Area. In that message, he encouraged "aggressive play" from the onset of Phase Two. He repeated his disappointment with the "slow pace and passive conduct" of all the participants in the first phase. (As we were the defenders in Phase One, I took his criticism to be directed at the Green forces.)

Nonetheless, I took careful note of the admiral's admonishments, and as the exercise was set to begin at the stroke of midnight of October 2, my staff developed a targeting plan to simulate "hits" on all the Green ships in the first minutes of live action. The objective was to preempt any Green attacks on the carrier. To that end, we had dispatched our surveillance assets during the period between phases to detect and localize the Green ships just before the beginning of Phase Two. This activity was not prohibited by the rules, and it provided us with intelligence in the period between hostilities.

As it happened, a few minutes before midnight and the opening of "hostilities," a column of Green surface ships came over the horizon within visual range, overtaking *Saratoga* and *Thomas Gates*. *Gates* had been tasked to simulate engagements of all five Green ships in the column with standard SM-2 missiles and gunfire. While *Gates* was in the process of engaging the Green forces, the commander on watch in *Sara*'s combat decision center (CDC) came into flag plot as I was receiving results of the engagements by *Gates.* The officer in charge of the CDC requested permission to participate by simulating attack on the same combatants, who were now less than three miles away. These units had already been reported as "hits" by *Thomas Gates.* I replied to the watch officer that if the carrier chose to exercise weapons teams and to simulate attacks with NATO Sea Sparrow missiles for training purposes, I did not object.

What happened next was as unexpected as it was tragic. The carrier's watch team had awakened the NATO Sea Sparrow missile crew and ordered an immediate engagement of one of the Green ships on the visual horizon. The sailors responsible for maintaining and operating the missile battery on the carrier had been ready for "real" engagements of threats to the ship had they materialized in the preceding weeks while operating off the coast of the former Yugoslavia. After hurrying to their missile station, these young sailors were mistakenly given orders from the watch officer in CDC to "arm and tune" the missiles. The watch team, made up of poorly trained junior officers, did not understand the terminology they were using. To "arm and tune" required putting missiles in a ready position. The petty officers at the missile station even asked if this was a "real" engagement. After being told that the engagement was "real world," they assumed that they had been instructed to fire missiles at the target their radar had acquired, the Turkish destroyer *Muavenet.*

It is painful to recall the colossal tragedy that ensued. Although I was officially absolved of responsibility for what happened, I live with the thought of whether I should have denied the permission *Saratoga*'s watch officer sought.

Two of *Saratoga*'s missiles impacted the bridge of the destroyer, killing the captain and four others on watch, and causing a fire that burned for what seemed to be an hour. I ran up to my flag bridge to get a visual understanding of what had happened. I immediately terminated the exercise and ordered the carrier to employ airborne helicopters to evacuate any *Muavenet* wounded to the *Saratoga*'s sick bay. I also directed the *Thomas Gates* to close the Turkish ship and render assistance in extinguishing the fires.

With exercise play terminated, we spent the remainder of the night and well into the next day rendering assistance. We also prepared for a visit from the chief of the Turkish Navy. The following afternoon, we held a memorial service in the carrier's hangar bay, with senior Turkish admirals in attendance. As it happened, we had one of the first Muslim navy chaplains assigned to the staff. He conducted the service with appropriate readings from the Koran, standing just behind the five Turkish flag-draped coffins. In the late afternoon, a C-2A COD aircraft landed aboard *Saratoga*, and we loaded the deceased into the aircraft for the flight to Ankara. The wounded in *Saratoga*'s sick bay were treated by the carrier's doctors until they were deemed able to transfer to Turkish hospitals.

The following morning, Adm. Boorda and Vice Admiral Joe Lopez, who had relieved Admiral Owens as COMSIXTHFLT, came aboard, and we flew to Ankara to attend formal funeral services for the fallen. It was a difficult moment, to say the least.

What followed was a testament to Adm. Boorda's leadership and experience managing significant incidents and accidents. He had my immediate superior, Vice Admiral Lopez, appoint a formal board to investigate the circumstances surrounding the incident and the actions taken by those in positions of responsibility. Three US rear admirals embarked in *Sara* two days after the accident to conduct the formal investigation. They included an expert in missile systems, a surface warfare officer, and a naval aviator. The board included a Turkish flag officer so that Turkish authorities could observe the procedures, processes, and results of the investigation. I found it curious that the Turkish admiral was keenly interested to know the names of those responsible for the missile launch. Apparently, he wanted to know if there were any Greek or Armenian Americans on watch with responsibilities on that fateful night.

At the beginning of the investigation and a preliminary review of what had led to the inadvertent missile firings, the CO of *Saratoga*, the commander on watch in *Saratoga*'s CDC, and several other watch officers were designated as "interested parties." Others even remotely connected to the event were scheduled for interviews. Naturally, I was read my rights and interviewed, as were several other members of my staff, including the operations officer and the officers of my staff on watch at the time of the incident. The board did not find fault with my actions and decisions nor with those of my staff. The findings confirmed that the cause was poor training of the watch team aboard the carrier. All the other activity in *Saratoga* and in our battle group seemed almost surreal while the investigation progressed over several days. We finally resumed exercise play, which included an opposed transit of the carrier out of the narrow waters of the Aegean.

When in open waters again, we received word of an unrelated investigation, which would weigh heavily on the embarked air wing and all of us in *Saratoga*. This was the DOD Inspector General's second investigation into the 1991 Tailhook Convention and the incidents resulting therefrom. As directed, we had reported earlier that some seventy-nine of the eighty-six officers assigned to CVW-17 staff and all the assigned squadrons had attended the convention. A number had previously been interviewed during the navy's own investigation of the scandal. None of those in attendance from our air wing had been formally charged with wrongdoing by the navy investigators.

With the arrival of the DOD team, a group of more than ten civilian lawyers, the situation aboard *Saratoga* became rather tense. Several who had attended the convention were reportedly offered immunity if they could or would implicate others who had engaged in conduct "unbecoming an officer and a gentleman" and therefore prosecutable under the Uniformed Code of Military Justice (UCMJ). The buzz in the carrier's wardrooms and in the squadron ready rooms was one of concern and disgust. It was certainly not conducive to an environment in which pilots could be tasked to conduct "normal" carrier flight operations.[89]

On the recommendation of my chief of staff and the carrier air wing commander, I sent a message to COMSIXTHFLT, requesting an immediate schedule change for TF-60. Specifically, I requested permission to delay the start of a planned exercise with the Israeli Air Force and to proceed to a training anchorage and a "stand down" until the DOD investigators had finished their interviews. When the team left the ship, they did not report or charge any of our aviators of misdeeds at the convention. Later, we learned that Commander Bob Stumpf, one of our former squadron commanders and easily the most highly regarded "stick" in VFA-83, who had already detached with orders to command the prestigious Blue Angels, had been charged with conduct "unbecoming." Stumpf refused to accept nonjudicial proceedings or admiral's mast and insisted instead on a court martial, which ultimately acquitted him of all charges. After overcoming strenuous objections from several senators who blocked approval and confirmation of his selection by two captain selection boards, Commander Stumpf was finally promoted to captain. He had lost command of the Blue Angels,

89 For a complete and critical account of the Navy and DOD investigations into Tailhook '91, see Robert L. Beck, *Inside the Tailhook Scandal: A Naval Aviator's Story* (Meadville, PA: Fulton Books, 2016).

had been suspended from flight duty, and had been parked in a nonjob while awaiting trial. I was not surprised that Bob Stumpf chose to retire and instead went to work as an airline pilot. His case underlined for me the vindictiveness of certain members of Congress determined to ruin the reputations of a variety of those connected with the convention, ultimately including the SECNAV and the Chief of Naval Operations (CNO).

The remainder of *Saratoga*'s deployment and the battle group's trip home were, thankfully, less eventful. We returned for one more stint in the Adriatic as Serbian and Bosnian Serb offensives against Croatia and Bosnia continued. As before, our presence there, in support of new US sanctions against Serbia, was intended to demonstrate US concern. The effect was not apparent. The press reports from Washington regarding our presence in the Adriatic and the conflict seemed equivocal and confusing. As instructed, we did maintain immediate readiness to conduct strikes against Serbian air and navy facilities. We also undertook a plan to coordinate with the amphibious task group and the embarked Marine Expeditionary Unit (MEU) should we be required to conduct a humanitarian mission or the evacuation of US and allied citizens threatened by the civil war raging in the former Yugoslavia. We also conducted one final visit to the beautiful city of Trieste before turning over our responsibilities in the Adriatic in November to the *John F. Kennedy* battle group. On returning from deployment, my staff and I disembarked *Saratoga* and we flew home to Norfolk, where I resumed my duties as a full-time cruiser-destroyer group commander.

There was a lot of catching up to do after an absence of six months. While we had monitored progress in the state of readiness of units assigned to the group of the cruisers and the battleship and the USS *Wisconsin* (BB-62), all assigned to CRUDESGRU 8, as well as the destroyer squadrons DESRON

2 and DESRON 10, it was now necessary to delve back into the readiness of the ships preparing for deployment. It was also time to prepare for significant changes in the organization of the Atlantic Fleet and the changing responsibilities of commanders such as myself. It would not be long before the three cruiser-destroyer groups and the four carrier groups in the Atlantic Fleet would be disestablished and their commanders relieved of administrative responsibilities for ships. Instead, there would be six battle groups under the command of either a surface warfare officer or an aviator, and they would be responsible for the carriers, air wings, and cruisers on a full-time basis. A destroyer squadron commander would be assigned responsibilities for the battle group's destroyers. Thankfully, this change in a historic organization model occurred after my watch. I, for one, am convinced that the reorganization and the disestablishment of "administrative" commands such as the CRUDESGRUs has contributed to the marked decline in the matériel condition and the training readiness of our surface ships.

In the summer of 1993, before my relief as COMCRUDESGRU 8, my staff and I made one more short deployment to the Caribbean, embarked in the USS *Mississippi* (CGN-40), with responsibilities for naval ships and aircraft engaged in counter-narcotics operations. Included in this deployment were meetings with the Colombian Navy in Cartagena to urge improvements in the interdiction of maritime traffic originating in the Guajira Peninsula of Colombia. We also transited the Panama Canal and operated in the eastern Pacific area of concern, making stops in Balboa, formerly in the US-controlled Canal Zone. There, we met with the commander of the Southern Command. I had not been in Panama since my father's assignment as the US consul in Colón. I was amazed at the changes on the Atlantic side of the isthmus since the disestablishment of the "Zona" and the transfer of control to the Republic of Panama. What had been the zone and its well-kept subdivisions, schools, and recreational facilities were now trashed and overgrown. It was hardly recognizable. It resembled a third world ghetto.

While on the Pacific side of the isthmus, I took the opportunity to call on and visit with a childhood friend, "Pancho" Motta, and his father. The Mottas had been a prominent family in Colón in the mid1950s. Pancho's dad was an important businessman who owned multiple businesses. By 1993, the Mottas had moved to Panama City and their wealth had grown exponentially. Pancho was by then a principal in the operation of Panama's duty-free zone. It was fun in any event, reminiscing about our boyhoods and hearing the story of Panama's emergence as a performing Latin America economy and a model for development in the Caribbean. I listened to their proud account but could not help contrasting it with what I had seen on the other side of the isthmus.

There remained one additional operational task before my change of command. My good friend and mentor since our days in OP-603, Adm. Hank Mauz, now the commander in chief of the Atlantic Fleet, gave me one more memorable assignment. In July 1993, a Russian task group comprising a cruiser and two destroyers transited to the western Atlantic to conduct the first, and only, combined exercise with a comparably sized US Navy task group. I was the responsible US commander embarked in the USS *Gettysburg* (CG-64). My counterpart was none other than the commander of the once-formidable Russian Northern Fleet, Admiral Oleg Alexandrovich Erofeev, embarked in a *Slava*-class cruiser. Looking back, there is a certain irony in the fact that after participating in what was arguably the last incident of the Cold War, I led the US group in what was the only combined US–Russian naval exercise during the thaw in US-Russian relations.

Following a rendezvous at sea, while steaming for three days in formation, we conducted a series of basic exercises, including surface gunnery, small boat and helicopter transfers, and basic maneuvers.

I was also given one last assignment by the fleet commander rather unrelated to my duties as a group commander. Admiral Mauz and I had commiserated over the impending prospect of a reduction in the size of the navy because the administration planned to reap a "peace dividend" by cutting defense budgets after the Cold War. He was determined to show that the navy should be the guarantor—the insurer—of our economic vitality and thus exempt the fleet from the drastic reductions under discussion in Washington. My assignment was to write a paper that made the case. After some research, I estimated the fraction of international commerce borne in ships on an annual basis and calculated the fraction of GDP represented by this seaborne commerce. This admittedly crude measure might serve as one argument that the size of the navy's budget should be tied to the value of national wealth the navy protected. I cautioned that my rough estimations on which the argument was based were subject to expert confirmation. Admiral Mauz enjoyed my paper and encouraged me to extend it. (In my next assignment, I commissioned a study by the Center for Naval Analyses that refined and elaborated the case.) Alas, while successive navy leaders have made traditional arguments about protecting freedom of the seas, the notion of tying the *value* of commerce to the means to protect it has not been advanced. Contemporary arguments for a larger fleet reflect a fixation with discrete competitors and joint "war fighting." They lack the permanence of Mahan's case for sea power, valid in any era and in the face of any challenge to our command of the seas.

The series of memorable experiences in what was my last at-sea assignment ended in August 1993, when I relinquished command of both CRUDESGRU 8 and the *Eisenhower* battle group to Admiral Hal Gheman. Because my flagship, the *Eisenhower,* was in the shipyard undergoing an overhaul, I chose to conduct the change of command in "the Battlecruiser," *Yorktown.* I used a pier reserved generally for cruisers and destroyers, immediately opposite my shore headquarters. The only other vessel on the pier that morning was my first command, the *Comte de Grasse.* Both ships were "dressed," immaculate in appearance and decked out with ceremonial signal flags, and their crews in dress white uniforms. CVW-17 conducted a flyover with the mix of jets I had while aboard *Saratoga.* All in all, it was a spectacular setting. I remember before the ceremony during my meeting with Captain Mike Mullen, a future CNO and Chairman of the Joint Chiefs of Staff (CJCS), who was then commanding *Yorktown,* I said to him, "Mike, I really appreciate the effort you and your crew have made to provide a memorable setting for what is probably an early retirement ceremony." He looked at me quizzically and asked, "Why do you feel that way?" I explained, presciently as it turned out, that the *Muavenet* tragedy had "probably complicated any opportunity for another command at sea."

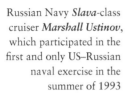

Russian Navy *Slava*-class cruiser *Marshall Ustinov*, which participated in the first and only US–Russian naval exercise in the summer of 1993

Russian cruiser *Marshall Ustinov* and my flagship *Gettysburg*, 1993

Russian helix helicopter preparing to land aboard *Gettysburg*, 1993

Donald Rumsfeld introduces me to his predecessor, Robert McNamara, April 1995

CHAPTER 14

PUTTING IT ALL TOGETHER

Office of the Chief of Naval Operations, Director, Strategy Division and Assistant Deputy Chief of Naval Operations (Plans, Policy and Operations)

Following the change of command in Norfolk, I drove north to my home in Washington and took several weeks of leave before reporting for duty at the Pentagon. The job assigned to me was director of the Naval Strategy Division in the Office of the Chief of Naval Operations (OPNAV), N-51. This had once been considered among the most important positions on the navy staff. My predecessors in this job when it was still known as OP-60 included several Chiefs of Naval Operations (CNOs) (Admiral David McDonald and Admiral George Anderson) as well as Vice Admiral James Stockdale.

This, however, was clearly not the assignment I had asked for after leaving command of my battle group. Instead, I had hoped for orders to command a numbered fleet, specifically the Sixth Fleet. Before I received these orders, I had communicated my preferences to Vice Admiral Ronald "Zap" Zlatoper, the chief of naval personnel, as well as to Admiral Mike Boorda, who was still in Naples as Commander in Chief US Naval Forces Europe (CINCUSNAVEUR). Adm. Zlatoper was not optimistic, and Adm. Boorda cautioned me to "sit tight" and to take my posting as N-51 "gracefully." Accordingly, on July 10, 1993, I relieved the incumbent, Rear Admiral Scott Redd (who "fleeted up" to be the assistant deputy CNO [N3B/5B]). Somewhat grudgingly, I settled into a familiar routine of working on strategy papers and policy options for the N-3/5, the DCNO for Plans, Policy and Operations, Admiral Leighton "Snuffy" Smith, and the CNO, Admiral Frank Kelso.

In one of my early calls on my seniors, Admiral Stan Arthur, it was explained to me in a rather direct manner that my quest for a numbered fleet command had been premature. Admiral Arthur had always been a friend, and I had gotten to know him well when I was in the secretary of the navy's (SECNAV) office. I suspect that my run-ins with senior aviators while in command of the *Saratoga* battle group had contributed to what was a rather frosty reception from the Vice Chief of Naval Operations (VCNO), then the "dean" of naval aviation.

When I had been on the job for only a few weeks, an exciting opportunity came our way in the strategy division. The most recent naval strategy concept, "From the Sea," published in 1992, advanced a new concept following the collapse of the Soviet Union and after Desert Storm. With no putative enemies to challenge us at sea and with a major conflict with Russia and the countries of the former Soviet Union now a seeming impossibility, the navy was now determined to justify using carriers and precision long-range cruise missiles as principal means to deliver power from the sea in a joint campaign. This rather straightforward and time-honored argument for carriers was clearly intended to protect what remained of the carrier force against budget cuts being labeled as "peace dividends."

As the prompt defeat of Iraq had shown, and notwithstanding the "tanker wars" with the Iranian Revolutionary Guards, one significant shortcoming of the "From the Sea"strategic concept was that the document discounted the peacetime value of naval forces operating *forward* in strategic ocean areas. Forward presence as an instrument of deterrence and crisis management was a mission set that was not adequately addressed in "From the Sea."

In addition, Marine Corps strategists believed that the contribution of deployed Marine forces in amphibious assault shipping had also been discounted in what the corps considered a "blue suit" navy document, and not a "naval" strategic concept. In fact, the failure to assign more credit to the Marine Corps and to amphibious lift in "From the Sea" may well have been the result of the navy's experience in Desert Storm. Although the United States feigned an amphibious assault on Iraqi positions in Kuwait, this was apparently never seriously contemplated by the Joint Chiefs of Staff (JCS) or General Schwarzkopf, the coalition commander in Desert Storm. I remember discussing prospects for combined amphibious assault with the French chief of the General Staff, General Schmitt, in the month before offensive ground operations were launched. He told me in strict confidence that General Powell had made clear to him that there would be no amphibious assaults from the sea.[90] That was news to me at the time, as I had been working hard to enlist the French in coalition planning for an amphibious assault in Kuwait.

As a result of the Marine Corps' unhappiness with the strategic concept put forth in "From the Sea" and after an emphatic push from the SECNAV, James Dalton, and his undersecretary, Richard Danzig, the navy and Marine Corps staff were formally

90 Powell allegedly told Schmitt, "We will not do an Okinawa." See Schmitt, *De Dien Bien Phu a Koweit City*, 205.

tasked by the secretary to prepare a sequel to "From the Sea" to address some of the aforenamed deficiencies.

Among the first initiatives we undertook to refine the department's thinking on the importance of the presence mission was a "presence" workshop, conducted at the direction of the secretary. To that end, I asked my old branch, N-513 (formerly OP-603, Strategy and Concepts), led by then-Captain (later Vice Admiral) Joseph Sestak, to begin preparing the workshop. It was held in Quantico, Virginia, at the Marine Corps base. Not surprisingly, the conclusions reached were, in sum, that naval presence was still a legitimate mission and vitally important to preserving US influence in Europe and Asia.

It was also apparent to me and to others that absent a peer competitor at sea, unless the navy and Marine Corps returned to stressing the value of deployed naval forces and forward presence both in periods of relative peace and in crisis situations, arguments important to maintaining our force structures would be seen as weak—the leadership of the army and even the Joint Staff clearly appeared content with the reduced emphasis on the importance of the navy's presence in situations short of war. Some of the navy's critics were also using "From the Sea" to downplay the relative "war winning" contribution of naval forces in their power projection role during Desert Storm, thereby reducing their priority in the hierarchy of the future needs of the "Joint Force."

In addition to arguments within the DOD, there was the matter of the direction the DOD had received from Congress in 1992 to conduct a comprehensive reexamination of the roles and missions of the armed services. This review was intended to address alleged issues of redundancies in force structure as well as opportunities for reallocation of resources to fund roles and missions that were arguably underresourced (e.g., special warfare forces). The navy and Marine Corps staffs rightly saw this congressional review as a clear and present danger. The number of ships, aircraft, and personnel in 1993 and the modernization of the principal elements of naval power were clearly at risk.

As I was taking up my responsibilities as N-51 and as a member of the newly established Roles, Requirements and Resources Board (R3B) in OPNAV, the sizing algorithms for the DOD in 1993 were to calculate the forces required to prosecute two major regional conflicts (MRCs) simultaneously. One MRC was a Middle East conflict with Iraq; the other was a major Asian contingency (i.e., Korea). After Desert Storm, and especially with the collapse of the Warsaw Pact toward the end of 1992, the Bush administration had ordered the services to take a hard look at the size and composition of their forces, with a view to reducing the DOD budget. The stated objective was to exact a "peace dividend." As a result, knives were being sharpened in relation to all service programming and budget directorates, and so major efforts were undertaken by each service to protect the most important programs and elements of force structure. Adding congressional pressure to the climate in the DOD made for a crisis atmosphere in the Pentagon.

In sum, the operative assumption driving budget considerations were that victory in Desert Storm, the collapse of the Soviet Union, and the increasing scrutiny of Congress required the navy and Marine Corps to preemptively reduce the costs attached to maintaining the "Cold War force." This logic applied a fortiori to "support" forces. The tactical imperative was to recapitalize and replace obsolescent systems with modern intelligence sensors, robust communications, and precision munitions. These were tall orders for the R3B, to say the least. As mentioned, concern explicit in the contrarian direction from the secretariat to emphasize requirements for forward presence as a critical mission of the navy–Marine Corps team was one that I shared.

Participating in the deliberations of the R3B with representatives of all the OPNAV codes and debating priorities on resource allocations, I found myself increasingly at odds with arguments made by representatives of the programming and budgeting directorate (N-8) being led by Vice Admiral Bill Owens, who was also the chairman of the R3B. From the perspective of plans and policy, we were cutting and decommissioning critical elements of the force structure such as cruisers, destroyers, logistics ships, and aircraft squadrons; all were essential to maintaining and sustaining the level of our naval presence in the Pacific, Atlantic, and Mediterranean. Although Admiral Owens claimed to recognize the importance of that very mission, which he had come to appreciate while serving as Commander of US Sixth Fleet (COMSIXTHFLT), he was determined to apply cuts to forces we in N3/5 felt were required to support the presence mission. Managing the R3B with typical determination and politely dismissing contrarian views with a "wave off," Admiral Owens had his way. Draconian cuts were made.

At this time, I was able to gain the support of seniors in OPNAV, including the VCNO and my boss, Admiral Smith, to charter and fund a Naval Presence Symposium in conjunction with the Edmund A. Walsh School of Foreign Service at Georgetown University. With the support of Dr. Charles Kupchan, the dean of that highly respected school, we assembled more than fifty representatives of academia, policy think tanks such as the Brookings Institution, the State Department, and Washington-based representatives of allied navies.

The three-day symposium was designed to discuss the importance of forward naval presence from a foreign policy or diplomatic perspective. The discussions were animated, and the points of view varied. Most speakers were supportive of our objectives to gain more recognition for the contribution of deployed naval forces in the furtherance of foreign policy and diplomatic objectives.

Some critical voices, representing institutions such as Brookings and the Center for Strategic and International Studies (CSIS), argued that although the presence of naval forces abroad mattered, the exact composition and capabilities they incorporated were less important. Representatives of the foreign navies attending also debated the issue at length.

Our argument regarding capabilities inherent in forward deployed forces was that expert and informed perceptions of the capabilities in a deployed force were roughly proportional to the influence the force had on diplomacy and policy objectives. We argued that this was especially true during periods of crisis and heightened tension. (I will note in passing that the crown prince and now the king of Spain, Felipe, and his cousin Prince Pavlos, pretender to the Greek throne, who were both students at Georgetown at the time and participating, expressed their support in the exchanges on the impact and importance of strong and capable naval forces in a peacetime presence role.)

In short, we argued that emphasis on credible and capable forces was as critical a consideration as presence itself. We were determined to convince skeptical audiences in the navy, in the DOD, and in Congress that absent *credible* deployed forces in peacetime, we did not have a useful measure of adequacy for sizing and configuring the navy and Marine Corps for an uncertain future.

As things turned out, many of the arguments developed during these workshops and symposia, and in a series of strategic war games we conducted in 1993–1994, were ultimately useful in the development and approval of a new strategic concept for the Navy Department, "Forward...From the Sea."

That revised statement of the navy and Marine Corps strategic concept was only issued to update the power-projection-in-wartime arguments advanced in "From the Sea" and was not intended to replace it; the navy and Marine Corps leadership recognized a parallel need to elaborate on the enduring utility of capable naval forces in times of peace and as instruments of crisis management—in other words, in situations short of major conflicts. The following excerpts from the document are pertinent:

> Forward...From the Sea addresses these naval contributions to our national security. Most fundamentally, our naval forces are designed to fight and win wars. Our most recent experiences, however, underscore the premise that the most important role in naval forces in situations short of war is to be **engaged** in forward areas with the objectives of **preventing** conflicts and **controlling** crisis. [Emphases added]
>
> Naval forces thus are the foundations of peace time forward presence operations and oversees response to crisis. They contribute heavily during transition from crisis to conflict and to compliance with terms of peace. At the same time, the unique capabilities inherent in naval expeditionary forces have never been in higher demand from US theater commanders.

One paragraph in the strategic concept earned pointed criticism from a future army four-star general:

> A US warship is sovereign US territory whether in a port of a friendly country or transiting international straits and high seas. US naval forces operating from highly mobile "sea bases" in forward areas are therefore free of

the political encumbrances that may inhibit and otherwise limit the scope of land-based operations in forward theaters. The latter consideration is a unique characteristic and advantage of forward deployed naval forces. In many critical situations, US naval forces alone provide theater commanders with a variety of flexible options—including precise measures to control escalation…to respond quickly and appropriately to fast breaking developments at the operational and tactical levels.

The reaction of then-Lieutenant General Wesley Clark (a future Supreme Allied Commander Europe [SACEUR]), who held the position as the strategy director, J5, on the Joint Staff was telling. After the navy and Marine Corps had published "Forward…From the Sea," he stopped me in one of the passageways in the Joint Staff area of the Pentagon and asked, "What in the hell are you and the Marines trying to do—undo Goldwater-Nichols?" I replied, "Not at all, General. Merely trying to underline the unique capability of forward deployed naval forces." In reply, he grunted, "Whatever."

My Marine counterpart while working the revised strategic concept was Major General Tom Wilkerson. We collaborated closely for more than a year, advancing the arguments for the unique and enduring importance of deployed naval forces. This included several briefings in Washington and beyond. Our work was the entrée into the "roles and missions" effort mandated by Congress, which became critically important in the fall of 1994. It seemed to be even more critical because the staff director of the Congressional Commission on Roles and Missions was none other than Michael Leonard, a long-standing critic of naval forces, both navy and Marine Corps, when he had served in the Program Analysis and Evaluation (PA&E) Directorate of the Office of the Secretary of Defense (OSD).

The navy and Marine Corps had good reason to worry about the direction taken in the work of the commission. Although "overseas presence" was one of the thirty-four issues that the commission staff identified for study, that term curiously did not include forward deployed forces or even forward based forces. This omission caused a great deal of concern. Our objective was to underline the *unique* ability of the navy and Marine Corps to deploy and maintain combat-ready forces in critical overseas theaters, independent of foreign basing and extensive land-based support. The objectives of the army and several unified commanders of the other services were rather different. As Secretary of the Army Togo West put it, "While other services provide lesser degree of influence or influence that is more transitory, the influence generated by Army forces will continue to be a central element of our national security strategy...The soldier remains this nation's sincerest and ultimate expression of commitment and will."

And the presence argument was not the only point of friction with the army. While discussing "army and Marine Corps capabilities," Secretary West sought to limit the contribution of Marine ground elements to "service with the fleet in the seizure or defense of advanced naval bases, and the conduct of such land operations as may be essential to the prosecution of naval campaigns." Secretary West was in effect arguing for a congressional finding that would limit the Marine Corps to a role to that was prescribed in the original Key West Agreement of 1947; in 1994, it was still the official description of the Marine Corps' role and mission as had been agreed following the rancorous interservice debates following World War II.

For our part, working closely with Undersecretary Danzig, Wilkerson and I drafted a letter for the SECNAV that he would send to Dr. John P. White, the chairman of the commission. In that letter, the secretary asked that the commission "assess our requirement for sea-based forces overseas for presence and crisis response and assign the navy and Marine Corps *primary functions* in providing combat ready forces forward for deterrence of conflict, promotion of interoperability, crisis control and to *enable* the deployment of heavier CONUS-based forces." A contest was looming as we sought recognition of the unique qualifications of sea-based forces.

The debates and the competition to obtain favorable consideration from the commission continued until the spring of 1995. A look at the final report to Congress, published on May 24, 1995, reveals that although we gained some recognition for the arguments we had advanced, the commission was nowhere as supportive as we had hoped. My impression of the final report was that it was a recantation of the virtues of "jointness" as codified in the Goldwater-Nichols Act. The commission emphasized the need for a more interservice, or "joint," approach to roles and mission. It stressed a difficult and unrealistic platitude: the importance of trusting the unified commanders with "much greater responsibility in the shaping, and training of the Armed Forces." By implication, the services would take a reduced role in that responsibility.

Although recognizing the importance of preserving "the core competencies" of each service,[91] the commission stressed the role of the unified commanders in "adapting" each service's capabilities to the demands posed by threats and objectives in their respective areas of responsibilities (AOR). To our chagrin, the discussion of "overseas presence" did not recognize the clear importance of naval forces and their relative independence of

91 As viewed by the commission, service core competencies included the following: "For the Navy, carrier-based air and amphibious power projection, sea-based air and missile defense, and anti-submarine warfare; for the Marine Corps, amphibious operations, over the beach forced entry operations, and maritime prepositioning."

shore bases. As we had feared, the report called for overseas presence requirements to be reviewed by the unified commanders with a view to reducing "automatic" deployments, which were regarded by the commission as artifacts of the Cold War.

Reviewing and digesting the report of the commission and its treatment of the navy and Marine Corps, one cannot discount the impact and influence of its executive director, Michael Leonard, and the deputy executive director, Gene Porter. Both had been assigned to PA&E for many years, and both were historically severe critics of every department of the navy Program Objective Memorandum (POM) written between 1977 and 1994. Together, they had argued incessantly—but not convincingly—for a navy configured only for strategic deterrence, anti-submarine warfare (ASW), and "sea lane defense." They had authored frequent Office of the Secretary of Defense (OSD) critiques of navy POMs. The constant argument was for reduced funding for aircraft carriers and large amphibious ships. I had jousted with them personally in memoranda written during earlier assignments on the navy staff and during my own stint in the OSD policy branch.

Looking back on my days on the OSD staff, where we had argued against the efforts of Leonard and Porter and won support for an offensive sea control and power projection navy, it seemed ironic now to be advancing forward presence and crisis response as critical missions with our Marine Corps allies. We were really arguing for undiminished force levels in the aftermath of Desert Storm. Although the Soviet Union was not the challenge it had been in 1979, our instincts told us that former critics would probably not become advocates for naval forces. We were also mindful that although Russia was still a challenge, a more portentous development as early as 1994 was a rising power in the Pacific, the People's Republic of China.

Preparing the navy's response to the questions of the Roles and Mission Commission and rewriting the navy's Strategic Objective Statement had occupied much of my time as N-51. My focus changed abruptly late in 1993, when I relieved Rear Admiral Scott Redd as the assistant deputy CNO (N3B/5B) for Plans, Policy and Operations. The immediate superior, when I took the position as his assistant, was Vice Admiral Leighton W. Smith (N3/5).

The most demanding responsibilities of Admiral Smith were serving as the operations deputy (OPDEP) and representing the CNO in the JCS arena. The Goldwater-Nichols Act of 1986 had dramatically increased the scope and responsibilities of the Chairman of the Joint Chiefs of Staff (CJCS) and the Joint Staff. We now had what was tantamount to a "General Staff," which the navy had historically—and successfully—opposed. The influence of service chiefs and their staffs was reduced commensurately. Ensuring that the navy's equities were adequately advanced and protected in the joint arena became the most significant dimension of our work in N3/5. As Admiral Smith's deputy, my role was to help ensure that the divisions and branches in the N3/5 organization were supportive of the many objectives and policies in staffing. This required reviewing a plethora of staff papers and correspondence before they were presented to the DCNO. In addition, I had my own work to do in joint matters as the deputy OPDEP. Each service had a two-star flag or general officer who met in the JCS "tank" on matters delegated to us by the OPDEPs.

While in this position and working for Admiral Smith, I did have some time to pursue other interests, including leading the navy's delegation in staff talks with the navies of the Federal Republic of Germany and France. I traveled to France in September 1994 to participate in a war game labeled Alliance '94. The purpose of the game, held in Toulon at the Marine

Nationale's Mediterranean headquarters, was really to explore how the Marine Nationale might fit into our strategic concept and to explore how and where our combined fleets could act in concert in a crisis or contingency. As I remember, the Middle East and the Persian Gulf were the settings for most of our gamed interaction. The talks with the Marine Nationale staff in December 1994 offered me an opportunity to build on the good relationships I had established with senior French naval officers during my tour in Paris as the defense attaché. The talks were hosted by the French at their headquarters in Paris on the Place de la Concorde.

In this setting, we discussed operational subjects that included advanced tactical concepts for ASW against diesel-electric submarines. Our contrasting approaches to ASW led to several important classified initiatives within OPNAV following our return. We also discussed the logistics challenges confronting both navies, especially the maintenance and repair of ships deployed at long distances from their homeports.

A highlight of our visit to Paris was an opportunity to attend a dinner in our honor at the residence of the French CNO, Admiral Jean-Charles Lefebvre. I had met the admiral several years before when he was a division director at the Marine Nationale headquarters (EMM). We had a good discussion, in French, summarizing the results of our staff talks and preparing for a subsequent visit to Paris by our CNO. I have little doubt that my election to the *Académie de Marine*, a year or so after my retirement in 1995, was orchestrated by three former Marine Nationale chiefs, Admirals Alain Coatena, Bernard Louzeau, and Jean-Charles Lefebvre. I also had the support of my great friend, now the chief of the French General Staff, Admiral Jacques Lanxade.

The staff talks with the Federal Republic of Germany Navy in January 1995 were much more modest in content and detail.

This was in part the result of the rather limited geographic reach of the *Bundesmarine*, whose focus and AOR was the Baltic and North Sea. We did encourage the Germans to continue the practice of sending their missile ships to our weapons range in Puerto Rico, where live EXOCET cruise missiles were fired by the Germans as targets to be engaged by US and German missile ships. At our instigation, after these talks the Germans also continued contributing to the standing naval forces of NATO, including the force in the Mediterranean (STANAVFORMED) that since 1993 had undertaken operations in the Adriatic Sea as tensions between Serbia and NATO had escalated.

A memorable moment in the German talks occurred during the dinner I hosted as the head of the US delegation. After a very good meal and several glasses of wine at a restaurant in Great Falls, Virginia, a slightly inebriated German admiral raised his glass to offer a toast. Ignoring the usual protocol—namely, toasting our respective leaders and our sailors, which I was prepared to reciprocate—the good admiral raised his glass, toasting the establishment of the European Union (EU). That would certainly have been appropriate, but he followed that salute with the following: "Finally, all the German-speaking peoples of Europe will be gathered under one roof." I was momentarily stunned, and by way of reply, I toasted European unity, the collapse of the Berlin Wall, and the continuing integration of the two Germanies.

I was also able to participate in several fascinating joint war games in the Pentagon that were meant to gauge the effectiveness and readiness of US forces for contingencies in the Pacific area and the Korean Peninsula. One war game that remains vivid in my memory involved a scenario centered on the Democratic People's Republic of Korea (DPRK) acquiring and deploying a deliverable nuclear warhead on a long-range missile. The crisis we were "gaming" escalated quickly to a decision on whether to neutralize what we suspected were missile launching sites with nuclear weapons capability. One reason that I remember the game so well is that the senior participant, who had taken the role as the National Command Authority (NCA) or president was none other than Joseph Nye, then the assistant secretary of defense (ASD) for International Security Affairs (ISA). Nye had been a professor at Harvard while I was working on my PhD in the early '70s.[92] (He was well known then for very liberal views and for his advocacy of conciliatory foreign policies, including the transfer of the Panama Canal Zone to the Panamanian government. As discussed earlier, the latter objective was realized during the Carter administration and a student/protégé of Nye, Robert Pastor, led the negotiations that resulted in the transfer of the canal.)

As the clock wound down to a decision, play was stopped to review our options and to consider the next move very carefully. The game never really progressed beyond the pause. Foremost among the concerns were the decisions to order the evacuation of all military dependents from the Republic of Korea (ROK) and the need to urge all civilian US citizens to leave the ROK. Options were complicated by the presence of literally thousands of DPRK artillery tubes within range of Seoul. In addition, we were made to consider the effect of radiological hazards to Japan and the US forces stationed there, which would likely result were we to preempt the DPRK missile sites. The set of unattractive options was staggering in its impact on the assemblage at the briefing. As I reflect today on the scenario and the circumstances we gamed in 1994, I am mindful that we may soon face very similar and even more complicated options dealing with a nuclear-armed DPRK.

---

92 See my account in Chapter 3 of Les Aspin's visits to the Institute of Politics at Harvard while I was a PhD candidate.

* * *

During most of my career, I was very fortunate to have had a close relationship with Admiral Mike Boorda, who ultimately came to a tragic end by taking his own life while serving as CNO. The admiral had first befriended me in 1970 while I was a lieutenant attending the Naval Destroyer School (DesTech) in Newport, Rhode Island, while he was serving as the executive assistant (EA) to Captain Al Sackett, the commanding officer (CO) of the school. Later, when I was a lieutenant commander, he was my detailer, and he facilitated my assignment to graduate study at Harvard. As Chapter 10, recounting my assignment in *Yorktown*, details, Mike Boorda, as my immediate superior, also became a close friend and mentor. This extended to my assignment as the SECNAV's EA and through the remainder of my career.

As others have noted, Adm. Boorda was a sailor's admiral. In the early '60s, he was in a relatively small group of enlisted men to gain officer commissions in the unrestricted line through the Integration Program. He was also among a very few of these to reach flag rank and the only former enlisted person to become CNO. A former enlisted personnelman, his concern for sailors and interest in career management led him to choose this sub-specialty as an officer. He served successive tours, culminating in his assignment as the chief of naval personnel. Boorda was well respected on the waterfront. He believed himself to be an expert ship handler, and he was critical of those he felt were lacking in what he considered the mettle of the surface warfare profession. As CO of a destroyer, commander of a destroyer squadron, and a cruiser-destroyer group, he was as exacting of juniors as he was demanding of himself. He was famous for his surprise inspections and tests of the combat readiness of units under his command. If he had a flaw as I saw it, it was insecurity about how his prior enlisted service affected his opportunities. He mentioned to me on several occasions that his commissioning source had counted against him. I don't believe it ever did, and in at least one case, it served to his advantage.

While serving together on the 1994 flag officer selection board of which he was the president, he signaled to me that if he acceded to the CNO position for which he was a candidate, he would support a promotion for me to vice admiral. He expressed concern that he might not be chosen as CNO, however; he explained that many senior admirals, active and retired, did not favor him to become the CNO. He was also mindful that he would be the first non-Naval Academy graduate to accede to the position. Instead, he explained that Admiral Charles Larson, the four-star superintendent of the Naval Academy, was the favored candidate of the "establishment." What the seniors opposing Boorda did not reckon with at the time was the determination of Secretary Dalton and Undersecretary Danzig to nominate Boorda, precisely because of his remarkable progression from the enlisted ranks and the record of accomplishments throughout his career. As it turned out, notwithstanding his premonitions, Boorda was named as CNO, and I was naturally overjoyed. Then fate intervened.

In the negotiations that typically occur during a change in CNOs, Adm. Kelso, the incumbent, Adm. Boorda, the nominee, and Secretaries Dalton and Danzig met to negotiate the replacement of other four-star admirals on the verge of retirement or reassignment. One such impending retirement was that of the CINCLANTFLT, Admiral Hank Mauz. The favorite of the secretaries for this assignment and promotion to four-star rank was clearly Vice Admiral Paul Reason, then Commander of Naval

Surface Forces, Atlantic (COMNAVSURFLANT). Reason was the navy's senior African American naval officer and the Clinton administration seemed determined to see the promotion of the first Black naval officer to four-star rank.

Admiral Boorda confided to me that he could not hide his concern about Adm. Reason's qualifications. He claimed to know him very well. As he explained things to me later, with the support of Adm. Kelso, he had argued that before being nominated for four stars as Commander in Chief Atlantic Fleet (CINCLANTFLT), Adm. Reason needed "at least" one tour in a demanding three-star billet in Washington. Reason had not served in any senior Washington jobs, and he was not qualified as a "joint" flag officer; his only Washington duty had been as naval aide to President Carter while a commander. Boorda's arguments were apparently persuasive in deferring the nomination.

To my bitter disappointment, however, the three-star Washington assignment that was negotiated for Reason was the N3/5 (DCNO Plans, Policy and Operations) position that Boorda had told me he would nominate me for. Shortly after this dramatic turn of events, he called me into his "flag cabin," as the CNO's office is known, to console me, while advising me to be patient. He assured me that I would get the three-star nomination that I deserved at the "next opportunity" and within a year. In the meantime, he said, "You'll be my real N3/5." He explained that he expected me to help Adm. Reason in protecting the navy's equities in the joint and interagency arenas.

And so I had come to an awkward interval in my career. I had a good working relationship with the SECNAV and especially with Undersecretary Danzig, established during the presence and roles and mission efforts. Although I had the obvious support of—and more importantly, unfettered access to—the new CNO, I was uncomfortable doing his bidding by working around my nominal superior, Adm. Reason. I did the best I could under the circumstances, but clearly, this arrangement did not please Reason. I can't remember how many times I had to "back brief" him on instructions that I had received directly from the CNO. Each time it happened, I could sense his frustration and occasionally his anger. To his credit, Reason never blamed me.

By late 1994, I despaired that a three-star assignment would be forthcoming any time soon. My desperation was fueled when I learned that a friend, colleague, and contemporary, the late Admiral Don Pilling, had been nominated for a third star and assignment as commander of the Sixth Fleet. I felt that command of that fleet was the job I had prepared for my entire career. I had served successive shipboard tours in the Mediterranean, including command of two surface combatants as a commander and as a captain. I had commanded a battle group and served as the carrier strike force commander in the Sixth Fleet two years before. I had written my doctoral dissertation at Harvard on the Sixth Fleet. I spoke fluent French and Spanish and had working knowledge of Italian and Russian. Finally, since naval diplomacy is a constant in a numbered fleet commander's business, I had cut my teeth as the defense attaché in Paris.

All of that notwithstanding, the job was going to another, and it would not open again for nominally two years. When I raised this with Admiral Boorda over dinner at Tingey House, his quarters in the Washington Navy Yard, he explained that I was his "and everyone else's first choice," but he was certain that the Turkish government would have balked at my selection to command the Sixth Fleet. Precisely because the job was double hatted with a NATO command of Striking and Support Force South (COMSTRIKFORSOUTH), the Turks had a veto on our nominations for the command. Recalling the *Muavenet* incident described earlier and despite the Court of Inquiry's finding that

I was not responsible for that tragic accident, Boorda explained that the Turks had not absolved me of responsibility. Moreover, he mentioned that they would not forget me, as my last name, *dur*, meant "stop" in Turkish, as evidenced on every stop sign in Turkey.

After that exchange, I expressed an interest in pursuing opportunities outside the navy to a good friend, Tom Neff, then a managing partner in the prestigious executive search firm Spencer Stuart. That expression of interest subsequently led to a call from Dana Mead, the president, CEO, and chairman of Tenneco, Inc., the major conglomerate headquartered in Houston, Texas. At the time, Tenneco consisted of seven highly diverse divisions ranging from the transmission of natural gas to shipbuilding. Annual revenues were on the order of $35 billion.

I accepted an invitation to visit Houston and discuss opportunities at Tenneco with Dana and several of his division heads and staff vice presidents. The meetings, or what were really interviews, went very well, and not long after my return to Washington, I received a rather generous offer to join Tenneco as a corporate vice president. The letter offered me an assignment in Houston to learn about the corporation, to be followed by a profit and loss (P&L) position in one of the divisions. Coming so soon after my meeting with Mr. Mead, the offer took me by surprise. From its tone, I knew I could not delay long in responding. I agonized for several weeks about whether I should discuss this opportunity with my superiors. I decided against it, convincing myself that I had to make this choice without appearing to be leveraging an offer from industry for a promotion in the navy. Accordingly, I decided I would accept the offer before informing the navy and requesting retirement.

The decision made, I wrote Mr. Mead accepting his offer, asking that I delay joining the company until I had completed thirty years of service in May 1995. On the same day that I put the letter to Mr. Mead in the mail, I called Captain John "Boomer" Stufflebeam, the CNO's EA, requesting an appointment with Adm. Boorda.

The following day, I reported to the flag cabin and informed the admiral of my decision to leave the navy. Being the proud and often humorous correspondent that he was, Adm. Boorda seemed a little surprised, and after a long pause, he remarked, "It's about the money, isn't it?" I replied that although the "money" was certainly an element in my decision, the driver was my conviction that my time for promotion to vice admiral had passed. I told him that the barrier to promotion in the case of the Sixth Fleet had convinced me. Shortly after my call on Adm. Boorda, I received a telephone call from the chief of naval personnel, Vice Admiral Skip Bowman, who expressed surprise at my decision. He quipped, "You could have knocked me over with a feather."

There was also the undeniable fact that the very nature of naval and military operations after the Cold War had diminished the attraction of the career that I had chosen thirty years before. I explained to Admiral Boorda how unseemly and trivial the planning for an invasion of Haiti seemed to me. I had worked as the navy planner to restore the deposed Haitian president, Aristide, to the presidency of that historically ungovernable country. Our generation of naval officers had stood down and forced the capitulation of the Soviet Union by fielding superior superbly trained forces, especially naval forces. Now we were embarking on "nation building" exercises in the Caribbean and the Balkans. In a real way, the business of the navy had changed and changed dramatically. In the post-Cold War era, the navy might need fresh leadership.

Boorda listened attentively, agreeing with most but not all of my logic but finished by expressing what seemed sincere disappointment. He expressed regret that he had invested considerable effort promoting my career. I was saddened by that reaction, but I assured him that I would never forget the example he had set for surface warfare officers, and I expressed the gratitude I felt for his enduring support of me personally. Leaving his office, I secured an appointment with Undersecretary Danzig, who had also been complimentary and helpful to me in the preceding two years.

Secretary Danzig's reaction was one of incredulity and what seemed sincere disappointment. After hearing me, he countered that I should bear in mind that I would have to get the SECNAV's approval of my request for retirement, adding that he would advise the secretary to disapprove my request. Returning to my office shortly after meeting Danzig, I received a call from the office of the SECNAV, advising me that Secretary Dalton would see me early the same afternoon. That meeting was memorable because Secretary Dalton began by asking me why I was leaving despite the "brilliant future" the navy had in mind for me. I politely explained to Mr. Dalton that I had commanded a carrier battle group, served in a variety of demanding billets at sea and ashore, and that I had awaited my turn for an opportunity to continue serving in the grade of vice admiral. Without mentioning contemporaries who had gone on to three-star assignments, I noted that it seemed to me that my opportunity had passed. He assured me that even though the timing for my promotion had lagged somewhat, I was still very much under consideration for a three-star assignment. I thanked the secretary and tried to explain that I had decided to try my hand in the private sector and hoped that he would approve my request to retire the following May. The secretary replied by telling me that I would soon hear directly from the CNO regarding future opportunities for me in uniform.

Early the next day, the CNO's office called me, saying that Admiral Boorda wanted to see me "immediately." I hurried to his office, expecting to be chewed out for having taken my case to the secretary. My expectations were met. Boorda was clearly upset that the secretary had directed him to challenge my decision to retire and not accept an assignment at the three-star level. Admiral Boorda then proceeded to "offer" me five different three-star assignments: COMNAVSURFLANT, COMNAVSURFPAC; N-6, N3/5; or COMSEVENTHFLT. The only numbered fleet assignment mentioned was command of the Seventh Fleet based in Yokosuka, Japan. After offering the latter, he dismissed that possibility with the assumption that my wife at the time would not want me to accept that assignment. He said, "She wouldn't move to Japan, I'm sure." (He was probably correct.) Boorda finished by telling me to get back to him within twenty-four hours. That unpleasant meeting, promising as it was meant to be, did not change my decision. As the Romans were wont to say, I had crossed the Rubicon.

I remained in my assignment as N3B/5B until the end of May 1995 and my thirty-year anniversary as a naval officer, making ready for my departure and my new career in corporate life. On my last day in the Pentagon, I was met in the passageway at the door to the CNO's office by Captain John Stufflebeam, who asked me to come in for a brief meeting with the CNO.

Admiral Boorda was in a much better frame of mind, as I recall. We had a pleasant chat over a cup of coffee, reminiscing about our times together. Then he asked if I would accompany him for a walk down the "E" ring toward my office. We turned into Adm. Reason's office adjacent to mine, and assembled there were all the branch and division heads in N3/5. After a few pleasantries, Adm. Boorda himself began reading the language in a citation accompanying award of the navy's highest noncombat decoration, the Distinguished Service Medal. I was proud to receive the award and even prouder that the CNO and my very good friend, Mike Boorda, read the citation. It read in part, "*Rear Admiral Dur was singularly responsible for the development of the navy's latest statement of strategy, 'Forward...From the Sea.*" As a strategic planner for so many years, I was honored to receive that tribute.

I left the Pentagon that afternoon satisfied that I had made the tough decision to leave the navy on my own terms. I had earned command at sea after successive assignments that allowed me to develop and apply skills in a setting that I loved. I had received the best education available to officers aspiring to positions of responsibility and influence in national security affairs. I had been able to contribute to the development of naval strategy and had contributed directly to promoting the president's objectives in the Reagan administration.

Finally, I believed that I had met my father's expectations for me, which was a special gratification.

A conversation with Admiral Carl Trost, the CNO, July 1989

Secretary of the Navy William Ball, myself, and Marine aide Colonel David Richwine, USMC, leaving Brussels, NATO headquarters

My mother and wife helping to pin my rear admiral shoulder boards in Admiral Mike Boorda's office, July 1989

"To Phil: To an enormously talented and dedicated officer who I hope will go all the way. Your friend, Donald Rumsfeld" July 1989

Formally attired US defense attaché, Paris, 1990

Secretary of the Navy Larry Garrett, American embassy, Paris, 1991

Generals Colin Powell and Maurice Schmitt, chief of the French General Staff, 1991

Briefing Secretary of Defense Richard Cheney aboard *Saratoga*, April 1992

Signing the visitor log at SETAF headquarters during the Bosnia crisis in the fall of 1992

The team at COMCRUDESGRU 8 in the fall of 1991

The Turkish destroyer *Muavenet*, damaged by Sparrow missile accident with *Saratoga*, October 1992

The STARS and STRIPES

1942-1992 · 50 YEARS OF SERVICE

Vol. 51, No. 170   50¢   Sunday, October 4, 1992   A   D 8693 A

Human error likely cause of missile firing, report says

For wire services

WASHINGTON — Human error was responsible for launching two U.S. Sea Sparrow missiles that killed five sailors and injured 15 aboard a Turkish destroyer late Thursday night, according to The Washington Post, which quoted sources familiar with the Navy's preliminary inquiry.

However, the Anatolia news agency quoted Gen. John M. Shalikashvili, supreme allied commander Europe, as saying that while he couldn't make an "advance guess," "human error or mechanical failure" were among possible causes that he couldn't be ruled out at that point.

Earlier, asked about reports by The Washington Post and The New York Times that human error caused two missiles to be fired, a NATO spokesman, U.S. Navy Capt. James Mitchell, called the news accounts "speculations."

"We do not yet know what has happened," said Mitchell, who is chief of information for Allied Forces Southern Europe.

Whoever fired the fatal salvo, The Washington Post's sources said, had to power up the missile launcher and the fire control console, raise a spring-loaded red safety cover and throw a toggle switch to close the firing circuit. The two missiles blew out the doors of their common launcher — one after another, in rapid sequence.

Sources said the aircraft carrier Saratoga's Combat Information Center, from which the ship's captain or tactical action officer must authorize weapons release, did not issue or simulate an order to fire the missiles.

Instead, the firing sequence began in a closet-sized "local operating station" on the outer hull of the 60,000-ton warship, adjacent to a Mark 29 missile launcher. There is no evidence so far of mechanical failure, the sources said.

Such local operating stations, typically manned by petty officers and senior enlisted sailors, routinely conduct autonomous drills and maintenance procedures

Continued on Page 2

Rear Adm. Philip A. Dur walks aboard the Saratoga on Friday after the aircraft carrier accidentally fired upon a Turkish destroyer, killing five sailors and injuring 15. The Navy is trying to determine the cause of the incident.

THE STARS AND STRIPES   Stars and Stripes Headlines 4 October 1992   Sunday, October 4, 1992

AT A GLANCE

Country music disc jockey Gene Price (left), seen here with singer Willie Nelson, says his show on Armed Forces Radio "has meant more to me than any show I've ever done." See SUNDAY magazine.

Setback for C-17

Wings of a ground-test model of McDonnell Douglas Corp.'s new C-17 cargo jet buckled during a stress test.
— Page 4

'Painful' program

"There will be pain everywhere," presidential candidate Ross Perot said of his program for deep spending cuts and higher taxes.
— Page 6

Iraqi oil assets seized

The U.N. Security Council ordered the seizure of frozen Iraqi oil assets to help pay for that which Iraq owes the United Nations under the ceasefire resolutions.
— Page 9

Report blames human error

From Page 1

that mimic the firing sequence of an actual launch. But safety procedures dictate that the missiles be disabled first, according to active and retired officers with expertise in the Sea Sparrow system.

Friday, as a high-ranking investigative panel arrived aboard the Saratoga, the U.S. government and the military chain of command tried to contain the diplomatic and public relations damage.

President Bush telephoned Turkey's President Turgut Ozal to express regret for the accident, and senior officers praised the Turkish crew's heroic efforts at damage control — even after the missiles killed their captain and gravely wounded the executive officer and chief engineer.

A Court of Inquiry, a fact-finding panel of three Navy rear admirals with a Turkish rear admiral observing, was due to convene Saturday aboard the Saratoga.

"We will go after this with a zeal to find out exactly why this happened so it won't happen again," Adm. Mike Boorda, commander-in-chief of Allied Forces Southern Europe and of U.S. Naval Forces Europe, said in a telephone interview from his Naples, Italy, headquarters.

The panel will report to Vice Adm. T. Joseph Lopez, commander of the U.S. 6th Fleet, and has the power to recommend changes in safety procedures and disciplinary action ranging from non-judi-

The Turkish destroyer Muavenet shows the damage caused when it was hit by a Sea Sparrow missile from the Saratoga, launched accidentally during NATO exercises.

cial punishment to court-martial.

Chances are that the Muavenet never knew it was in danger.

The Sea Sparrow travels 2.5 times the speed of sound and had only three miles to fly.

Muavenet's "lookout would have seen a flash coming from the Saratoga and said, 'Gee, I wonder what that is,' and, about the time he was probably reporting, it the missile was on top of him," said a well-placed Navy official.

RELIEF

From Page 1

satisfaction with the way the Federal Emergency Management Agency, the lead civilian agency for domestic disaster relief, reacted to the situation in Florida.

Critics lambasted the agency after it was caught unprepared for the magnitude of Hurricane Andrew's destruction and then was slow to organize relief.

Sen. Barbara Mikulski, D-Md., is so unhappy with the response of FEMA

then it is incumbent upon the Guard to configure themselves more appropriately for state missions."

For their part, military officials seem reluctant to join in the debate. Gen. Colin L. Powell, chairman of the Joint Chiefs of Staff, and Gen. Gordon R. Sullivan, Army chief of staff, both declined interviews through spokesmen.

However, in a brief Sept. 10 news conference in Miami after getting a firsthand look at the military's relief efforts in the wake of Hurricane Andrew, Powell downplayed the issue of an expanded role for the military in domestic crises.

Stars and Stripes article following *Saratoga* accident with TGS *Muavenet*, October 4, 1992

POSTSCRIPT

A respected reader of an earlier draft of this book commented that although the book will be an enlightening read for those interested in a Cold Warrior's career, he was left with questions about its relevance for future strategic thinkers and those interested in pursuing a naval career. Recognizing the importance of that premise, I have added the following reflections, which may be useful to those who will deal with a future that is still unfolding.

Developing and pursuing an interest in maritime strategy and national security policy was comparatively easy during the Cold War. Although there were many crises that characterized the era, in fact the world and the strategic context were simpler. After all, the United States was the unquestioned leader of alliances with the major European and Asian democracies. We created the alliance systems, led them, and funded them for the most part. There were only two putative enemies, China and the Warsaw Pact, and the nuclear balance of terror bounded the field of play. Looking to the future and the geostrategic context that contemporary aspirants face, there are many complicating factors to consider.

In the first place, the "global order" that characterized the post-World War II period seems to be in inelegant retreat. Agreement regarding the value of transnational and international organizations and alliances is in precipitous decline. The declared policies of the Trump administration, British exit from the European Community, Chinese militarization of reefs and archipelagos in the South China Sea, and the reaction of several countries to the coronavirus pandemic provide abundant proof of resurgent nationalism. Even before the pronouncements of the last administration, it was clear that American leadership in multinational organizations and economic fora was increasingly being called into question.

Although geostrategic complexities abound and some of the multitude of challenges we face may appear insurmountable, there will be an enduring need for uniformed leaders to shape future strategies and policies important for the security of the United States. Political leaders with experience in military service are in short supply. Many leaders' understanding of weapons, their application, and the limits of their application are accordingly shallow. I will argue that the digital age and the technology it has spawned may have exaggerated the instrumentality and potential of raw military power. The wide use of Tomahawk missilery and precision aerial strikes by recent administrations against adversaries in the Middle East, for example, had little, if any, effect on the course of events.

The advent of robotic systems, artificial intelligence, and the dawn of high-energy weaponry may mask the need for good strategic thought, mastery of the operational art, and the development of workable tactics. There will be an enduring requirement for talented military thinkers who understand the impact, and the limits, of these capabilities and who can then help develop strategies and policies to deal effectively with putative enemies and peer competitors.

There will be a concomitant need for military thinkers educated in the softer sciences of political organization, economics, sociocultural trends, foreign languages, and area studies, to name a few. But the education of strategic thinkers should not come at the expense of their mastery of military specialties. This argument should be made because the trend in officer careers today tends to overemphasize "joint" staff experience which in turn may limit opportunities for graduate education or the development of service-specific skills.[93] The important point is that some line careers should be selectively managed to afford education and strategic planning experience without compromising professional development, especially tactical and operational prowess. Too many required "wickets" (i.e., "joint" qualifications) may limit opportunities to develop strategic thinkers.

There is general agreement among experts regarding major threats to our national security in the next decade or two, though the severity of climate change may be the exception. Given the partisan fracture and the ideological divide that characterize contemporary American politics, the deliberations required for achieving agreement on sound national strategies appear impossible. In short, unlike the Cold War period, we are far from attaining bipartisan consensus on policies and measures that will successfully address the challenges that lie ahead.

The most daunting security challenges all have significant bearing on our maritime interests in general and our navy in particular:

The reemergence of Russia and its irredentist claims to control territory that once comprised the Soviet Union.

PRC hegemony in East Asia and its global designs to control avenues of commerce across Eurasia and Africa.

Iran's emergence as a regional power with nuclear and ballistic missilery and the resulting impact on Arab oil producers and on European dependence on energy from the Middle East.

93 The service-specific skills that come to mind are seamanship and airmanship as well as tactical proficiency. The recent spate of collisions involving Navy ships are said to reflect lapses in training and development, for example. The required exposure to joint duty is seen as onerous by many in all the services.

Rising tension between Russia and the United States, and between Russia and the newest NATO Allies in the Baltic region and Eastern Europe, is an area of increasing concern, precisely because US leadership of the alliance has been in marked decline. Although of pressing concern to our European allies, Russian incursions against Ukraine and Georgia did not result in bold, US-led responses by the alliance. The simple facts are that Russia's inheritance of the Soviet nuclear arsenal and Germany's obvious unwillingness and inability to contribute to offsetting Russia's conventional military power make a purely Euro response to Soviet aggression virtually impossible. The failure of the United States to respond adequately to Russian aggression has diluted the value of our leadership. This was true even before the broadside of criticism directed at our major allies reached a crescendo at the 2017 NATO mini-summit. For instance, Germany's insistence on continuing to fund the Nord Stream 2 gas pipeline from Russia, even after sanctions were imposed following Russian occupation of Crimea and its violent interventions in Ukraine, provided early proof of our declining influence among our major European allies.

Further proof may be found in Russia's continuing pressure on the Baltic nations with large Russian minorities, Ukraine, and the Asian republics once part of the USSR. To be clear, the extension of NATO's mantle to Estonia, Latvia, and Lithuania, as well as to Poland, the Czech and Slovak Republics, and Hungary resurrected long-standing Russian insecurity. As the noted Sovietologist Adam Ulam has argued, this insecurity over invasion routes from the west was the causal factor that led to the Communist order in Eastern Europe.[94] Concern for the political orientation of Ukraine, Georgia, Belarus, and the Central Asian Republics will be an enduring preoccupation of Russian leaders.

94 Adam B. Ulam, *Expansion and Coexistence: Soviet Foreign Policy, 1917–1973* (New York: Praeger, 1974).

This decline has serious implications for the future of collective security in Europe and the adjacent ocean areas. The challenge for American and European leaders then is to develop a collective response that will confront a martial Russian Federation. The continuing reduction in US military presence in Germany and the proposed redeployment of a token force to Poland are clearly not serious deterrents to Russian aggression and influence. (The reduction in US forces based in Germany may exacerbate the historic concerns of several smaller West European allies.)

Of special relevance for maritime policies is the impact of receding ice floes and the laws or regulations governing the access to routes across the polar seas north of the Russian and Canadian land masses. Finally, the modernization and growth in the capabilities of Russia's northern and Baltic fleets point to a pressing need to address Russia's naval dominance of these ocean areas. Strategies to deal with these issues are sorely needed, but they will not be developed without active US participation.

China's emergence as a strategic competitor to the United States in the western Pacific basin may be the most profound challenge in the immediate future. It is clearly one the United States will have to manage. Much has been written on the emergence of the PRC as a global power, but the responses have been woefully short of the mark. The heralded "pivot" toward Asia announced by the Obama administration was anything but. The rebalancing of our submarine fleet favoring the Pacific and the deployment of a Marine battalion to Australia have proven insufficient. Looming before us is the Gordian knot that is Taiwan and our commitment to that island's defense. (We need only imagine the risks that would attend a US response to Chinese aggression against Taiwan.) The establishment of the informal Quadrilateral Security Dialogue (Quad) arrangement with Japan, India, and Australia is a good point of departure to signal multilateral resistance to a Chinese design for the Indo-Pacific region, but it is not enough. The relevant partner for the United States in containing Chinese expansion is Japan.

The stability of our relationship with Japan turns on that country's perception of the durability of its formal alliance with the United States. Although created as a deterrent to Soviet aggression and nuclear blackmail, the Mutual Security Pact and its "nuclear umbrella" also serve to encourage Japanese compliance with the strict terms of the MacArthur constitution, which limited Japan to self-defense, narrowly defined. That logic, including the limitations imposed by the United States after World War II, appears overtaken by more recent events. China's stated designs and its naval power are Japan's concern. A Taiwan crisis would be watched with great interest in Tokyo, and a US failure to defend Taiwan against China would have portentous consequences. A loss of confidence in the reliability of US commitments could be reflected in changing attitudes in Japan and in the ROK regarding appropriate steps to improve their defenses, including the heretofore unmentionable—the acquisition of nuclear weapons by Japan.

We might begin by encouraging the Japanese to break out of the constitutional limits we imposed and begin investing in a much larger defense capability, including offensive weaponry. Such a transition (including the 1 percent of GDP ceiling on defense spending) should go into effect now. The challenge for strategists will be to recast the pact with Japan in terms that specify the objectives of our cooperation against China. It will also be up to the United States to mollify and reassure other Asian friends and allies still wary of the Japanese that contributions to containing China are also in their collective self-interest.

Finally, there is the Belt and Road strategy of the PRC, which has provided ingress and encouraged dependence on Chinese economic munificence in sixty-eight countries, many far afield from China, such as Djibouti and Sri Lanka. This global strategy is particularly important to Chinese interest in maintaining a significant presence in the Indian Ocean by drawing on access to distant naval bases. Chinese spokesmen readily concede the intent to gain positions astride the commercial lanes linking the Mediterranean, Red Sea, the Persian Gulf, and the Indonesian straits. Notably, these bold moves have motivated India's leadership to respond programmatically, albeit rather quietly for the time being. Strategists should promote a consortium of Western democracies (Europeans included) to meet and best economic development advanced by the Chinese.

The burning question of Iran and that country's future nuclear and military posture in general has been brought into sharp focus by US withdrawal from the nuclear "deal," the Joint Comprehensive Plan of Action (JCPOA). Whether the current strident positions of the theocratic regime regarding Israel, Saudi Arabia, and the United Arab Emirates (UAE) could have consequences over time is a worrisome question. Specifically, where does Iran's eventual coupling of nuclear warheads with a family of ballistic missiles, and its rapid progress in space-based sensing and communications lead? What does Iran's demonstrated capability in cyber warfare portend?

The relative independence of US consumers and our country's reduced dependency on energy resources in the Middle East have altered our strategic calculus regarding access to foreign sources of fossil fuels. Europe, on the other hand, in the face of dwindling production in the North Sea, is ever more dependent on Russian sources and those in the Persian Gulf. China, Japan, and the ROK clearly have few alternatives to Persian Gulf sources. This dependency may explain why the four other signatories to the JCPOA remain supportive of this agreement. As of this writing, the Biden administration appears committed to rejoining the Iran deal. Hopefully, reason will prevail, and the countervailing and overriding strategic arguments and actions by the Iranians will constrain those advancing the case for rejoining the JCPOA.

Having outlined some of the most vexing issues in the near- and midterm, I recognize the need to assess and strategically address their implications for future generations of officers interested in the development of appropriate and responsive strategies and policies. At the same time, future uniformed operators will also deal with the emergence and proliferation of new technologies, sensors, and weapons that will define the environment in which our forces will operate. These developments will bear heavily on the development of viable strategies.

In terms of intellectual preparation for the geopolitical maelstrom before us, we can postulate obvious needs. Area studies and foreign language expertise will remain important to understanding the impact of history and culture on the motivation of Chinese, Russian, and Persian actors, inter alia. Thankfully, the formal establishment of a Foreign Area Officer (FAO) community in the navy provides some assurance that we will meet some of this need. Similarly, facility with digital processing for statistical inference, the application of artificial intelligence algorithms, and big data analytics will invariably be part of the strategist's tool kit. This demanding menu of skills requires caution to ensure that education and specialization does not hinder or preclude commensurate attention to warfare specialties and preparations for command.

In sum, we are in the middle of a transformation characterized by the gradual abandonment of global solutions to geographically distinct problems, pandemic disease spread, and emerging nationalism. The world that is evolving will put a premium on those with solid grounding in history and demographics. My own experience suggests to me that education will be critical to producing individuals able to develop workable regional strategies and policies for the decades ahead. We need only to consider the amazing penetration of the PRC in so many countries and the growing economic dependency of these "clients." American policy makers unfamiliar with Chinese designs and the objectives of the Communist Party were either oblivious or unwilling to anticipate this portentous challenge. Wishful thinking that the adoption of a "mixed" economy and some liberalization would lead to responsible participation in a global economy and international organizations is being belatedly recognized for what it was.

As to developments that bear on the operational art and doctrine, understanding the importance of advances in sensors, communications, and weapons technologies will be important to the development of uniformed strategic thinkers. Dwelling only on the maritime realm, advances in technology will affect both the capabilities of our naval forces and their vulnerabilities. Foremost among these will be dealing with the proliferation of ballistic and hypersonic missile technologies and their precision targeting and terminal guidance from an array of space-based sensors. The emerging technological capabilities of Russia, China, and even Iran portend dangerous operating environments in the relatively near future.

Second, and only slightly less portentous, is the proliferation of nuclear weaponry. The DPRK and Iran are regarded as the next nuclear-capable states, but one can only speculate about the reactive proliferation likely when these countries field offensive capabilities. A question seldom asked is, Which countries that have foresworn nuclear weapons will nevertheless arm themselves when weapons proliferate among their enemies?

These, then, are representative—but by no means exhaustive—issues that must be considered in developing maritime strategies and building the capabilities required in US naval forces to support future strategies. It is important that we develop officers who can work hand in hand with civilian counterparts and leadership to formulate strategic approaches and policies that will address some of the challenges described above. This becomes even more important as it becomes increasingly evident that civilian national security experts lack direct experience with service and joint capabilities and operations.

The challenge before those who aspire to careers as uniformed strategic thinkers and operators will be to develop the requisite intellectual reach and pertinent operational skills. Predictably, the rewards will provide an attractive return to those who will chart courses **between land and sea.**

APPENDIX 1

Letter of commendation from the director of the Joint Staff

THE JOINT CHIEFS OF STAFF
WASHINGTON, D.C. 20301

THE JOINT STAFF

DJSM 1737-78
30 October 1978

MEMORANDUM FOR VADM WILLIAM J. CROWE, JR., USN

Subject: Letter of Commendation for Commander Philip A. Dur,

1. On 7 September 1978, the Joint Chiefs of Staff approved "Review of US Strategy Related to the Middle East and the Persian Gulf." This paper provided the Secretary of Defense with a review of existing strategy in the region and recommended an improved national strategy including military initiatives.

2. The paper was developed by a working group composed of OJCS, Service, and DIA representatives, and represents an innovative approach to the complex situation in the Middle East/Persian Gulf region.

3. As the representative of the Navy on the working group, Commander Dur analyzed the existing US national strategy and conceived innovative concepts which were the basis for developing a recommended national strategy. His insight into Soviet concepts and strategy and complete familiarity with the region were instrumental in developing the military initiatives presented in the paper. Commander Dur is highly commended for his active participation and valued judgments which are reflected in the approved paper.

JOHN A. WICKHAM, JR.
Lieutenant General, USA
Director, Joint Staff

APPENDIX 2

Letter to the author from General Richard Boverie

Citibank, N.A.   **Richard T. Boverie**
399 Park Avenue   Vice President
New York, NY
10043

November 13, 1984

Captain Philip A. Dur, USN
National Security Council Staff
The White House
Washington, D.C. 20506

Dear Phil:

Thank you very much for your letter informing me that the time
has come for you to complete your NSC Staff duty and return to the Navy.
I also appreciate the meaningful thoughts and kind words you offered.
It was very considerate of you to write.

When I was on the NSC Staff a couple of years ago and we asked
you to come there, I knew that it was a very difficult decision for you
to make. While you recognized the critical importance of the NSC Staff,
your first professional love had always been -- and continues to be --
the Navy, and so you were understandably reluctant to take an assignment
away from the Navy. However, you have contributed enormously to the
country as you have carried out your extremely difficult and challenging
NSC Staff responsibilities, and this clearly has been in the finest
tradition of the Navy.

We had asked you to come to the NSC Staff because you are the
cream of the crop. As you return to the Navy, I am absolutely confident
that your extraordinary qualities -- leadership, intelligence,
dedication, integrity, industriousness, and many others -- will continue
to serve the Navy exceptionally well. I fully expect to see you rise to
the highest levels of the Navy as your career progresses. You deserve
it, and the Navy deserves it.

My very best wishes to you, Phil. Godspeed.

Sincerely,

Dick

Richard T. Boverie

RTB/md

cc: The Honorable John Lehman
     Secretary of the Navy

APPENDIX 3

Letter to Caspar Weinberger from Vice President Bush regarding DOD contribution to drug interdiction

THE VICE PRESIDENT
WASHINGTON

December 2, 1982

The Honorable Caspar W. Weinberger
Secretary of Defense
Washington, D.C. 20301

Dear Cap:

I want to take this opportunity to acknowledge the splendid performance of the military units assigned to assist in the current interdiction operations of the South Florida Task Force in response to my request to you of September 29.

The contribution of Patrol Squadrons from Navy Patrol Wing Eleven and Reserve Patrol Wing Atlantic has been simply outstanding, as have been the contributions of the entire NIMITZ battle group and the USS MISSISSIPPI in particular. It is clear that several of our recent off-shore seizures could not have been possible without the locating information these units provided.

The recent aerial surveillance of the Bahamas has yielded extremely valuable information on the patterns of suspicious air activity in the Islands and between the Bahamas and the East Coast. Working with the Bahamian government, we will now use this data to intensify our joint law enforcement efforts.

I want to make special note of the professionalism of the air crews from the Navy's Carrier Airborne Early Warning Squadron 126 from Norfolk, Virginia, and the Air Force's 552nd AWACS Wing from Tinker Air Force Base, Oklahoma which assisted in the Bahamas surveillance operation. Their perfect record of availability and around-the-clock coverage were testimony to the superb readiness of these units. I would be most appreciative if you would convey my gratitude to the officers and men and women of these units for their contribution to our continuing "war" against drugs.

In light of the success of our operations to date, I would like to request that the military support you have been providing in response to my September 29 request be extended for another thirty days. I will again review the need for further assistance at the end of that period. I sincerely appreciate your cooperation in this important effort.

Sincerely,

George Bush

CPH:sac

APPENDIX 4

Memorandum for the president from Robert C. McFarlane, drafted by the author

~~TOP SECRET~~

MEMORANDUM

~~TOP SECRET~~   THE WHITE HOUSE   SYSTEM II
                            WASHINGTON   91357 add on

ACTION

MEMORANDUM FOR THE PRESIDENT   SIGNED

FROM: ROBERT C. McFARLANE

SUBJECT: General Kelley's Report on Security for the U.S.
               MNF Contingent in Beirut

Issue

Improvement of security measures for Marine contingent in Beirut

Facts

General Kelley has forwarded a report of his visit to Beirut with
recommendations to improve security measures for our Marine
contingent.

Background

As you directed at the NSPG meetings immediately following the
bombing attack, General Kelley visited Beirut to assess the
security situation and prepare recommendations on how to improve
security in the wake of the attack. General Kelley's report has
been endorsed by General Vessey and Secretary Weinberger, and it
is attached at Tab A.

The recommended security improvements should reduce the risk to
our Marines substantially. Improved coordination with the
Lebanese and other MNF contingents, particularly in the intelligence area, has been effected and the physical security of the
airport perimeter has been increased by restructuring the road
access, more stringent search procedures, and more aggressive
participation by the LAF. The disposition of Marines at the
airport has been revised to emphasize sound defensive tactics
instead of administrative expedience.

Of some concern is General Kelley's conviction that more attacks
using different tactics are very likely even as we improve the
physical security of the perimeter at the airport. The problem
is the traffic congestion in and around the airport and the urban
setting for the Marine (and other MNF) deployments. One means to
mitigate the risks inherent in the environment in which the
Marines are deployed is to redeploy the Headquarters and support
elements of the Marine Amphibious Unit (MAU) to a more secure and
less congested site. General Vessey's endorsement notes that the
JCS are examining such a measure.

~~TOP SECRET~~
Declassify OADR

~~TOP SECRET~~

DECLASSIFIED
NLRR M370/1 #38643
BY KDU NARA DATE 1/10/13

2.

~~TOP SECRET~~

~~TOP SECRET~~   2   SYSTEM II
                                                91357 add on

There are two additional points of note in the Kelley report.
One is the recommendation that we move logistical and support
forces for the MAU back to the ships off shore to the degree
feasible, which has already begun, and that we further reduce the
number of <u>line</u> personnel in tactical dispositions. This latter
step is under review by the JCS. My concern here is the impact
such reductions may have on both the Lebanese and the other MNF
contingents which, by the nature of their deployments, do not
have the capability to redeploy forces to support ships
off-shore. I am especially concerned that these reductions in
personnel could send the wrong signals to the French and Italian
MNF units, whose positions in Beirut are at least as vulnerable
as ours and whose numbers exceed our own.

The second point is that the security improvements proposed will
enhance the perception that our MNF unit is a force which is dug
in for self-defense and therefore increasingly less visible to
the Lebanese people. Congress has been very critical of our
static deployment at the airport on the grounds that it creates a
veritable "bull's eye" for artillery, rocket and sniper fire.
Neither the basic report nor the endorsements come to grips with
this criticism, principally because a more mobile and tactically
aggressive deployment is regarded by the JCS and the responsible
commanders as inconsistent with the mission of our MNF. I
believe that a statement clarifying the mission of our MNF in a
way which would allow regular training exercises and civic
actions in the greater Beirut area might encourage the JCS to
give more consideration to this type of activity.

From my experience I think that a more active and mobile
deployment which would permit regular tactical training exercises
could go a long way toward reducing the continuous exposure of
our Marines, increasing their visibility and deterrent effect and
improving their training readiness. An NSC staff paper which
makes this argument is attached at Tab B for your consideration.

Recommendation

On the basis of the foregoing, I recommend the following:

OK   NO
✓ 🖉🖉 ___ 1.   That you approve the near-term recommendations as
                submitted in General Vessey's endorsement while
                placing a floor on the extent of the reductions in
                total numbers ashore.

~~TOP SECRET~~

~~TOP SECRET~~

3

2. That you approve and sign the decision directive
   at Tab C which would clarify the mission of our
   MNF.

3. That you authorize me to transmit the foregoing
   decisions while encouraging the Department of
   Defense to recommend additional measures to
   enhance the mobility, visibility, and training
   readiness of the MNF. (I would do this in the
   correspondence which forwards the NSDD on the MNF
   mission to State and Defense.)

Attachments:

Tab A   General Kelley's report on the security situation in
        Beirut.
Tab B   NSC staff paper: Improving Security, Training
        Readiness and Visibility of the MNF.
Tab C   Draft National Security Decision Directive: Mandate
        and Mission for the U.S. Contingent of the
        Multinational Force in Beirut, Lebanon.

                                    Prepared by:
                                    Philip A. Dur

APPENDIX 5

Letter from President Reagan to the author

THE WHITE HOUSE

WASHINGTON

October 31, 1984

Dear Phil:

As you complete the demanding assignment as
Director of Political-Military Affairs on the
National Security Council Staff, I want to
express my personal thanks for your exceptional
contributions to our great nation. For over two
years, your imagination, experience, and tireless
energy have been crucial to protecting our vital
interests in the Middle East.

The thoughtful and articulate briefings and
papers you provided have been invaluable to me
and the other members of our national security
community. I am particularly grateful for the
insights and perspectives you developed during
your frequent and often protracted trips to the
region. I know that these ventures, particularly
those to Lebanon, were not without personal risk.
Despite the hardships and hazards of your mission,
you were able to proffer skillful advice and
sound judgements that were essential to our
efforts in stopping the bloodshed in that
tortured country.

The nation cannot repay you for your dedicated
commitment to the noble task of bettering our
security and our hopes for peace. You can,
however, be assured of my personal gratitude and
that of the American people for what you have
done to advance our cause. This Republic has a
long heritage of benefit from officers of the
naval service. You are among those in this
gallant tradition. Thank you and God bless you
in your future assignments.

Sincerely,

Ronald Reagan

Captain Philip A. Dur, U.S. Navy
Director, Political-Military Affairs
National Security Council
Washington, D.C. 20506

APPENDIX 6

Letter from Vice President Bush to the author

THE VICE PRESIDENT
WASHINGTON

June 1, 1987

Philip A. Dur, Captain USN
Commanding Officer
USS YORKTOWN (CG 48)
Fleet Post Office
New York, New York   09594

Dear Phil:

I was delighted to receive your letter about the YORKTOWN's visit to Maine waters on July 25-26. It happens, by chance, that Barbara and I will be there on that weekend.

I would like very much to pay a visit to YORKTOWN to salute her Captain and crew. Further, Barbara and I would like to have a reception at our house for whatever officers and men might be designated to attend -- only two miles as the crow flies from Cape Porpoise. Tide is high around noon on both Saturday and Sunday. I would like to propose that perhaps 20-30 from YORKTOWN come by launch to our house. We have a dock and pier right at Walker's Point. I would invite some family and friends, and we could have a relaxed swim, cookout, etc. You choose the days.

When we are in residence, the Coast Guard usually has a vessel standing off Walker's Point. They have a strong mooring out there, about a mile off our house. Perhaps YORKTOWN could fasten onto that for a few hours. We would welcome several shifts of your officers and men, if that seems appropriate.

I am the proud owner-driver of a fast 28-foot Cigarette, so I would plan to come alongside YORKTOWN in that vessel, if that meets with your approval. And, yes, I would like at a later date to suggest some others who could come aboard YORKTOWN for a visit. Also, Barbara and I would love to have Kathie be our guest at Walker's Point for Saturday night. Perhaps you could leave the Exec. in charge of YORKTOWN and have a pleasant Saturday evening on shore.

Please let me know which of the two dates fits for a reception.

Warm regards,

Most sincerely,

George Bush

APPENDIX 7

Message from Lt. Gen. Robert Chelberg (US Europe Command) to author on completion of Paris assignment

INCOMING UNCLASSIFIED INCOMING

AMEMBASSY PARIS

```
          PAGE 01              USCINCEURVAIHIN  101434Z  XMB343     10/1335Z
          ACTION: DAO (03)

          INFO:  DCM (01)  MIL (01)  CPU (01)
          -------------------------- 10/1335Z  A0       (TOTAL COPIES: 006)
          VZCZCTAI738PAO420  JAB
          RR RUFHFR
          DE RUSNTCB #3861 1001332           10-APR-91  TOR: 13:31
          ZNR UUUUU                                     CHRG: DAO
          R 101434Z APR 91                              DIST: DAO
          FM USCINCEUR VAIHINGEN GE//ECCS//
          TO RUFHFR/USDAO PARIS FR
          RUSNNOA/USCINCEUR VAIHINGEN GE //SPACOS//
          BT
          UNCLAS
          0000
          MSGID/SYS.RRM/ECJ4//
          AMPN/PERSONAL FOR RADM DUR FROM LTG CHELBERG
          SUBJECT:  CONGRATULATORY NOTE TO RADM DUR//
          1.  UPON YOUR DEPARTURE FROM PARIS I WOULD LIKE TO PERSONALLY THANK
          YOU FOR THE SUPERB JOB YOU HAVE DONE DURING YOUR TOUR OF DUTY.
          2..  THE CLOSE COOPERATION YOU HAVE ESTABLISHED BETWEEN THE USDAO AND
          THE OFFICE OF DEFENSE COOPERATION IN FURTHERING US-FRENCH MILITARY-
          TO-MILITARY COOPERATION IS COMMENDABLE.  YOUR PARTICULARLY SUCCESSFUL
          EFFORTS IN COORDINATING FRENCH SUPPORT DURING OPERATION DESERT
          SHIELD/STORM CONTRIBUTED IMMENSELY TO THE SUCCESS OF THE WAR EFFORT.
          3.  AGAIN, PLEASE ACCEPT MY SINCERE APPRECIATION FOR A JOB WELL DONE,
          AND  THE BEST OF LUCK IN YOUR NEW ASSIGNMENT.//
          BT
          #3861
          NNNN
```

SPECIAL

APPENDIX 8

Award of the French *Ordre Nationale du Merite* to the author

Ambassade de France
aux Etats-Unis

Washington, D.C., le 2 November 1993

After entering the United States Navy in 1965, Rear Admiral DUR received surface officer training and gained a broad experience at sea, highlighted by the commands of the USS COMTE DE GRASSE, USS YORKTOWN, and finally CRUISER DESTROYER GROUP EIGHT, in which he deployed in the Mediterranean as of June 1991.

His proficiency in foreign languages and his deep interest in politico-military affairs, for which he obtained graduate degrees at the Universities of Notre-Dame and Harvard, made him a top candidate for high-level positions both in the United States, at the Pentagon and the National Security Council, and overseas.

His thorough knowledge of the French language and of our country made him the perfect choice to assume the duties of Defense Attache at the American Embassy in Paris, where he served from July 1989 until April 1991. In the course of that assignment, during the Gulf crisis, he distinguished himself by playing an outstanding spirit of cooperation sustained by great competence and remarkable efficiency. While in that position, he consistently contributed in a perfect francophile spirit to the strengthening of trustful relations between our Armed Forces.

In recognition of his untiring and successful efforts at developing a closer French-American military cooperation, the President of the Republic of France has named Rear Admiral Philip Dur "Commandeur de l'Ordre National du Mérite".

Brigadier General Guy POULIQUEN
French Defense and Air Attache

APPENDIX 9

Covering pages of *Forward...from the Sea*

"FORWARD ... FROM THE SEA"

The Strategic Concept for the Employment
of
NAVAL FORCES

CONTINUING THE PREPARATION OF THE NAVAL
SERVICES FOR THE 21ST CENTURY

19 September, 1994

19-Sep-94

"FORWARD . . . FROM THE SEA"

The Navy and Marine Corps White Paper in September 1992, titled ". . . , From the Sea," defined a strategic concept intended to carry the Department of the Navy beyond the Cold War and into the 21st Century. It signaled a change in focus and, therefore, in priorities for the Naval Services towards power projection and the employment of naval forces to influence events in littoral regions of the world.

The purpose of U.S. Naval forces remains to project the power and influence of the Nation across the seas to foreign waters and shores in both peace and war. This White Paper updates and expands the strategic concept to address specifically the unique contributions of Naval expeditionary forces in peacetime operations, responding to crises, and in regional conflicts. In short, this latest edition amplifies the scope of our strategic concept, while confirming the course and speed for the Naval Services as defined in the original document.

John H. Dalton
Secretary of the Navy

J. M. Boorda
Admiral, U.S. Navy

Carl E. Mundy, Jr.
General, U.S. Marine Corps

1

ACKNOWLEDGMENTS

My wife, Judy, encouraged and assisted me in every step of this project. Every word was transcribed by her from my pen to understandable typescript, and she provided the administrative discipline to get this done. Captain Peter Swartz, USN, first persuaded me to complete the record of my experience in hopes of attracting current and future generations to careers as operators and strategic planners. I am also indebted to dedicated public servants and longtime colleagues Dr. Phil Depoy; Admiral Hank Mauz, USN; Vice Admiral Doug Crowder, USN; Major General Tom Wilkerson, USMC; Rear Admiral John Bitoff, USN; the Hon. William Ball; and the Hon. John Lehman, all of whom reviewed early drafts. Shipmates Rear Admiral Mark (Buz) Busby, USN, Captains Brent Gooding and Rick Easton, USN, and Capitaine de Frégate Aimery Fustier, FN, all helped refresh my memory of our times together at sea.

The events and circumstances recorded herein are based entirely on my personal recollections and the copious notes I made during my career. Of course, I alone am responsible for the views and opinions expressed unless otherwise noted and attributed.

GLOSSARY

AAW: anti-air warfare

AAWC: AAW commander

ACM: anti cruise missile

AEW: airborne early warning

AFWTF: Atlantic Fleet Weapons Training Facility (Puerto Rico)

AGI: Soviet (Russian) intelligence collection ship

ALESCMED: admiral commanding French naval forces in the Mediterranean

ANGLICO: Naval gunfire spotting team

AOR: area of responsibility

ASD: assistant secretary of defense

ASW: anti-submarine warfare

ASWGRU: ASW group commander

AUTEC: Atlantic Undersea Test and Evaluation Center

AWACS: Airborne Warning and Control System (USAF)

BDA: bomb damamge assessment

BuPers: Bureau of Naval Personnel

CAP: Combat Air Patrol (USN, USAF)

CDC: combat decision center (carrier combat information center)

CDO: command duty officer (USN)

CEC: cooperative engagement capability (USN network linking ship and airborne radars)

CECLANT: Commander French Naval Forces in the Atlantic

CG: Consolidated Guidance (DOD guidance to service programs and budgets)

CIC: Combat Information Center

CINCAFMED: Commander in Chief, Allied Forces Mediterranean (NATO)

CINCCENT: Commander in Chief, US Central Command

CINCCHAN: Commander in Chief, Channel Command (NATO)

CINCLANTFLT: Commander in Chief, US Atlantic Fleet

CINCPACFLT: Commander in Chief, US Pacific Fleet

CINCSOUTH: Commander in Chief, Allied Forces Southern Europe (NATO)

CINCUSNAVEUR: Commander in Chief, US Naval Forces Europe

CINCUSREDCOM: Commander in Chief, US Readiness Command

CIWS: close-in weapons system

CJCS: Chairman, Joint Chiefs of Staff (US)

CNO: Chief of Naval Operations

CO: commanding officer (navy)

COCOM: unified combat commanders

COMCRUDESGRU: Commander, Cruiser Destroyer Group (US Navy)

COMDESRON: Commander, Destroyer Squadron (US Navy)

COMECON: Council for Mutual Economic Assistance (Soviet led)

COMNAVAIRLANT: Commander, Naval Air Forces US Atlantic Fleet

COMNAVSURFLANT: Commander, Naval Surface Forces US Atlantic Fleet

COMNAVSURFPAC: Commander, Naval Surface Forces US Pacific Fleet

COMSECONDFLT: Commander, US Second Fleet

COMSEVENTHFLT: Commander, US Seventh Fleet

COMSIXTHFLT: Commander, US Sixth Fleet

COMSTRIKFLT: Commander, Striking Fleet (NATO)

COMSTRIKFORSOUTH: Commander, Striking and Support Force South (NATO)

CSCE: Commission on Security and Cooperation in Europe

CSEDS: Combat Systems Engineering Development Site

CSN: Confederate States Navy

CSS: Confederate States Ship

DCM: deputy chief of mission

DDG: guided missile destroyer

DEA: Drug Enforcement Agency

DESRON: destroyer squadron (US)

DesTech: Naval Destroyer School

DIA: Defense Intelligence Agency

DLG: guided missile frigate

DMZ: demilitarized zone

DOD: Department of Defense

DPG: Defense Policy Guidance

DPRK: Democratic People's Republic of Korea (North Korea)

DUSD: deputy undersecretary of defense

DUSD/PR: DUSD policy review

EA: executive assistant

EOD: emergency ordnance disposal

EW: electronic warfare

FLEETEX: Fleet Exercise (major predeployment milestone)

FOG: flag officer Gibraltar (British naval command in Gibraltar)

FYDP: Five Year Defense Plan

Gig: A small boat carried on a naval ship intended to convey ship commanding officers

Gitmo: Guantánamo naval base

GIUK: Greenland-Iceland-United Kingdom

HF: high frequency

HICOM: high command network

IAF: Israeli Air Force

IDF: Israel Defense Forces

INF: intermediate nuclear forces

ISA: international security affairs

ISP: International Security Policy

JCPOA: Joint Comprehensive Plan of Action (Iran nuclear deal)

JCS: Joint Chiefs of Staff

JP-5: aviation jet fuel

JPMG: Joint Political Military Group

LAF: Lebanese Armed Forces

LAMPS: Light Airborne Multipurpose System

LF: Lebanese Forces (Christian militia of the Phalange Party)

LONGEX: exercise sponsored by the Royal New Zealand Navy

MAU: marine amphibious unit, later renamed MEU

MEU: Marine Expeditionary Unit

MNF: multinational force (Lebanon)

MOD: Ministry of Defence (Britain) / Ministry of Defense (France)

MRC: major regional conflict

N-6: Navy Staff Directorate for Command, Control, Communications, Computers

NATO: North Atlantic Treaty Organization

NAVCOMMSTA: Naval Communications Station

NAVSOUTH: Naval Forces Southern Europe (NATO naval command in the Mediterranean)

NGFS: naval gunfire support

NROTC: Naval Reserve Officers Training Corps

NSC: National Security Council

NSDD: National Security Decision Directive

NSFO: navy standard fuel oil ("black" oil)

NSPG: National Security Planning Group

NSSD: National Security Study Directive

NTPI: nuclear technical proficiency inspection

OC: Operations Communications

OCE: officer conducting the exercise

ONI: Office of Naval Intelligence

OOD: Officer of the Deck

OODF: Officer of the Deck Fleet qualified

OPDEP: operations deputy (deputies to service chiefs responsible for joint matters)

OPNAV: Office of the Chief of Naval Operations

OPPE: operational propulsion plant examination

OSD: Office of the Secretary of Defense

OTC: officer in tactical command

PA&E: Directorate for Program Analysis and Evaluation in the Office of the Secretary of Defense

PCI: Italian Communist Party (*Partito Comunista Italiano*)

PG: patrol gunboat

PIM: plan of intended movement

PLF: Palestinian Liberation Forces

PLO: Palestinian Liberation Organization

POM: Program Objective Memorandum

POMCUS: prepositioning of matériel configured in unit sets (US Army equipment stored in Europe)

PRC: People's Republic of China

PSP: Parti socialiste populaire, aka Progressive Socialist Party (Lebanese Druze political party and militia)

RDJTF: Rapid Deployment Joint Task Force

RN: Royal Navy

ROC: Republic of China (Nationalist Chinese government in Taiwan)

ROCN (or ROC): Republic of China Navy, aka Taiwan Navy

ROE: rules of engagement (military rules governing the use of deadly force)

ROK: Republic of Korea (South Korea)

SAC: strategic air command

SACEUR: Supreme Allied Commander Europe

SACLANT: Supreme Allied Commander Atlantic

SAG: surface action group

SASC: Senate Armed Services Committee

SECNAV: Secretary of the Navy

SLOC: sea lines of communication

SNA: Soviet Naval Aviation

SOA: speed of advance

SOSMRC: Senior Officers Ship's Material Readiness Course

SSBN: strategic ballistic missile submarine

SSG: Strategic Studies Group (navy group reporting to the CNO charged with studying strategic options)

STRIKFLT: NATO Striking Fleet

STW: strike warfare

SWOS: Surface Warfare Officers' School

TAO: tactical action officer

UCP: Unified Command Plan

USCINCEUR: US Commander in Chief Europe

USCINCLANT: US Commander in Chief Atlantic

V/STOL: vertical/short takeoff and landing

VANDALEX: missile exercise featuring retired TALOS missiles simulating sea-skimming cruise missiles

VCNO: vice CNO

VHF: very-high-frequency

VLS: vertical launch system

WEU: West European Union

XO: executive officer

INDEX